Enrich Series on China-India Issues

Enrich Series on China-India Issues

CHINA-INDIA COOPERATION PROSPECTS

Papers presented at the 1st Academic Summit on China-India Cooperation in 2011

Editor: Victor F. S. Sit

Enrich Professional Publishing

Published by

Enrich Professional Publishing (S) Private Limited
16L, Enterprise Road,
Singapore 627660
Website: www.enrichprofessional.com
A Member of Enrich Culture Group Limited

Hong Kong Head Office:
2/F, Rays Industrial Building, 71 Hung To Road, Kwun Tong, Kowloon, Hong Kong, China

China Office:
Rm 1800, Building C, Central Valley, 16 Hai Dian Zhong Jie, Haidian District, Beijing, China

United States Office:
PO Box 30812, Honolulu, HI 96820, USA

Project editor: Victor F. S. Sit

Edited by Barbara Cao and Glenn Griffith

ISBN (Hardback) 978-981-4402-30-9
ISBN (ebook) 978-981-4402-31-6 (pdf)
978-981-4402-32-3 (epub)

Enrich Professional Publishing is an independent globally minded publisher focusing on the economic and financial developments that have revolutionized New China. We aim to serve the needs of advanced degree students, researchers, and business professionals who are looking for authoritative, accurate, and engaging information on China.

Printed in Hong Kong with woodfree paper from Japan

Contents

Foreword

A good friend of mine established the China Fortune Foundation Limited under the mission statement of "Gathering the Strengths of the Chinese People to Realize a Prosperous China." The foundation aims to contribute to a better China by providing manpower, economic knowledge, and resources to support various sectors, including welfare, education, healthcare, as well as environmental protection. This has always been my goal and the mission of my company, GCL-Poly Energy Holdings Limited.

Being a socially responsible international energy enterprise group, GCL-Poly surveys market trends and gives active support to new energy strategies and the development of a low-carbon economy in China, whilst adhering to the philosophy of "Bringing Green Power to Life and Creating a Better Living Environment" in the development and production of green and renewable energies, with developing "green energy" as its core business. GCL-Poly has turned itself into a large and integrated green energy enterprise up to a world-class standard, especially within the solar photovoltaic industry. Capitalizing on ever-improving technology, product innovation, and efficient implementation under streamlined management, together with its customer-oriented service which is guided by the simplistic concept of "quality + cost = market," GCL-Poly has become a global, top-notch supplier of photovoltaic material in just five years. The company has helped to create a brand new standard for the healthy development of the industry and participation in fair trade worldwide.

In the course of GCL-Poly's development of new energy business, we noticed that our neighbor India was confronted with similar questions in environmental protection, including the quickening pace of urbanization, and a growing population, which made environmental protection and energy saving the major challenges for India. It is the imperative for China and India to step up efforts in adjusting energy structure, safeguarding energy supply, and improving energy efficiency. From my perspective, developing green energy and a low carbon economy serves as one of the important approaches to realizing sustained economic growth and the prosperity of China and India in the future.

My fellow colleagues and I are full of confidence and enthusiasm at the prospect of participating in this new energy industry. We will continue to push the envelope to enhance the quality of products and lower the cost of production in order to produce affordable solar products for the residents of China, India, and the whole world. We envision a greener living through the use of green energy so as to genuinely "Bring Green Power to Life!"

Zhu Gongshan
Hong Kong, 2012

Preface

China and India are the world's oldest surviving civilizations. They are also currently the world's fastest growing economies and typical examples of global emerging powers.

In addition to gaining the world's attention for these reasons, the two countries have demonstrated other traits. They share a land border, have value systems and social hierarchies distinct from the West and the so-called "industrialized economies," and have low levels of economic development, and heavy burdens of huge populations combined with fragile ecologies. Besides the need for domestic stability and friendly and benign foreign relations, both countries need to forge closer cooperative ties and complement each other for long-term stable development. At present, they are key members of the BRIC countries and are developing multifaceted cooperation.

The Advanced Institute for Contemporary China Studies (ACCS) of the Hong Kong Baptist University has taken on a small role in this broad and significant global trend by hosting an annual Research Summit on China-India Cooperation. It shares a platform for the exchange of views and discussions between Chinese and Indian researchers on issues of mutual interest related to cooperation for development in both countries. The present volume contains papers presented at the First Summit in Hong Kong in November 2011 and it is published in both Chinese and English.

The Summit is to be held in rotation in the big cities of the two countries. It is hoped that this and future volumes that constitute the "Series on China-India Issues" will be an important reference for researchers and governments interested in the growing importance of China and India in global development.

Victor F. S. Sit
Director, ACCS
Hong Kong Baptist University

Preface

Introduction of the China India Fortune Foundation

As China and India, two of the BRIC (Brazil, Russia, India, and China) countries, rise in tandem, the world will soon see global shifts in the terms of political and economic power in Asia. After years of misunderstanding and dormancy in diplomacy, China and India should now strengthen bonds and create synergy in the long run for the betterment of the welfare of the people of the two countries.

The China India Fortune Foundation takes the initiative to rekindle friendship and foster cooperation between these two major countries on a non-governmental level, especially through exchanges in education and views on future development and cooperation.

Objectives of the China India Fortune Foundation

- To improve mutual understanding among China, India, and Hong Kong
- To foster dialogue and strategic collaboration among the three partners on a non-governmental level
- To discover opportunities for cooperation and the potential paths to co-prosperity
- To provide a comprehensive economic and social outlook for the governments of these regions to consider

List of Contributors

Dr. Basudeb Chaudhuri, Director of the Centre de Sciences Humaines, New Delhi, India, and Associate Professor of Economics, Center for Research in Economics and Management (CREM), University of Caen, France

Professor Chen Fenglin, Department of Diplomacy, Institute of Diplomacy, China Foreign Affairs University

Dr. Rup Narayan Das, Senior Fellow at the Institute for Defence Studies and Analyses (IDSA), New Delhi, India

Dr. Srikanth Kondapalli, Professor in Chinese Studies, Centre for East Asian Studies, School of International Studies, Jawaharlal Nehru University, New Delhi, India

Dr. Li Li, China Institute of Contemporary International Relations

Ms. Li Ting, postgraduate student majoring in International Trade at Fuzhou University

Dr. Liu Jian, researcher at the Institute of Asia-Pacific Studies, Chinese Academy of Social Sciences

Dr. Velayoudom Marimoutou, Institut Français de Pondicherry, India, and Groupement de Recherche en Economie Quantitative d'Aix Marseille (GREQAM), Université de la Méditerranée, France

Dr. Jagannath P. Panda, Research Fellow at the Institute for Defense Studies and Analyses (IDSA), New Delhi, India, Associated Research Fellow at the Institute of Security and Development Policy (ISDP), Stockholm (Sweden), and Research Associate at the Institute of Transnational Studies (ITS), Italy

Professor Quan Yi, researcher at Fujian Academy of Social Sciences, Chief Editor of *Asia Pacific Economic Review*, and Deputy Director of Asia Pacific Economy Studies of the Fujian Academy of Social Sciences

Dr. Rajeswari Pillai Rajagopalan, Senior Fellow at the Institute of Security Studies (ISS), Observer Research Foundation, New Delhi, India

Professor Kishan S. Rana, former Indian ambassador, author, and teacher

Professor Sudhakara Reddy, Indira Gandhi Institute of Development Research, Mumbai, India

Professor Shang Huipeng, School of International Studies, Peking University

Dr. Shen Kaiyan, Research Professor at the Institute of Economics, Shanghai

Academy of Social Sciences

Ms. Sun Wei, Executive Director, GCL-Poly

Professor Ting Wai, Political and International Relations Department, Hong Kong Baptist University

Professor Yu Jianhua, Director of the Institute of Eurasian Studies, Shanghai Academy of Social Sciences

1

Chapter

A Comparative Study of Economic Reform and Development between China and India

Shen Kaiyan

In recent years, more and more concern has been raised to compare the economic development between China and India. Indeed, from the perspective of the economic scale, China and India, the two largest developing countries, are now experiencing an unparalleled economic expansion. The economies of the two countries are projected to rise continuously up the global GDP ranking, and China will have a growing share of imports and exports in the world market. Meanwhile, the market scale has expanded notably. Specifically, the process of economic growth, the enormous increase of labor productivity, the great domestic demand, the huge Foreign Direct Investment and the Domestic Investment all together have brought about the miracle of a fast developing China.

From the perspective of development quality, China and India, once at the low levels of economic development, are now shouldering the challenges from the double-edged sword of the fast development of the economy. The country is getting richer with the income gap widening; industrialization is developing with the urbanization lagging behind; the economy is developing with higher environmental and resource pressures. The Economic Modernization Index is rising while human concerns and social development are neglected. From the perspective of economic structure, China and India both possess distinct evolutionary characteristics which vary to some extent. China is on the track of traditional industrialization development, i.e. driving the development of other industries with the manufacturing industry development at its core, thus bringing the development of the whole national economy and the adjustment, optimization, and upgrading of the industrial structure. McKinsey & Company holds that the development of the manufacturing industry having turned China into a "World Factory" within only 20 years. China has found in the manufacturing industry a sustainable development mode. India, however, hopes to rely on its development in the information industry and modern service trade to enter directly into the Post-Industrial Period without entering into the development stage of industrialization. The paradigm shift of the industrial structure of India wins it the reputation as the "World's Office." From the perspective of social economic system, there are significant differences between the Chinese government-led economic system and the market-oriented one in India in the determination of equity structure, the definition of legal system, and the ownership of the political system. However, the final economic achievements of the two countries are not merely the results of these major differences.

From the perspective of economic development process, as a matter of fact, the significance and effectiveness of the comparative study are based on the analysis of historical development.

The Historical and Economic Factors for the Choice of a Planned Economy in China and India

The choice of economic development mode and strategy is deeply restricted by the epoch and social conditions with the path dependent on the process of economic development. This has a significant long-term impact. China and India, in the early periods after independence, both chose the planned economy as their development mode. It is not a coincidence, but it has deep historical and economic reasons.

China and India had been the two cradles of human civilization and once were the two richest nations in Asia. However, the Western colonialists, led by the U.K., opened the door of the two empires with firepower following the Industrial Revolution. The colonialists brought the Chinese and Indians not only bloodshed but also the destruction of the self–sufficient economic basis of the agriculture and handicraft industry. We learn from history that the countries which suffered more from the brutal colonial rule were more likely to take the road of a Soviet-style planned economy after independence. The reason is related to the strong, or even radical, nationalism which gets embedded for a long time in the minds of the leaders and people of these countries. The Soviet Union, with the help of the highly centralized political system and the planned economic system, was turned into a world class economic power after being a second class or third class economic system which made the Socialist Road seem feasible. To the late-developing countries eager to achieve modernization, the Soviet model exerted a strong attraction. At that time, people believed that Socialism was not only connected to a planned economic system, but also to the strategy of giving priority to heavy industry.

After the independence of China and India, the motive force of revolution was turned into economic construction. Both countries adopted a catch-up development strategy of giving priority to heavy industry. This form of a planned economy had great advantages in pulling together the labor power and financial and material resources. It was, therefore, the first choice for China and India and it raised people's enthusiasm for production at the primary stage.

In economic construction, Mao Zedong Thought is almost a copy of a highly concentrated and planned economic system of the Stalin Pattern. Through the Socialist transformation of capitalist industry and commerce in China and land reform, China built a highly planned Socialist industrial and agricultural foundation. Seven or eight years were taken to implement the nationalization and collectivization of the rural land nationwide. The industrialization in China was also similar to the Stalinist Pattern of the former Soviet Union, i.e. put priority on developing heavy industry, use the scissors gap between the prices of the industrial and agricultural products, and get industrialization capital from agriculture.

With the effort of all Chinese people, the First Five-Year Plan, started in 1953, was successfully accomplished and it gained worldwide attention. The Plan also laid a concrete basis for the industrialization of Socialism in China and basically formed the highly concentrated planned economic system of China. This system had some positive effects for pulling together human labor and material resources in the construction of the major programs under the conditions of material shortage and the then-current weak economic basis.

After independence, India practiced the development mode of Nehru-style Socialism. The former Soviet Union had defined Socialism for countries on the track of non-capitalist development,[1] but, in the meantime, India was allowing the development of the private-sector economy and constantly building and expanding the public economy and this occupied the "commanding heights" of the Indian economy. Till 2010, India practiced 11 Five-Year Plans. Since India had long practiced federalism, each state had the freedom to choose the personalized development mode which was more suitable to local development. The state of Kerala and West Bengal, for example, are under the long-term governance of the Communist Party which advocates the Communist development road, not the practice of capitalism.

The economist, economic advisor, and now the prime minister of India, Mr. Manmohan Singh once wrote that "adopting the policy of planned construction is to accelerate the industrial growth, to effectively use the limited resources, and to achieve a balanced economic development."[2] The independent Indian leaders headed by Jawaharlal Nehru cherished the limited resources of the country, and so wanted to use them in the right way for economic development. After independence, India was noted for its mixed economy and the government put its efforts towards developing the state-operated industry, without neglecting the private sector of the economy. Because of the balanced development mode, the industrial policy of India had two restrictions, i.e. restrict the foreign capital and restrict monopoly.

From the Planned Economy to the Market-Oriented One: A Comparison on Economic Reforms and the Development Process between China and India

By the year 1978, the Third Plenary Session of the 11th CPC opened a new era of reform and opening up. China was then on a path of high speed economic growth for 10 successive years. The year 1978 was a milestone for the history of economic development in China. Thirteen years later, in 1991, India announced with a positive stance to the world that it would start its economic reform. Their achievements could compete with those of China. The year 1991 was a milestone for the history of economic development in India.

First, the reforms of both countries are quite concerned with agriculture. The rural reform of 1978 was of vital importance to the economic reform of China. The success of the rural reform not only laid a solid foundation for the reform in other areas, but prepared for the further liberalization of minds. The major measure for the rural reforms was to practice the Household Contract Responsibility System in rural areas; raise the prices of farm products; reform the purchasing and marketing system, and encourage the development of township enterprises. These measures had promoted the peasants' enthusiasm in farming and further emancipated the productive force of the rural areas. This greatly increased the output of the agricultural products and the income of the peasants.

Since 1991, India had started large-scale economic reforms. Agricultural reform was also highly valued. The government policies for agricultural reform made the agricultural production of India stay on a high standard for six successive years. The country's production areas achieved food self-sufficiency, and still had some more food for export. The reforms, however, had not changed the previous policy framework. For instance, there are still some restrictions in the production and circulation of the agricultural products, e.g. the processing and refining of oil and sugar, the price of sugar and trade in grains, etc.

Second, from the content of the economic reform of the two countries, we can see that China and India both changed their past economic development modes and policies.

First, both countries had put marketization as the orientation for the reform of economic systems. After learning the lessons and experience from a decade of reform, China in 1992 clearly stated in the Fourteenth Congress of the Chinese Communist Party that the general objective for China's economic restructuring was to establish a Socialist system of a market economy. India's reform had abolished most of the economic restraints and gradually achieved economic liberalization. The new industrial policy adopted in 1991 had basically exempted a variety of licenses for newly constructed and expanded business industries. The *Antimonopoly Act* was abolished; there were no restrictions on the total asset value of enterprises. And, according to the policy, the types of industry monopolized by the public sectors shrank to eight types closely related to strategy and security and partial privatization was granted within the public enterprises.

Second, the two countries both positively encouraged the development of the private economy. The 15th National Congress of the Communist Party of China held in 1997 emphasized that China was still at the primary stage of Socialism. The Non-State Owned Sector is an important component part of China's Socialist market economy. It is China's basic economic system to retain a dominant position for State ownership and to develop diverse forms of ownership side-by-side.[3] In order to let the private sectors play a bigger role and join in the important economic activities, the Indian government opened more departments to the private sector. The number of the specialized departments only reserved for the state-owned enterprises was cut from the previous 17 to 6. Even in such areas, the private sectors can choose to participate. In the past, it was forbidden for the private enterprises to invest in the infrastructure departments. But later, private enterprises were encouraged to join in the development and construction of electric power, iron and steel, mining, oil refining, and development, roads, airports and port construction, as well as telecommunications and shipping services. At present, the retained departments are limited to the industries closely related to national defense and strategy making.

Third, the two counties had both adopted the policy of opening up to the outside world, emphasizing the importance of economic globalization and integration into the world economy. China's economic reform and opening up had entered a new stage after Deng Xiaoping's "Southern Tour Speech" in 1992. India was then encouraging exports, and 60% of the foreign exchange income was discretionary to the exporters. Import and export trade licenses were replaced by the customs administration, and tariff reduction or exemption was also granted. In 1993, the Indian government declared that the rupee was then to become a freely convertible currency in the current account transactions, and they were working for the free convertibility of capital account. Access policy opened the stock market to foreign investment, allowing the foreign investors to subscribe for shares of the stocks of Indian companies, and to set up exclusively foreign-owned enterprises.

Comparing the Achievement of Economic Reform between China and India

Both of the two countries have their uniqueness and advantages in the progress and effects of the economic reform.

The characteristics of China's economic reform are the rapid economic growth and high degree of opening up. China has greatly promoted the industrialization and made great achievements. And now it has become an important base for world processing industry and so achieved the name of the "World's Factory." From Table 1.1, we can see that since the 1990s, the secondary industry accounted for up to 45% of China's total GDP or more, of which most came from a share of manufacturing output. Since 1990, China's industrial output value accounted for the proportion of an average of 40% of GDP or more. The proportion of the manufacturing industry has accounted for more than 85% of the industry, and the proportion reached about 37% of the total GDP in recent years. In the advanced process of industrialization, China had consciously absorbed a large number of rural labor forces. It in one way raised the income of the farmers, and in another promoted the development of urbanization.

Table 1.1 The ratio of three industries and other major industries in GDP

Year	China				India			
	Primary industry (%)	Secondary industry (%)		Tertiary industry (%)	Agriculture (%)	Industry (%)		Service sector (%)
			Of which: manufacturing (%)				Of which: manufacturing (%)	
1990	27.1	41.3	34.2	31.6	29	28	16.7	44
1991	24.5	41.8	34.6	33.7	30	26	15.7	45
1992	21.8	43.4	35.8	34.8	29	26	15.9	45
1993	19.7	46.6	36.0	33.7	29	26	15.8	45
1994	19.8	46.6	36.0	33.6	29	27	16.7	45
1995	19.9	47.2	36.3	32.9	26	28	17.9	46
1996	19.7	47.5	36.6	32.8	27	27	17.5	46
1997	18.3	47.5	36.6	34.2	26	27	16.4	47
1998	17.6	46.2	35.5	36.2	26	26	15.5	48
1999	16.5	45.8	35.2	37.7	25	25	14.8	50
2000	15.1	45.9	35.4	39.0	23	26	15.6	50
2001	14.4	45.1	35.1	40.5	23	25	15.0	51

(Cont'd)

Year	China				India			
	Primary industry (%)	Secondary industry (%)		Tertiary industry (%)	Agriculture (%)	Industry (%)		Service sector (%)
			Of which: manufacturing (%)				Of which: manufacturing (%)	
2002	13.7	44.8	35.0	41.5	21	26	15.3	53
2003	12.8	46.0	36.3	41.2	21	26	15.3	53
2004	13.4	46.2	35.6	40.4	19	28	15.7	53
2005	12.1	47.4	36.8	40.5	19	28	15.8	53
2006	11.1	47.9	37.4	40.9	18	29	16.3	53
2007	10.8	47.3	37.5	41.9	18	29	16.3	53
2008	10.7	47.4	37.3	41.8	18	28	15.8	54
2009	10.3	46.3	35.5	43.4	18	27	16.0	55

Notes: 1. Before and including the year 2004, the proportion of the manufacturing sector refers to the proportion of enterprises above a designated size. After 2004, the proportion of the manufacturing sector to the proportion of all the industrial enterprises.

2. Industrial enterprises above a designated size refer to those with annual revenue from principal business over RMB5 million.

Sources: 1. China's data is from *China Statistical Yearbook*; data of China's manufacturing industry is based upon the author's own calculations according to the original data from the *China Statistical Yearbook*, with current price.

2. India's data (except the manufacturing sector) is from the World Bank's website: www.worldbank.org.cn; the data of India's manufacturing sector is based upon the author's own calculations according to the Central Statistical Organization, Ministry of Statistics and Programme Implementation, Government of India (CSO, MoSPI, GoI), with current price. The website: http://www.mospi.gov.in/cso_test1.htm.

China has been very successful in opening up to the outside world. First, it has made outstanding achievements in attracting foreign investment. Since 1979 to 2008, the average speed of China's absorption of Foreign Direct Investment (FDI) has been more than 30% per year's growth, which is rare in other countries with FDI after World War II. Until 2009, China had, for four successive years, become the second largest country of Foreign Direct Investment inflows, just second to the U.S. The foreign enterprises running business activities in China are over 300,000. With only a small part of the world's top 500 enterprises[4] which could not invest in China because of the Chinese government's restrictions in certain areas (though the majority of companies did invest in China). Second, the development of foreign trade has been very fast. In 2008, the total value of imports and exports amounted to USD2,207.3 billion, ranking the third in the world. Third, the Chinese enterprises made great progress in investments in foreign countries. Generally, China's foreign investment is still at the primary stage of development, but from 2001 to 2005, the total amount of China's capital outflow reached USD22.6 billion.[5]

Fig. 1.1 A comparison between the total FDI value and its proportion of GDP between China and India

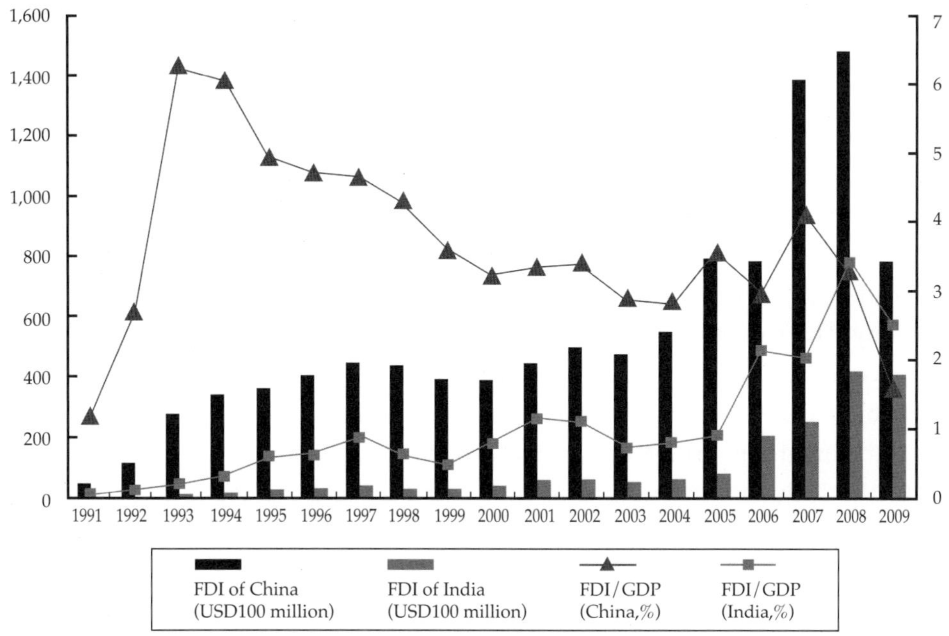

Note: The data released by this website has minor differences with that released by the Ministry of Commerce of China and *China Foreign Economic and Trade Yearbook* and the *China Statistical Yearbook*.

Source: Drawn according to the figures from www.worldbank.org.cn.

China has made great achievements in infrastructure construction. In recent years China continued to increase the investment in infrastructure. The situation of infrastructure construction had been greatly improved. The areas of energy, transportation, steel, telecommunications, and computer industries were developing rapidly, thus creating favorable conditions for the quick and sustainable development of the economy. China's present power generation capacity ranks the second in the world; and the railway mileage ranks the third in the world; the road mileage ranks the fourth in the world, with the highway mileage ranking the second in the world. The Civil Aviation Routes reached 2.4618 million kilometers (data of 2008); and the postal and telecommunications industry has grown by leaps and bounds. At present, the fixed telephone users exceed 340 million and the mobile phones users are 48.53 per 100 (data of 2008), ranking the first in the world.[6]

The economic reforms of India can be summed up as having produced a perfect financial system and a leading tertiary industry. The financial reforms of India are fast and successful. First, India basically accomplished the reforms in interest rate liberalization and exchange rate liberalization. These liberalizations not only become a useful means for the Indian government to regulate the economy, but also make the allocation of resources more rational and effective. In 1994, India declared that its currency is convertible under the current system, thus the currency liberalization had taken a big step forward. Second, India has formed a relatively complete system of commercial banks. The government banks, private banks, foreign banks, and urban and rural cooperative banks are properly placed with orderly competition which has greatly improved the efficiency of the banking system and guaranteed the rapid and stable development of the economy. The successful reform in financial sectors promoted the development of the capital market, stimulated the growth of the competitive enterprises and ensured the orderly operation of the securities market, thus playing an active role in optimizing the allocation of social resources.

In the industrial structure of India, the service industry is of a higher proportion. India is relying on the development of the service sector to promote economic growth on the condition that there is no broad-based revolution in the manufacturing sector. The proportion of India's service sector in the last 10 years is over 50% of the total GDP value (see Fig. 1.2), 12–13 percentage points higher than that of China, within which mainly is seen the rapid development of the modern service industry.[7] At present, India's modern service sector accounts for about 40–50% of the entire service industry, about 50–60% of the traditional service sectors. In recent years, the average growth rate of India's service sectors was 9%, within which the increased level of the modern service industry was more than 10%, nearly 3 percentage points higher than that of the traditional service industries. In India, the IT service sector is a model of the modern service industry, with the support of the national policy, and the advantages of sufficient human capital and language, India's software services industry rose greatly in the 1990s, maintaining a growth rate of more than 50%. This high value-added, knowledge-intensive service sector is a typical modern service industry. It is an important growth point for driving the development of the tertiary industry. China is leading the manufacturing industry, thus India won its reputation as the "world's office."

Fig. 1.2 The proportion of GDP in three industries[8] in India

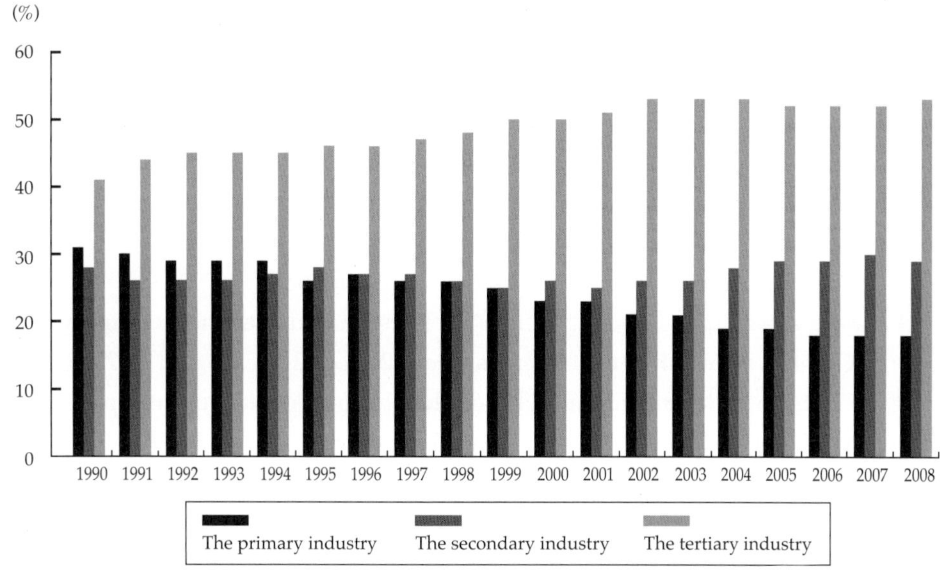

Source: Drawn according to the figures from www.worldbank.org.cn.

Problems of China and India's Economic Reform and Development

Different kinds of contradictions and obstacles will inevitably arise with economic reform and development. Any country may encounter such difficulties on their way forward, even China and India.

First, unemployment and wealth disparity become major obstacles to the social progress of the two countries. Although the previous Indian government aimed at increasing employment and eradicating poverty in the ruling, and one of the objectives in economic development was to eliminate unemployment and provide gainful opportunities to millions of the unemployed, unemployment and poverty still trouble India's economic development.

The unemployment problem is leading to India's impoverishment. The Indian population grows rapidly, increasing by 2% annually. An annual increase in both population and labor force is over 15 million people.[9] As the Indian manufacturing industry develops slowly, it can provide few employment opportunities. Generally speaking, the service sector can create more opportunities. But in India, it is not the case: Their service sector supplies fewer opportunities, for the Indian service industry requires high-quality employees. There are very limited opportunities in these enterprises, which make it rather difficult for the Indian economy to pull together the growing labor force, so the Indian unemployment problem is increasingly critical.

Known as "the world's factory," China's manufacturing industry really draws more workers than the Indian counterpart, however, there are quite a few laid-off workers of state-owned enterprises due to the early 1990s reform. Together with hidden and structural unemployment, the total number of the unemployed is by no means small. Recently, the employment of university graduates appeared rather difficult. According to the *Social Blue Book of 2009*, published by the Chinese Academy of Social Sciences, it is estimated that the unemployment rate for Chinese university students was over 12% , and by the end of 2008 there were 1.5 million college students who could not find jobs. The unemployment, on one hand, expands the hundreds of millions of poor people, and on the other hand, it increases the difficulty of solving the employment problem, which will continue to hamper China's economic development, especially the progress of modernization.

Table 1.2 Comparison of unemployment rates between China and India

Year	China (%)	India (%)
2002	—	8.8
2003	4.0	8.8
2004	4.1	9.5
2005	4.2	9.2
2006	4.2	8.9
2007	4.3	7.8
2008	4.0	7.2
2009	4.0	6.8

Notes: 1. China's unemployment rate is defined as the registered unemployment rates in urban areas.
2. India's unemployment rate is defined as the percentage of the labor force without jobs.

Source: 1. China's data is from *Chinese Statistical Yearbook*.
2. India's data is from the website: http://www.indexmundi.com/g/g.aspx?v=74&c=in&l=en.

China has solved the problem of poverty better than India, but the gap between rich and poor has grown. The social divide between the rich and poor has continued to widen since the deepening of reform in the 1990s. Some data shows that since 2000, China's Gini coefficient of income in the urban and rural residents has exceeded the internationally recognized warning line of 0.3–0.4, and it increases each year. In 1981, China's Gini coefficient was only 0.288; in 1990, 0.343; in 1999, 0.397, in 2006, it rose to 0.496.[10] There is no sound and credible estimate to China's Gini coefficient in people's income distribution and the conclusions are quite different. The estimated value is between 0.39 and 0.55. But most researchers think the 0.45 is a realistic one to China's current income distribution Gini coefficient. Anyway, China's Gini coefficient now has exceeded a reasonable margin.

Compared to India, the seriousness of the disparity in income distribution in China is underestimated and covered up because of China's specific conditions. These special features refer to the income gap between the regions and between the urban and rural areas. Compare India with China, in fact, and China's degree of polarization between the rich and the poor is the same as that of India. People think that the gap between the rich and poor is larger in India for it exists in the same area, in the same city, but it may exist in any place. While in China, the gap is between different regions, between the urban and rural areas.

Second, the reform of enterprises and property is extremely difficult. In recent years, China's state-owned enterprise reform has been questioned a lot because of assets loss and the appearance of numerous laid-off workers in the property right reform. In 2006, the change in the layout of state-owned property laid waste to the reform of the enterprises. To a large extent, it dashed expectations to increase employment and fair income distribution by way of developing state-owned enterprises. More importantly, on one hand, state-owned enterprises are in a monopoly position and participate in the competition unequally, while, on the other hand, foreign direct investment pours in with the opening policy. China's domestic organizations and the private sector feel that it is very difficult to grow in a landscape of state-owned enterprises and transnational corporations. With the outbreak of the 2008 global financial crisis, the Chinese government strengthened the macro-economic control and regulation, a new round of "state-owned enterprises in privately-owned businesses" emerged, and China's non-governmental and private businesses become even worse.

At present, China must face the challenge on how to deepen the property right reform and how to solve the worsening of the divide between rich and poor. China's rural reform has continued to progress and the biggest problem is that the land property right cannot be transferred. It is the case with the state-owned enterprises. The reform of distinct property rights is not yet complete. In addition, China's capital survives, despite repeated prohibition and the short-sighted behavior in the private business, which, without exception, relates to the inadequacy of the property rights reform.[11]

The privatization of state-owned enterprises of India has proven effective, yet the reform in the state-owned enterprises is not complete. The public enterprise only sold some shares, and shutting or selling the loss-making state-run enterprises lacks adequate means and methods. India's public enterprises have undergone reform over 20 years, but there is still a substantial loss, and the effectiveness is low. It is the bottleneck in India's economic development.[12]

Third, the construction of the infrastructure lags behind, the investment environment is not satisfied, and this has a negative effect on the pace of economic development. China's FDI had been top in the world but, even so, China's investment environment needs constant improvement. Compared with China, India needs to improve the investment environment. The main aspects: 1) Inefficiency. The Indian government sector is low in efficiency. The World Bank report shows that the setting-up of an enterprise in India usually requires 89 days, while in China, it requires just 41 days. India's labor productivity is very low. Although the average wage is 25% lower than that of China, yet the output per worker is 50% lower. 2) Energy shortage. India's power infrastructure is primitive; the average rate of the electricity shortage is over 10%, and there is even no nationwide 24-hour power supply system, which seriously affect the profitability of enterprises. Shortage in capital makes India unable to purchase a large quantity of imported oil in the short term, or to build more nuclear power stations, which holds back the increase of investment in India. 3) Strict labor laws. India is probably the only country where dismissing employees must be approved by the State Government, the closing down or "shutting off" of the enterprises is strictly controlled, which objectively may restrict the enterprise investment initiative.

Many economists believe that the insufficiency in India's infrastructure can be redeemed, but the problems in China's system and other "soft" powers will be difficult to overcome. Therefore, in the long run, the developing potential of India is stronger than China. For this point of view, some of China's economists, such as Hua Min from Fudan University, do not agree. He thinks that although the economic growth in developing countries often faces a double constraint, there are both soft restrictions, such as system and technology, and rigid constraints, such as infrastructure. But the key to the problem is that in these two different kinds of constraint factors, one should try to find out what kind of constraint will constitute the greater obstacle to economic development. The 2005 World

Development Report from the World Bank showed through surveys and studies that among various constraints to economic growth in developing countries, the first factor is not system, technical, financial, or some other soft elements, but the infrastructure that is usually considered unimportant. Therefore, Hua Min believes that the reason is that the infrastructure is rigid. It is impossible to obtain the infrastructure from the outside world but the technology can be introduced and the system can be adopted, and both can be improved through "learning by doing." That is the reason why China, even with more soft restrictions than India, develops faster.[13]

Fourth, the imbalance of economic development structure may easily lead to "growth" poverty. China's economic development pattern depends on investment and net exports to promote economic growth. This model, in the historical circumstances, is in agreement with China's national development. But in today's new international and domestic economic situation, China's domestic consumption is under a continuous downturn, while too much investment and exports may cause an imbalance in the economic and social development. Especially since 2008, due to the global financial crisis, China's exports have fallen sharply; China's structural economic imbalance is more and more evident. As the consumption rate is low, China can only rely on investment growth to make up the exports, so the investment spurs economic growth. And because of the obvious extension of China's investment and the rough growth mode in the investment itself, this leads to the insufficient internal impetus in economic growth and therefore seriously affects sustainable economic development.

Table 1.3 China: Contribution share and contribution of the three components of GDP to the growth of GDP

Year	Final consumption expenditure		Gross capital formation		Net exports of goods and services	
	Contribution share (%)	Contribution (Percentage points)	Contribution share (%)	Contribution (Percentage points)	Contribution share (%)	Contribution (Percentage points)
1978	39.4	4.6	66.0	7.7	–5.4	–0.6
1979	87.3	6.6	15.4	1.2	–2.7	–0.2
1980	71.8	5.6	26.5	2.1	1.8	0.1
1981	93.4	4.9	–4.3	–0.2	10.9	0.5
1982	64.7	5.9	23.8	2.2	11.5	1.0
1983	74.1	8.1	40.4	4.4	–14.5	–1.6
1984	69.3	10.5	40.5	6.2	–9.8	–1.5

(Cont'd)

Year	Final consumption expenditure		Gross capital formation		Net exports of goods and services	
	Contribution share (%)	Contribution (Percentage points)	Contribution share (%)	Contribution (Percentage points)	Contribution share (%)	Contribution (Percentage points)
1985	85.5	11.5	80.9	10.9	–66.4	–8.9
1986	45.0	4.0	23.2	2.0	31.8	2.8
1987	50.3	5.8	23.5	2.7	26.2	3.1
1988	49.6	5.6	39.4	4.5	11.0	1.2
1989	39.6	1.6	16.4	0.7	44.0	1.8
1990	47.8	1.8	1.8	0.1	50.4	1.9
1991	65.1	6.0	24.3	2.2	10.6	1.0
1992	72.5	10.3	34.2	4.9	–6.8	–1.0
1993	59.5	8.3	78.6	11.0	–38.1	–5.3
1994	30.2	4.0	43.8	5.7	26.0	3.4
1995	44.7	4.9	55.0	6.0	0.3	—
1996	60.1	6.0	34.3	3.4	5.6	0.6
1997	37.0	3.4	18.6	1.7	44.4	4.2
1998	57.1	4.4	26.4	2.1	16.5	1.3
1999	74.7	5.7	23.7	1.8	1.6	0.1
2000	65.1	5.5	22.4	1.9	12.5	1.0
2001	50.0	4.1	50.1	4.2	–0.1	—
2002	43.6	4.0	48.8	4.4	7.6	0.7
2003	35.3	3.5	63.7	6.4	1.0	0.1
2004	38.7	3.9	55.3	5.6	6.0	0.6
2005	38.2	4.0	37.7	3.9	24.1	2.5
2006	38.7	4.5	42.0	4.9	19.3	2.2
2007	39.4	4.7	40.9	4.9	19.7	2.3

Notes: 1. Three components of GDP by expenditure approach are final consumption expenditure, gross capital formation, and net exports of goods and services.

2. Contribution share of the three components to the increase of the GDP refers to the proportion of the increment of each component of GDP by expenditure approach to the increment of GDP.

3. Contribution of the three components to GDP growth refers to the growth rate of GDP multiplied by the contribution share of the three components.

4. Data in value terms in this table are calculated at constant prices.

Source: *Chinese Statistical Yearbook* over the years.

Furthermore, we will find that the lower share of domestic consumption in China in recent years is responsible for insufficient domestic demand in China, slow improvement in national welfare, and the polarization between the rich and the poor. And, if the private consumption needs cannot be realized for a long time, even though the quantity of the economy increases, people's living standards may decline in the meantime. This is known as the "growing poverty" trap.

Summary of the Economic Reform and Development between the Two Countries

Many people tend to evaluate China's and India's economic reforms and development modes. In fact, the evaluation of a country's economic reform and development pattern is to judge whether this mode is adaptable to their national conditions. China and India have different opportunities to promote their businesses and the entire national economy to achieve prosperity and development, but the key is to grasp the chance to develop.

In view of the effectiveness of economic reform and development in China and India, the two countries, after a long period of trying, under the premise of maintaining political stability, have each found ways suitable to national status to promote the economic development according to the specific historical conditions. Both China and India will make full use of their own advantages and the opportunities in the global economic development, lose no time in developing their economies, and promote the growth of the entire national economy. "All roads lead to Rome," as they say, although the mode of the development in the two countries is quite different, yet the achievements are greatly beneficial to the world.

China's economic reform and development mode is largely based on high-savings, high-investment (including a large number of international capital flows), high export, and the construction of basic infrastructure. To promote a strong manufacturing sector in the industrialization process is a Chinese developing pattern combined with domestic demand and foreign trade development. While India's development mode is characterized by establishing a perfect capital market and banking system to solve investment sources by stimulating domestic demand and domestic investment to promote the economy to increase their national income as a way of increasing domestic demand and encouraging the development of the high-tech industry. In this way, the Indian economy may not rely on the international market too much and it is able to resist the shocks of external risks.

After in-depth analysis, we find that the significant and decisive factor of China's and India's future economic development lies in whether the traditional system can make timely adaptation to modernization, as well as whether the two economies in the world economic globalization process can apply advantages and avoid disadvantages. There are unfavorable conditions in the development of the two countries, of which, the problems in institutions and policies are relatively easy to overcome, but it is hard to resolve some inherent social traditions that are against modernization within a short period of time. For China, to improve the future system is to remove the system and mechanism that are incompatible with the market economy in order to promote political civilization and to realize the target of governing the country by law.

The impact of world economic integration is a common problem to the future development of China and India alike. Both China and India are developing countries. During the long period of economic development, they need an external modification of modernization to change their traditional economy and make up for the shortage of domestic modernization factors. India's opening to the outside world is not as complete as China, but the level of internationalization of Indian companies is very high, with a number of local enterprises bearing relatively strong international competition. China's opening success is mainly reflected in the import and export of merchandise trade as well as large-scale overseas investment. India needs to expand opening up under the premise of maintaining a competitive advantage in the local community and gradually increase the foreign trade and attract more foreign investment. China needs to expand domestic demand and to improve the quality of opening up on the basis of the quantity scale.

Notes

1. Qin Hui, "Visions and long-term considerations: A comparison of the economic development of China and India," *Magazine of Humanities* (2005).
2. J.N. Mongia, *India's Economic Development Strategies 1951–2000 A.D.* (New Delhi: Allied Publishers), 112.
3. Jiang Zemin, *The Report on the Fifteenth National People's Congress of the Communist Party of China* (Beijing: People's Publishing House, Sep. 12, 1997).
4. The world's top 500 enterprises released by *Fortune Magazine* of the U.S. in 2001.
5. The figures are based upon the author's own calculations according to the original data from the *China Statistical Yearbook*.
6. The figures are upon the author's own calculations according to the original data from the *China Statistical Yearbook*.
7. India's service sector generally can be divided into two categories: The modern services and traditional services. Modern service industries, including telecommunications, finance, business, education, health, etc.; traditional service industries, including retail, transportation, community, and family services.
8. The three industries are agriculture, industry and service sector, corresponding to China's primary industry, secondary industry, and tertiary industry.
9. Datt Ruddar, *Indian Economy* (New Delhi: Chand (S.) & Co Ltd, 1996), 10.
10. "The income of the highest is 33 times [that] of the lowest, [and] high hopes are on the third distribution," *China Economic Weekly*, Jun. 2006.
11. Hua Min, "A comparison of economic development patterns of China and India: Similar principles and different methods," *Journal of Fudan University* (Social Science Edition), vol.6 (2006).
12. During 1994–1995 among India's 240 central government enterprises, 109 ones suffered loss. The management of the 700 state-level enterprises was even worse. During the year of 1996–1997, the capital gains of the state power business averaged –13.3%.
13. Refer to Hua Min, 2006.

References

Babu, D. Shyam. 2003. *Observer Statistical Handbook: India 2003*. New Delhi: Rupa Company.

Hua Min. 2006. "A Comparison of Economic Development Patterns of China and India: Similar Principles and Different Methods." *Journal of Fudan University* (Social Science Edition) 6.

Huang Yasheng, and Tarun Khanna. 2003. "Can India Overtake China?" *Foreign Policy*, Jul.-Aug.

Pant, K. C. 2003. *India Development Scenario*. New Delhi: Academic Foundation.

Qin Hui. 2005. "Visions and Long-Term Considerations: A Comparison of the Economic Development of China and India." *Magazine of Humanities* 5.

Shen Kaiyan, and Quan Heng. 2008. *A Comparative Study of the Economic Development Mode: A Comparison of the Economic Development of China and India*. Shanghai: Shanghai Academy of Social Sciences Press.

Shen Kaiyan, and Sheng Wei. 2009. "China and India: Analysis and Thoughts on Economic Reforms and Developments." *Guangdong Social Sciences* 1.

Sun Peijun. 2007. *Study on Economic Development of China and India*. Beijing: Economic Management Publishing House.

Sun Shihai. 1998. "Comparison of the Economic Reforms between China and India." *South Asian Studies* 1.

Wang Haiguang. 2000. "Mode and Strategy: Historical Reflections on China's Modernization Development Path." *Lingnan Journal of Chinese Studies* 3.

Wang Liqian. 2006. "Economic Reform of India and a Comparison of the Economic Reforms between China and India." *Journal of Henan College of Financial Management Cadres* 1.

Whang Dehua, and Wu Yang. 2003. *Dragon and Elephant: A Comparison of the Rise of China and India in the 21st Century*. Shanghai: Shanghai Academy of Social Sciences Press.

Zuo Xuejin. 2007. *Dragon's Dance with the Elephant*. Shanghai: Shanghai Academy of Social Sciences Press.

Yue Zhanren. 1997. "The Economic Development of India after Independence." *Historical Research* 5.

2

Chapter

The Prospect of China-India Cooperation and the Special Function of Hong Kong

Liu Jian

The relationship between China and India is one of China's most important foreign relationships. This is not only because the two countries are geologically close to each other, nor because both are ancient civilized countries with long histories, but because they are both the biggest developing countries in the world, whose populations and economies are similar to each other. Furthermore, they are rising in the age of globalization, and will play more and more important roles in the world in the twenty-first century. Due to Hong Kong's geographical and historical advantages, and other favorable factors, Hong Kong will play a positive role in Sino-India cooperation and, in turn, also benefit from this kind of cooperation.

The History of China-India Relations

India was known to the Chinese people no later than the late Han Dynasty. The contact between China and the Western Regions [typically defined as Central Asia] was the beginning of the cultural exchanges between China and the outside world. Zhang Qian, as an ambassador of the Han Dynasty, went to the Western Regions at the order of Emperor Wudi in the Han Dynasty for the very first time in 138 BC. On the way, he was imprisoned by the Huns. After struggling to escape from the Huns, he went to Da Yuan and other Central Asian countries. In 126 BC, he returned back with exciting tales of Sindhu, now called India.[1] Zhang Qian's exploration extended the Chinese people's knowledge of geography and enlarged their horizons.

In the subsequent 2,000 years of exchanges between China and India, Buddhism has become the bond which connects the two countries. After Buddhism was introduced to China, it began the long process of localization, and then it was gradually integrated into mainstream Chinese culture. Buddhist culture, together with local Confucianism culture and Taoist culture, had become a necessary part of traditional Chinese culture.

A late scholar on India, Ji Xianlin once observed, "Since Buddhism was introduced to China, it has exerted a deep and profound influence on China. Its unprecedented influence is widely known to all and covers various fields in China, such as philosophy, religion, literature, language, music, painting, architecture, sculpture, customs, [etc.]...It is a fact that Buddhism has influenced Chinese people's faith."[2] In the ancient times, especially in the flourishing period, the influence of Buddhism upon China was expressed both in the spiritual civilization and the material civilization.

Since Buddhism was introduced to China in the East Han Dynasty, it has gradually been accepted by the rulers and most Chinese. "In this process, Buddhism also constantly adapts to the Chinese culture and eventually becomes a part of Chinese culture."[3] From a philosophical perspective, Buddhism's grand thinking on time and space has enlarged Chinese horizons towards the world and the universe as a whole. After confirming the existence of India and realizing that Buddhism represents a great civilization, some insightful people doubted whether China was the center of the world. During the Three Kingdoms period, a famous Confucian, as well as a Buddhist scholar, Mouzi expressed his ideas in his book *Master Mou's Treatise Dispelling Doubts*, saying that "It is said that 'The North Star is the center of the sky, but it is considered to be in the north of the sky in people's view.'[4] From this perspective, Han territory may not be the center of the whole world."[5] Therefore, Mouzi recognized that it was groundless to divide the world into *Yi* [barbarians in the eastern China], *Di* [ethical groups lived in northern China], and *Huaxia* [China]. Amartya Sen, after reading the relevant literature, highly appreciated this breakthrough in the Chinese people's understanding of this ideology: "One of the positive contributions made by Buddhism in China is to reach a consensus, that is, to some extent, [that] the Chinese people must explore outside. In fact, Buddhism not only implies that beyond China also exists the source of wisdom, but [it] also leads to a tendency for many Chinese scholars to go abroad, especially to India, to gain an enlightenment and understanding of Buddhism. In addition, visitors returning from India bring back [stories] about the wonderful things they have seen in India, which makes it difficult for people to totally hold the view of [the] China-centered world civilization."[6]

Since Buddhism was introduced to China, the ancient Chinese monks had been looking for truth from the West, as the West had a far-reaching and extensive impact on Chinese culture. Buddhism not only expanded the Chinese people's concepts of space and time, enabling Chinese people to understand the geography, history, and customs of the countries in South and Southeast Asia, but it also transmitted China's brilliant material and spiritual civilization to outsiders. Buddhism has greatly enriched the culture of China and it "effectively defines Asia as a unique space to explore," and, in the long-term, "links Asia in a unique way."[7]

In essence, Buddhism is a moderate religion. No war in the world has been caused by Buddhism. The basic doctrine of Buddhism encourages followers to be free of greed, anger, and devoted to doing good works. The core doctrine of Indian Buddhism is the "Eightfold Path," which is fully accepted by Chinese Buddhism, in particular, the Zhengye Doctrine has had a profound impact.

For example, the concept concerning "no harm" is popular. It requires people to be merciful and not do any harm to living beings, which is of great benefit for keeping one's inner peace, establishing a harmonious relationship between humans and even between man and nature. Over the years, Buddhism has been playing its part in maintaining the Chinese nation as a peace-loving nation.

In the course of the development for thousands of years, India and China have undergone many similar stages. For example, Sakyamuni founded Buddhism in India, Confucius founded Confucianism in China; a different heterodoxy existed in India when Buddhism was founded, whereas in China, different schools of thought flourished in the Spring and Autumn Period. Soon after Ashoka unified India, Emperor Qin started the unification of China. The Gupta Dynasty in Indian history and the Tang Dynasty in Chinese history were once the golden ages when both of these two dynasties in their own respective histories had undergone blossoming periods in politics, economy, literature, arts, science, technology, etc. India's Mughal Empire and the Qing Dynasty in China contributed half of the world's total economy in their heyday. In the late 17th century or early 18th century, India was at the peak of the Mughal Empire and China was in the flourishing period ruled by Emperor Kangxi and Qianlong. At that time, India had a population of 165 million, the world's largest economy, while China had a population of 138 million, the world's second largest economy. It was not until modern times that the two ancient civilizations gradually declined.

In the early 13th century when the funds for Buddhism in India were unavailable, communications between China and India gradually reduced. Since Zheng He voyaged to the Atlantic Ocean in the Ming Dynasty, the cultural exchanges between the two countries almost completely ceased. In the mid-19th century, the British invaded India, which aroused some patriotic citizens' reflection on the civilization of India and the Indian society; at the same time, the British invasion into China also caused loyal citizens to reflect on Chinese culture and Chinese society. China was reduced to a vulnerable country from an ancient civilization with a great history of over 2,000 years. What exactly caused such a great decline in China? How could China restore its former glory? New ideas to the study of Western civilization emerged. Lin Zexu organized some scholars to compile the *Law of Nations* and *Gazetter of the Four Continents* in order to understand the social system of Western countries and their basic national conditions. Translation of Western books, since then, has been an important way for Chinese people to learn the ideology of the West.

At the request of Lin Zexu, Wei Yuan, a great thinker and historian, compiled *Haiguo Tuzhi* (*An Illustrated Gazette of Overseas States*) by reference to *Gazetter of the Four Continents*. In the preface of *An Illustrated Gazette of Overseas States*, he wrote, "What is this book about? It is on how to fight against foreign countries, on how to treat foreign countries, on how to curb foreign countries by learning strong points from them." China never rejected positive outside cultural influences in its flourishing period. However, a declining dynasty tended to be conservative and rigid in terms of ideology, therefore, it was difficult for such a dynasty to make wise decisions. The feudal rulers always wrongly stressed "the Invariable Heaven, and the Invariable Tao" and they always insisted that "remaining unchanged will deal with all possible changes." Therefore, the idea proposed by Wei Yuan to "curb foreign countries by learning strong points from them" was really an advanced and valuable idea at that time. He advocated that the Chinese should equip themselves with advanced Western science and technology and build up Chinese military strength and wealth. After the publication of *An Illustrated Gazette of Overseas States*, many other books introducing the world to readers were published subsequently, such as Yao Ying's *Kang Qiu's Log* and *Introduction to Coastal Nations*. These books played a positive role in guiding the Chinese to have a correct understanding of the outside world (for example, India) and reflect the Chinese themselves.

More than 10 books published in China in the 19th century involved information about India in some chapters, such as *An Illustrated Gazette of Overseas States*, *Haiguo Jianwen Lu* (*Records of Sights and Sounds of Overseas States*) written by Chen Lunjiong, and *Records of Seas* written by Xie Qinggao. Through these books, the Chinese people realized that India had been completely conquered by the British. These authors generally showed sympathy to India, and meanwhile, they warned the Chinese to guard against the invasion of Western powers, and avoid making the same mistakes as India. A beautiful vision of a paradise world in India gradually faded away in the eyes of the Chinese people. With the degeneration of India, and along with the advanced thoughts of learning from the West to build up the East, the Chinese people began to turn their eyes and interest to the modern West, as well as Japan. The same is true with India. In modern times, they directed their attention to America and Europe, especially England. Two declining nations showed a tendency of alienation and an absence of mutual communications or understanding. This tendency lasted until the modern era.

Misreading Sino-India Relations in the Early 20th Century

In the early 20th century, Chinese people showed their sympathy for, and misreading of, India. Kang Youwei and Liang Qichao, leaders of the Reform Movement of 1898, famous scholar Zhang Binglin, Sun Yat-sen, and others were keen on Indian culture, and very concerned about the development of India. They showed their objective and friendly attitude towards Indian culture. While Zhang Binglin studied in Japan, he even got acquainted with revolutionary Indian friends, advocating the coalition between China and India, or the establishment of an alliance. He always reported on the Indian independence movement through the influential newspaper *Min Bao*, showing his support for the movement. However, Lu Xun and Chen Duxiu had a misreading of India, which was mainly reflected in their attitude towards the great Indian poet Rabindranath Tagore.

Lu Xun showed his great respect for ancient Indian literature. However, he was pessimistic about India in its modern times, considering that the Indian civilization had completely declined, without any hope of survival. In 1908, he published an essay titled *On the Poetic Power of the Satanical School*, in which, he expressed that "the fate of the national people will end up in misery if their own country is subject to another powerful country; the civilized history will be its past glory if reading its history makes you feel a sense of depression and arouses your anger. All declining countries that have a glorious past have undergone such a process. India is just such a typical case... Its national people are despised by the other country and are exiled anywhere, homeless." Obviously, in Lu Xun's view, the declined India in modern times became the "Shadow State" and was reduced to a British colony. India actually was only a failed state in name, and it was no longer a country where many great writers and works were known worldwide. In fact, history has repeatedly shown that the civilization of Indian has a regenerative capacity.

In September 1921, in his translator's postscript for *Narrow Cage*, Lu Xun again expressed his anger in words to attack India and condemn the Indian poet Rabindranath Tagore for the first time. In the book, Lu Xun criticized Indian people for their no bad feeling for not working hard, but being outraged over their customs Sati [the self-immolation of a widow on her husband's funeral pyre] being banned. Lu Xun also faulted Tagore's support for barbaric custom of Sati.

However, India had no shortage of enlightened people who opposed such barbaric customs. Many emperors in the Mughal Dynasty even prohibited Sati. In modern times, Roma Mo Luo, a pioneer in the Bangladesh Renaissance, launched the Hindu reform movement against the system of Sati in 1818. In 1829, the British Indian government issued a decree, formally abolishing this system. Tagore, as the best product and the greatest representative of the Bangladesh Renaissance, in fact, strongly opposed the Sati system.

In 1924, at the invitation of Liang Qichao, Tagore paid a visit to China. In general, the two-month visit was very successful and was widely popular with Chinese scholars in the literary field, but some dissenting voices were also heard. Some radical students even went to the venue to throw leaflets against Tagore who made positive comments on traditional Chinese culture and oriental culture that they denied completely. Some people who had appreciated Tagore in their early years, such as Chen Duxiu, also made a strong and unreasonable criticism of him.

Lu Xun, in his lectures and articles, mentioned Tagore several times, but had no positive comments. The reasons for this are complex. However, one of the most important reasons seems to be that Lu Xun had contempt for India, which was reduced to a "Shadow State" and therefore he naturally showed spontaneous contempt for Tagore who came from that very Shadow State. Luxun and Tagore were the greatest writers of the 20th century in China and India, respectively. But Lu Xun's prejudice against Tagore showed that the communication of different civilizations demanded ceaseless efforts.

Even today, a lack of an in-depth understanding between these two countries exists, and even in the academic field Contempt for each other also exists. Taking tourism as an example, the number of Chinese visitors to India seems smaller compared with the number of tourists going to other countries. This shows that China's middle class is not familiar with India and that the country cannot arouse their interest. According to related posts and comments on the Internet, Chinese citizens are not concerned about the rise of India and even, from time to time, show an air of contempt. Similarly, according to data from Pew's *Global Attitudes Survey*, the Indian public also shows the negative attitude towards the rise of China. Their favorable impression of China decreased from nearly 60% in 2005 to less than 30% in 2011.[8]

Realistic Relations: Competition and Cooperation

The national conditions in India and China have a lot in common. In the late 20th century, China and India promoted economic reform successively, and rose at the same time. In addition, there are obvious similarities in their basic national conditions both in their population and development.

The history of friendly exchanges between China and India lasted for about 2,000 years. However, Sino-India relations have also undergone ups and downs. The two countries jointly proposed the Five Principles of Peaceful Coexistence in the 1950s, but in the 1960s, conflict broke out due to border disputes. In the late 1970s, after a long period of estrangement, bilateral relations gradually returned to normal. From December 19 to 23, 1988, Indian Prime Minister Rajiv Gandhi paid an official visit to China. This was the first official visit of an Indian Prime Minister to China since 34 years earlier when the first Indian Prime Minister Jawaharlal Nehru visited China in 1954. In a meeting with Rajiv, Deng Xiaoping pointed out that, "China and India shoulder a common responsibility to mankind, that is, to take advantage of the existing favorable and peaceful international environment to develop ourselves...It cannot be called an Asian Century without the development of China and India. It can only be called a real Asia-Pacific century or Asian century when China, India, and other neighboring countries have become powerful...We both need to adjust our bilateral relations with our neighboring countries."[9] Since then, bilateral relations between China and India have begun to improve rapidly. Today, China's population reaches 1.3 billion, whereas India's reaches 1.2 billion, both accounting for nearly one third of the world's population. The development of normal relations and cooperation between these two rising powerful countries is absolutely of great significance.

Since the 1990s, the frequent high-level exchanges between these two countries promoted the development of Sino-India relations in the new historical conditions. In September 1993, China and India signed the *Agreement on the Maintenance of Peace and Tranquility along the Line of Actual Control in the China-India Border Areas*. From November 28 to December 1, 1996, China and India established a constructive and cooperative partnership in order to face the twenty-first century on the basis of the Five Principles of Peaceful Coexistence. The two countries also signed the *Agreement on Confidence-Building Measures in the Military Field along the Line of Actual Control in the China-India Border Areas* and other important documents.

With the advent of the new century, the high-level leaders of both countries took many measures to enhance mutual trust and dispel doubts in order to establish a constructive and cooperative partnership, with which to face the twenty-first century. On June 23, 2003, Indian Prime Minister Atal Bihari Vajpayee and Chinese Premier Wen Jiabao signed the *Declaration on Principles for Relations and Comprehensive Cooperation between the People's Republic of China and the*

Republic of India in Beijing. Subsequently, the relevant departments of the two countries also signed nine government-level cooperation documents, covering education, science and technology, culture, jurisdiction, and other aspects. This was a significant event in the history of Sino-India relations, marking a new era of comprehensive cooperation between the two countries. The Declaration serves as a guiding document, laying the legal basis for guiding the two countries to have all-round cooperation in various fields.

The China-India border issue has long been affecting the bilateral relations. It seems that, in the short term, this problem cannot be completely solved. The two countries have decided to maintain the border status and actively carried out comprehensive cooperation in other fields while striving for a delineation of boundaries as early as possible, which reflects that they are addressing the issue under a flexible and pragmatic principle. History has shown that China and India, as two vast neighboring countries, would benefit each other when they agree, but they would also harm each other when they disagree. The modernization of both countries requires mutual communication and cooperation in a peaceful international environment, rather than a hostile and vicious competition. Of course, it is true that competition exists between the two countries in the economic field, but they are more complementary. The trade volume between the two countries has always been increasing steadily

From April 9 to 12, 2005, the Chinese Premier Wen Jiabao paid an official visit to India. China and India announced the establishment of a strategic and cooperative partnership oriented towards peace and prosperity. Special representatives on the Sino-India border issue signed the *Agreement between the Government of the Republic of India and the Government of the People's Republic of China on the Political Parameters and Guiding Principles for the Settlement of the India-China Boundary Question*. Since then, the strategic, political, and economic relations of both countries have thus been pushed to a new level.

The comprehensive recovery of both China and India will have a significant influence on the development of the world economy, the political landscape, and culture. The long-term relationship between the two countries and their cooperation in important areas, of course, not only play key roles in their rise as powers, but also closely affect their relationships with their neighboring countries and regions. At present, Sino-India relations are in a sound and stable period in history, forming a competitive and cooperative relationship that is on a legal basis. The bilateral trade volume increased from less than USD300 million in 1991 to USD61.7 billion in 2010. The Prime Ministers of the two countries published a joint communique in New Delhi on December 16, 2010, determining to establish a strategic and economic dialogue mechanism and setting a goal of reaching USD100 billion for the bilateral trade volume in 2015. They have also made considerable progress in cooperation between the two countries in tourism, science and technology, education, culture, politics, military issues, and other fields. From a strategic perspective, the cooperation between the two countries is in the fundamental interests of the two peoples.

However, from the perspective of the development of China-India relations in recent years, competition exists in terms of the Chinese model and the Indian model in an objective manner. As the pain of the border war of 1962 still lingers, the border issue has not been solved in the long-term; some subtle frictions and discords have sprung up in recent years. Frankly speaking, the mutual political trust between the two countries is still unstable, and the nationalism existing in some private organizations is constantly attempting to interfere with the normal development of the bilateral relations.

Between China and India, however, there are many historical and realistic problems and fierce competition, such as a certain tension on the energy issues and water issues between the two countries. After all, sense gains the upper hand while the possibility of conflict is small. Dr. George Yeo, the Foreign Minister of Singapore, delivered a keynote speech in a meeting in Calcutta in December 2010 for commemorating the 150th birth anniversary of Rabindranath Tagore, which was titled "Realizing the Vision of Tagore, and Promoting the Friendly Relations between India and China."

Dr. Yeo asserted that war and peace in Asia would depend on the development trend of the relations between India and China in the coming years. Mutual pursuit of a better life would be an irresistible trend because of this reason. He said that he was optimistic about the normal development of Sino-India relations. I appreciate and agree with his ideas. Competition is bound to exist in the Sino-India relationship in the future, but cooperation is the mainstream goal, after all. Although CHINDIA between China and India may not become a reality in the short term.

Unique Position and Function of Hong Kong in the Sino-India Cooperation

Due to its unique geographical and historical conditions, Hong Kong will play a unique role in China-India cooperation.

Hong Kong was once a bridge connecting India and China in history. In 1916, Tagore visited Japan via Hong Kong. On the pier, he saw some hard-working Chinese workers, from whom he sensed the great strength of the Chinese nation. He wrote, "Having seen the strength, skills, and joy revealed in their working, I realized what kind of force was beneath this great nation. Who can stop the full exercise of the power when such a huge force was equipped with modern tools and science?" Tagore was full of confidence for the Chinese people and the future of China. He sincerely wished that China would awaken from sleepiness to become prosperous and strong. His prophecy showed his goodwill, but also revealed his wisdom and vision. Today, the great prophecy of Tagore on the rise of China is becoming a reality.

Hong Kong has been an important transition station between China and India. Its advantages lie in its advanced jurisdiction, finance, education, tourism, trade, service, and other aspects, which are highly developed and mature, and enjoy a sound reputation in China and India. Hong Kong is full of various professional talents who are very dedicated to work. In addition, local people in Hong Kong have an edge on language as they are good at English and can speak Mandarin as well. Therefore, in Hong Kong, both Mandarin and English are acceptable, without communication problems for mainland Chinese as well as the Indians. Geographically, Hong Kong is convenient for both Mainland China and India. The Indians can enjoy a two-week visa-free treatment when they travel to Hong Kong, whereas the procedures for Mainland Chinese to visit Hong Kong are also relatively simple. Because of these advantages, Hong Kong can fully play its role of establishing a bridge in Sino-India cooperation. I'd like to mention a few points in this regard.

First of all, like Singapore, Hong Kong is qualified to become a more important center of international conferences and academic activities. Those well-known universities in Hong Kong, including Hong Kong Baptist University, can play a greater role in organizing international academic conferences so that Hong Kong can become an important platform for exchanges among international scholars from China, India, and other countries. Dialogues, discussions, and even negotiations concerning Sino-India cooperation in various fields can be held in Hong Kong. The city is not only a financial and trading center, but it may also become an important and influential international academic center. In this way, it will be more attractive for students and scholars in mainland China and India, and meanwhile, it can continue to foster its own educational and academic resources.

Second, Hong Kong has a great potential in promoting tourism in China and India. China and India are abundant in tourist resources. Due to the steady development of India in modern society, a large number of ancient cultural heritage sites across the country have not been seriously damaged. Many Western tourists are fascinated by Indian culture, thus the prospects for the development of the tourism market in India are bright. The average stay for foreign tourists in India lasts 26 days, much longer than in many other Asian countries. This official statistic shows that the duration is six times longer than in Singapore (4.2 days). As early as 2006, the consumption of foreign tourists per capita in India reached USD1,470, almost twice the global average of USD844. The president of the National Committee of Tourism in India, Lavi Budalinmu once said, if India and China exchanged their tourists, accounting for only 2–3% of the population of each country, to the counterpart, either of them would have had about 20 to 30 million tourists because of their large populations. This can be completely achieved under the trend of tourism development. In the future, China and India will have a lot of cooperation in the development of tourism. However, due to the prejudice and misunderstanding of the majority of the two peoples, though the number of Chinese tourists to India has increased to more than 100,000 every year, the equivalent is only about one fifth of the number of Indian tourists to China. If Hong Kong can exercise its role in promoting the Sino-India cooperation in tourism, making itself a portal for Indian tourists to come in and out of Mainland China, it will be beneficial for Hong Kong's tourism and its related industries.

Third, Hong Kong can play many other roles in promoting the Sino-India cultural exchange. As a film industry base with an international influence, Hong Kong has the capacity to provide professionals for Indian and Chinese movies and other cultural industries. China and India have undertaken close exchanges in the film industry. For decades, India's film industry has made tremendous progress and boasted a considerable audience. And it has established its influence in the international arena. However, it seems that Chinese film-makers seldom understand and appreciate Indian films, including those with major international influence.

In addition, the publishing and sales industries in Hong Kong can cooperate with India as well. At least, Hong Kong can introduce some important English original materials from some well-known publishers such as Oxford University Press. These materials can serve as a window for the mainland tourists or scholars to Hong Kong to learn about India.

In short, China and India will become the top economic powers in the world in the middle of this century, and their international political and cultural status will be greatly improved. Sino-Indian cooperation is the inevitable trend in the development of history, and Hong Kong can put its own advantage into full play to better promote the cooperation between China and India. This will not only benefit China and India, but also will be favorable for Hong Kong's prosperity and development.

Notes

1. "Dayuan biography," Vol. I, II, and III of *Historical Records.*
2. *The Chinese Academic Dictionary of Religious Studies in 20th Century: Preface I*, ed. Ren Jiyu (Fuzhou: Fujian Education Press, 2002), 2.
3. Xue Keqiao, *Buddhism and Chinese Culture* (Beijing: Kunlun Publishing House, 2006), 2.
4. The source of the quotation following "It is said that" is unknown.
5. *Buddhism History in China* , Vol. I, ed. Ren Jiyu, (Beijing: China Social Sciences Press, 1981), 223.
6. Amartya Sen, *The Argumentative Indian: Writings on Indian History, Culture and Identity*, trans. Liu Jian (Shanghai: Shanghai Joint Publishing, 2007), 131.
7. "Buddhism: Drawing on Asian history and culture," *India Today*, comp. The Indian Embassy in China, vol. 112 (Jun. 2011):12–13.
8. Zheng Bin, and Xu Shaomin, "Cognitive of India on the rise of China," *Study on South Asia*, vol. 4 (2011):2.
9. *Selected Works of Deng Xiaoping*, vol. III (Beijing: People's Publishing House, 1993), 281–283.

3

Chapter

Economic Growth and Regional Disparities in India: Are the Challenges the Same or Different Compared to China?[1]

Basudeb Chaudhuri

Velayoudom Marimoutou

The Indian Context

A speech by Professor Jagdish Bhagwati on economic reforms in India, made to the Indian Parliament in December 2010, sparked a considerable debate in India on how to sequence policies in order to achieve economic growth and reduce poverty. In a nutshell, one can present the debate in a slightly condensed way. There were those who argued that it is only growth-oriented policies that can generate the tax revenue necessary to finance social infrastructure such as health and education. Hence growth should have first priority over social development. Others argued that a lack of investment in education, health, and social infrastructure ensured that poor people stayed poor, and an overemphasis on growth reduced the impact that the state could have had in reducing endemic poverty, by enabling people to take charge of their own lives and acquire social and economic mobility. India's experience could thus be contrasted with Japan, South Korea, and eventually that of China, where a greater investment in human resources had taken place over time, albeit in very different historical circumstances in these three countries, and that growth had come from outward-looking policies and state-led capitalism.

Indian planning, since its inception, was concerned with the idea of balanced growth, an idea that came naturally from the Solovian framework that economies can reach a balanced growth path that optimises their use of resources. The fact that a large economy with considerable heterogeneity can have different regions growing with widely different trajectories gave rise to concerns about "unbalanced growth" and regional disparities. This is lined up with the growth poverty debate outlined above, but it lays emphasis on geographical disparities also on top of the individual inequalities. Since the opening up of the Indian economy in 1991–1992, and its fairly impressive growth over the past decade led essentially by a certain number of Indian states, increasing concern has been raised about the fact that some states are growing too slowly or not at all, and thus falling behind or failing to benefit from the opening up of the Indian economy and the dynamism of certain sectors and regions. Specialists of growth economics have also tried to verify in the context of large economies like India or China, as to whether one of the predictions of growth theory, that less developed regions or countries will "catch up" with the more developed ones (through faster capital accumulation) is confirmed or not. This is often referred to as the "convergence" debate, and in the Indian context, empirical evidence points to the "divergence" in the growth path between Indian states, which is influenced by the initial conditions of social and economic infrastructure and human capital.

This convergence debate is obviously relevant in the Chinese context also, albeit in a different way. China, through its economic and political choices, assured its population of much better basic access to education and health, and a better livelihood, than India did, especially for the poorer population. Even with internal emigration restrictions, the policy of developing interior regions in order to survive external military threats had positive effects on development. However, with the opening up of the Chinese economy and the arrival of private foreign capital, the possibility of unequal regional growth was opened up and it did happen as is briefly documented further down. However, we shall first present some recent changes on growth and regional inequalities in India.

Recent Evolution in Growth and Regional Disparities in India and Some Remarks on Convergence in China

Physical, social, and economic infrastructure varies widely between regions in India. These are inputs into the economic process which subsequently affect the process of growth. However, it is obvious that we should not focus exclusively on growth when we talk about regional disparities. The modern approach to development increasingly considers good health, a high level of education, the equal rights of women or of previously oppressed social classes, and the possibilities for individuals to participate in social and political processes to be an integral part of development goals. Hence, understanding the full complexity of regional disparities implies that we not only look at the income (or growth of income) disparities between regions, but also at the disparities in the above-mentioned indicators between social categories and classes in the same region. In almost all regions, be they growing rapidly or slowly, social and spatial segregation is widespread, in urban agglomerations, between rural and urban areas (often separated by just a few kilometers or tens of kilometers) and between areas that are easily accessible by transportation and those that are not, such as hilly areas or the remote interiors. The Multidimensional Deprivation Index that is being increasingly used by international agencies and scholars[2] in order to compare international development. However, this approach, like the Human Development Index, still needs further theoretical and empirical refinement in order to understand long-terms trends in growth and development, because the underlying linkages and causality between growth and its potential explanatory social, economic, and political variables is still a matter of considerable debate in the academic and policy community.

Hence, the terms "regional disparities" cover many inequalities, and we try to cover the principal ones here. Ram and Mohanty (2005), in one of the most extensive studies on human development indicators for the states and districts of India, used a composite index of reproductive, child health, and census indices on literacy and gender, to classify India's districts and states. Based on this index, the 100 worst off districts in India were concentrated in the states of Bihar (35 out of 37 districts), Uttar Pradesh (32 out of 70), Jharkand (formerly a part of Bihar) (12 out of 18), Rajasthan (9 out of 32), Madhya Pradesh (9 out of 45), Arunachal Pradesh (2 out of 13), Orissa (1 out of 30). Considering Jharkand as part of the former state of Bihar, 79 of the 100 worst off districts in terms of the Ram-Mohanty index are concentrated in two of the most populous and poorest states of India. Among the 100 best off districts of India, there is a heavy concentration in Southern and Western India. For the South there is Tamilnadu (25 districts out of 30), Karnataka (11 out of 27), Kerala (14 out of 14), Andhra Pradesh (6 out of 23), and Pondicherry (4 out of 4). For the west, there is Maharashtra (12 out of 35), Gujarat (1 out of 25), Daman-Dui (1 out of 2), and Goa (1 out of 2). These 9 states make up 75 districts out of 100. In the North, Delhi (9 out of 9), Punjab (1 out of 17), Chandigarh (1 out of 1), and Himachal Pradesh (2 out of 12) make up 13, West Bengal (2 out of 18), Assam (2 out of 23), Mizoram (4 out of 8), and Manipur (1) make up another 9 . Hence, we find according to these social development indices that the South and the West are clearly doing much better than the North and the East. So this helps us to shed light on the controversy: Is there an East-West divide or a North-South divide? In fact, both divides exist.

Now, if we rank the States according to the Ram-Mohanty index, we have the following ranking (from the bottom upwards): Bihar (25.31), Jharkhand (30.77), Uttar Pradesh (32.00), Rajasthan (35.13), Arunachal Pradesh (35.13), Madhya Pradesh (40.18), Meghalaya (45.32), Chattisgarch (45.07), Nagaland (45.24), Orissa (47.39), Assam (47.96), Jammu and Kashmir (48.76), Manipur (49.75), Haryana (50.02), Uttaranchal (50.78), Sikkim (53.70), West Bengal (54.29), Gujarat (54.84), Tripura (55.90), Punjab (58.92), Mizoram (61.17), Maharastra (61.41), Karnataka (61.53), Andhra Pradesh (62.02), Daman and Diu (63.83), Himachal Pradesh (64.67), Chandigarh (70.30), Tamilnadu (71.49), Delhi (71.72), Andaman and Nicobar islands (73.27), Goa (76.22), Pondicherry (78.82), and Kerala (83.45). The ranking of the states follow globally the ranking of the districts (i.e., the poorest districts are in the poorest states), with the following caveat: Some of India's economically advanced (high per capita income) states such as Punjab, Haryana, and Gujarat are in the middle range as far as social development is concerned. Several middle ranking states in terms of per capita income are among the major performers in terms of social development (Karnataka, Andhra Pradesh, Pondicherry, Kerala). Maharashtra, and Tamilnadu are the only two large states in the top of the league on both counts.

The publication of the 2011 provisional census results makes it imperative to mention regional disparities in the sex ratio. Chinese readers would undoubtedly be interested in the gender problem in India, which is different from that of China. Mary John (2011) highlights that in the previous census (2001), several states of northwest India had a sharp fall in the child sex ratio, with Punjab at the top, in the negative sense of the term, with a child sex ratio falling below 800. Gujarat, Haryana, Delhi, and Himachal Pradesh also had declining sex ratios. These northern and northwestern states have been peaking or levelling off the practice of sex selection, and John emphasizes that these states have not yet come back to their 1991 levels of the child sex ratio, which was already a fairly unfavorable figure. Furthermore, the practice of sex selection is probably widening, even if it is less dramatic than in the north-west, to states and districts in western, southern, and eastern India. Further analysis of district level data from the 2011 census in the coming months will enable greater in-depth analysis of this question, but the slowness of social change in India and the persistence of male preference in relatively richer states of the northwest, aided by technologies of sex screening, also highlights that economic growth will not necessarily lead to better social indicators in the absence of both governmental policy at federal, state, and local levels, and a stepping up of societal debates on such questions. The availability and use of technology, in spite of government bans on sex screening, shows the state-society divide in India on such questions.

As far as the growth of per capita income and physical and economic infrastructure is concerned, a considerable body of work demonstrates the role of infrastructure in growth (Nagaraj, Varoudakis, Veganzones 1998; Bandyopadhyay 2002); and, in fact, one finds, that the ranking of the per capita income and the physical infrastructure ranking correspond closely. The per capita income ranking goes like this for India's largest states (2002–2003): Punjab, Maharashtra, Haryana, Tamilnadu, Gujarat have consistently been the rich states; Karnataka, Kerala, Andhra Pradesh, West Bengal, Rajasthan, Madhya Pradesh are in the middle; and Assam, Utar Pradesh, Orissa, Bihar are the poorest states. This ranking is very close to the ranking generated by Chevrou, Chaudhuri, and Marimoutou (2006) using the Classification and Regression Trees (CART) method that endogenously generates "clubs" of states (clubs in the sense that they have similar characteristics) according to the trajectories of their growth of per capita income. One observes the following phenomenon in these groups: The rich states stay rich, the poor states stay poor, but states that are in the middle can progress or regress; over the last decade, Karnataka, Kerala, Andhra Pradesh, and West Bengal have shown distinct signs of moving upward towards the richer states albeit along different growth trajectories, whereas Madhya Pradesh and Rajasthan, in spite of occasional progress, fell behind and became poorer. Also, in the long period, states have changed their relative position within the groups. Kar, Jha, and Kateja (2011), in an important and recently published paper, also using convergence models of distribution dynamics, emphasize the rather disquieting fact that in post-reform India, and especially in the period after 2000, there is evidence of a polarization in India around two groups of rich and poor state states. They point out that high and middle income states — Gujarat, Kerala, Himachal Pradesh, Karnataka, Tamil Nadu, and West Bengal — have a tendency to move up in the group of richer states while Punjab and Maharashtra, which are part of the same richer group, tend to fall behind. Bihar and Uttar Pradesh are members of the "poorer" club along with some middle income states like Assam, Madhya Pradesh, Jammu and Kashmir, and Rajasthan, and these latter states have actually moved down in the income and growth ladder, while Bihar has moved up within the poorer group in terms of income growth rates. This also highlights the fragility of the Indian growth story. Even if the overall growth story at the macroeconomic and aggregate level is a positive one and internationally and nationally visible, it also highlights the fact, as André Gunder Frank had stated, that before there was development, there was no underdevelopment. Growth can be fragile, temporary, or cyclical, if the underlying economic fundamentals are not strong. Competition between states, regions, and agglomerations can stimulate capital movements and the flight of human resources, as internal migration trends in India are showing, with the south, the west, and the northwest of India continuing to lead the way and attract the bulk of investible resources.

If one considers the percentage of the poor living below the poverty line, one finds that India's poorest states in per capita income terms — Bihar (43%), Uttar Pradesh (31%), Orissa (47%), Assam (36%), and Madhya Pradesh (37%) — are again the worst performers according to the 1990–2000 official calculations. The performance of the high and middle income states is mixed (Ram and Mohanty, 32). Poverty and its reduction, for these two groups, seem to be related more with the effort at social development rather than directly correlated with income levels in terms of per capita income. Kozel and Parker (2005) have carried out an important study of Uttar Pradesh, India's most populous state, and they point out that this state, which has a population of 175 million, of which approximately 60 million (34% according to the authors, who contest the official calculations) live below the poverty line, constitutes approximately 8% of the world's poor at that point of time. Their article underlines the varied dimensions of poverty[3] related to the lack of employment opportunities, property rights, access to finance, to public goods and services (notably education and health) that help to build up human capital, caste- and gender-related oppression, governance failures, and the lack of political voice. They stress the multidimensional nature of deprivation and the wide variations that exist in the conditions of the population that live below the poverty line within the state. The heterogeneity within and between states, and the possible reasons for the differences in performances that have been raised above, are also reviewed by Sachs, Bajpai, and Ramiah (2002).

In a work on social development similar to the Ram-Mohanty index analyzed in the previous version of the paper, Banerjee (2010) provides a well argued synthetic indicator of social and demographic variables, including contraceptive prevalence rate, total fertility rate, infant mortality rate, health indicators, educational attainment indicators, basic amenities indicators, and social and economic deprivation indicators. The overall results give the ranking of India's states in 2008 and 2010, the 2010 ranking in social development as the following: Kerala, Punjab, Tamilnadu, Maharashtra, Andhra Pradesh, Karnataka, Gujarat, Haryana, Assam, West Bengal, Orissa, Rajasthan, Chhattisgarh, Madhya Pradesh, Uttar Pradesh, Jharkhand, Bihar, taking into account only India's largest states. In this list, Andhra Pradesh, Karnataka, Orissa, Punjab have slightly improved their positions, Chattisgarh, Gujarat, Haryana, Rajasthan, and Tamilnadu have moved down slightly, and the positions of Assam, Bihar, Jharkhand, Kerala, Madhya Pradesh, Maharashtra, Uttar Pradesh, and Bengal remain unchanged. It has to be remembered that these are synthetic indicators that average out opposing movements in their individual components, some of which, such as income growth, demography, health or education, are extensively commented on in public debate where individual states are often highlighted. This paper would be incomplete without a mention of the demographic dividend, much commented on in recent debate. Projections from the Census (Aiyar and Mody 2010) seem to suggest that India's poorer states, which have not yet attained the population transition fully, are more likely to contribute to the working age (15–59) population in the coming decades as compared to better off or more socially developed states. This implies that if educational and job opportunities and infrastructures are not substantially developed in these states (and in neighbouring states) in the coming decades, the demographic dividend might boomerang into a Malthusian handicap.

To sum up, in India, the west, the northwest, and the south are progressing faster than the rest of the country in both growth and development indicators if one considers the long term. The east, the northeast, the center and parts of the north have been lagging behind, even though there are some positive evolutions over the last decade.

In rather stark terms, India is probably capable, in less than a decade, of having economic regions with the per capita income of middle income countries coexisting with regions with per capita income levels of current sub-Saharan Africa or the currently poorest regions of India.

There is at least one common feature in the structure of growth between India and China: There is a tendency towards the divergence of growth between regions, but a certain degree of convergence in clubs (Maasoumi and Wang 2006). They make the further point that in the Chinese context a different number of clubs exists in both the pre- and post-reform periods, with a greater degree of convergence in the post-reform period, even though the characteristics of these clubs in the Chinese context is not unique (in terms of regional groupings, policy choices, or other characteristics).

In another very interesting paper, Anderson and Ying Ge (2007) compare per capita income distribution between cities and show that while their incomes have increased over time, cities in advanced (coastal) regions tend to converge and compete with each other, less advanced regions can fall behind and polarization can take place at the two tails of the intercity income distributions. Again, China has the advantage that since its average per capita incomes and levels of living are much higher than they are in India, the problem of disparities does not require desperate measures as they often do in India.

Open Questions and Debates

Is it true that the controlled variety of capitalism that India and China are trying out while integrating into the world economy is not capable of, or not geared to, managing rising income inequalities or regional disparities? This is claimed by many critiques of globalization. Recent events and evidence in India in the last five years show that, in spite of the international economic slowdown that affected India and China and some of India's poorer states and regions, their performance in governance maintained a fairly good growth rate. One lesson of the Indian experience is that open migration within the country enables migrants from poor regions to send remittances to their home states and thus boost development in those places. However, migration towards cities is putting a severe strain on the infrastructure of cities, increasing urban inequalities, and posing difficulties for the development of sustainable cities. In some of the more developed regions of India, there is a resentment of poorer migrants coming into the city. Many experts and commentators feel that exacerbating social tensions and the breakdown of the "social contract" (i.e. social cohesion) challenges the legitimacy of the system, as is happening now in many countries. "Elites" need to reflect on this, on going beyond cosmetic mechanisms that try to cover up systemic failures.

In growing economies, relative deprivation can become as important as absolute poverty; if one just takes a figure as an example, USD10,000 or EUR10,000 annually is below poverty level income in the U.S. or Europe and people at this level of income are really badly off as compared to the average income level. This is where the European experience shows that access to public goods has an important impact on welfare, because it supplements income as a welfare indicator by directly providing education or health care at a relatively high level of quality.

International comparisons clearly show that poorer regions need to cross a critical threshold of investment, savings, infrastructure, and "agglomeration economies" in order to get on a sustained growth path. This has rarely happened without the strong involvement of the state.

There is nothing inevitable about growth; evidence from India and elsewhere (Latin America in particular) shows that growing regions can regress, and recent evidence from the West shows that social classes that progressed over more than half a century (the middle class, laborers) can regress sharply in terms of their overall shares of wealth and income in the space of a few decades.

The research agenda in this area probably needs to delve into the following question: Do regional disparities reflect underlying long-run structural differences in the initial economic conditions of the growth process, or are they more related to social, cultural, or political differences between the states and regions? The answer might be a combination of all these factors, but they need to be singled out in increasing detail.

Notes

1. Specific sections of this paper have appeared in the *New Oxford Companion to Economics in India*, eds. Kaushik Basu and Anemie Mertens (New Delhi: Oxford University Press, 2012).
2. Please refer to *United Nations Human Development Report 2010* and references therein.
3. See also Ravallion and Datt (2002), and Besley, Burgess, Esteve-Volart (2005).

References

Aiyar, Shekar, and Ashoka Mody. "The Demographic Dividend: Evidence from Indian States." IMF Working Paper, WP/11/38.

Anderson, Gordon, and Ying Ge. 2007. *Intercity Income Inequality, Growth and Convergence in China*, mimeo.

Bandyopadhyay, Sanghamitra. 2002. *Convergence Club Empiric: Some Dynamics and Explanations of Unequal Growth Across Indian States*. London: London School of Economics.

Banerjee, Kaustav. 2011. "Social Development Index 2010," Chapter 19. In *India: Social Development Report 2010*, ed. Manoranjan Mohanty. New Delhi: Council for Social Development / Oxford University Press.

Besley, Timothy, Robin Burgess, and Berta Esteve-Volart. 2005. *Operationalising Pro-Poor Growth: India Case Study*. London: London School of Economiscs, Jun.

Chaudhuri, Basudeb, Hélène Chevrou-Séverac, and, Velayoudom Marimoutou. 2006. *Growth and Convergence Clubs in Indian States, 1965–2002*. Working Paper, GREQAM.

Government of India. 2001 / 2011. *Census Reports*.

John, Mary E. 2011. "Census 2011: Governing Populations and the Girl Child." *Economic and Political Weekly* XLVI (16).

Kar, Sabyasachi, Debajit Jha, and Alpana Kateja. 2010. *Club Convergence and Polarisation of States: A Nonparametric Analysis of Post Reform India*. Working Paper 2010 of the Institute of Economic Growth. In the *Indian Growth and Development Review 2011*.

Kozel, V., and Barbara Parker. 2005. "A Profile and Diagnostic of Poverty in Uttar Pradesh." *The Great Indian Poverty Debate*, eds. Angus Deaton, and Valerie Kozel. New Delhi: Macmillan.

Maasoumi, Esfandiar, and Le Wang. 2006. *Economic Reforms, Growth and Convergence in China*, mimeo. Dallas: Southern Methodist University.

Nagaraj, R., A. Varoudakis, and M. A. Véganzonès. 1998. *Long Run Growth Trends and Convergence Across Indian States*. Technical Paper No. 131. Paris: OECD, Jan.

Ram, F., and S. K. Mohanty. 2005. *State of Human Development in States and Districts of India*. Mumbai: International Institute of Population Studies.

Ravallion, M., and Gaurav Datt. 2002. "Why Has Economic Growth Been More Pro-Poor in Some States of India Than Others?" *Journal of Development Economics*, 68:381–400.

Sachs, Jeffrey, N. Bajpai, and A. Ramiah. 2002. *Understanding Regional Economic Growth in India*. Centre for International Development Working Paper No. 88. Cambridge: Harvard University.

United Nations Human Development Report (UNHDR). 2010.

7th All India Educational Survey. 2005. Human Resources Ministry, Government of India.

4

Chapter

Developing China-India Trade Relations and Establishing the Bilateral Free Trade Zone

Quan Yi
Li Ting

China and India are the two oldest ancient civilized countries in Asia and the biggest developing, new economies in the world. The trade relationship and cultural exchange between them have had a long history. As early as 2,000 years ago, these two countries already had very close economic and cultural exchanges. In the late 1980s, after Rajiv Gandhi undertook the premiership, he changed India's diplomatic policy which led to the actual improvement in the China-India relationship. The most remarkable aspect in their economic relationship was the establishment of the bilateral free trade zone. Early in 2003, China and India organized a united research group studying its feasibility and finished the united research report in 2005. But so far, there have not been any government negotiations, and the establishment of free trade agreement (FTA) is still facing lots of difficulties and challenges. In the near future, both China and India should take active measures to promote the construction of the bilateral free trade zone. The author of this paper will make a primary discussion on it.

Present Development of China-India Trade Relationship

China-India Trade Relationship has been developing fast since 2000. At present, China has become the greatest trade partner of India while India has turned into China's No. 1 trade partner in South Asia and No. 10 trade partner in the world.[1]

Rapid increase in China-India bilateral trade volume

With the continuous development in the economies of the two countries, the economic relationship between China and India becomes closer, and their trade volume increases every year.

Table 4.1 China import and export volume to India

Unit: USD100 million

Year	Export volume	Growth rate (%)	Import volume	Growth rate (%)
2000	15.6	34.48	13.5	62.65
2001	19	21.79	17	25.93
2002	26.7	40.52	22.7	33.53
2003	33.4	25.09	42.5	87.22
2004	59	76.64	76.8	80.71
2005	89.3	51.36	97.7	27.21

(Cont'd)

Year	Export volume	Growth rate (%)	Import volume	Growth rate (%)
2006	145.8	63.27	102.8	5.22
2007	240.1	64.68	146.2	42.22
2008	315.9	31.57	202.6	38.58
2009	296	–6.1	137.1	–32.3
2010	409.2	38.0	208	51.7

Source: Sorted and edited based on *China Statistical Yearbook* (2001–2011).

According to Table 4.1, China's import and export volume to India presents a tendency to increase year by year. Significantly, the export volume to India increased prominently from 2000 to 2008 with an average annual growth rate of around 45%. Particularly, it increased most rapidly in 2004, an increase of 76.64%. And the import volume increased most rapidly in 2003 and 2004, and both import and export rates rose by above 80%. Overall, China-India bilateral trade volume increased from USD2.9 billion in 2000 to USD51.8 billion in 2008 with the high annual growth rate of 43%.

In 2009, due to the impact of the global financial crisis, the export volume from India to China was USD9.85 billion, a drop of 6.5%, while the import volume from China was USD28.72 billion, a drop of 14.3% according to the statistics from the Indian Commerce Department. And the bilateral trade volume was USD43.38 billion, a drop of 16.3%, based on the statistics from China's General Administration of Customs. But when it came to 2010, the bilateral trade volume recovered and increased rapidly at its previous pace. Based on the statistics from the Indian Business Information and Statistics Department and the Ministry of Commerce of India, China-India bilateral trade volume reached USD55.58 billion, up by 42.5% in 2010. Indian exports to China were USD17.42 billion, a rise of 71.5%, and the imports from China were USD38.16 billion, a rise of 32.3%. Now, China has surpassed the United Arab Emirates (UAE) to become India's biggest trading partner and it continues to be India's largest source of imports and the third largest export market.[2] From 15 to 17 December, 2010, the Chinese Premier Wen Jiabao led a big commerce delegation consisting of more than 300 members to visit India. During his visit, the leaders of the two countries agreed to enhance their economic cooperation and they were confident that bilateral trade would reach USD100 billion by 2015.[3]

As a whole, China-India bilateral trade shows a tendency of rapid development and there is comparatively large developing potential in their economic cooperation.

Rapid increases of the combination degree in bilateral trade

The trade combination / intensity degree is the index to measure how close the trade relationship is and how much the trade partners depend on each other. The formula is shown as follows.

$$T_{ab} = \frac{\text{Country A } \textit{to Country} \text{ B } \textit{impor} \text{ tan } d \text{ exp } \textit{orttotalvolume} \Big/ \text{Country A } \textit{impor} \text{ tan } d \text{ exp } \textit{orttotalvolume}}{\text{Country B } \textit{impor} \text{ tan } d \text{ exp } \textit{orttotalvolume} \Big/ \textit{impor} \text{ tan } d \text{ exp } \textit{orttotalvolume} \text{ int } \textit{heworld}}$$

T_{ab} shows the combination degree of Country A to Country B. If $T_{ab} > 1$, it means the trade relationship between these two countries is very close. The bigger the value is, the closer their trade relationship is. On the other hand, the smaller the value is, the more alienated their trade relationship is. The data sources used in this essay mainly come from *China Statistical Yearbook* on the China National Bureau of Statistics website. The result is as follows:

Table 4.2 China-India trade combination degree

Year	1993	1995	1997	1999	2001	2003	2005	2007	2008	2009	2010
Tci	0.6	0.666	0.834	0.777	0.955	1.186	1.158	1.38	1.4	1.2	1.14

Source: Based on *China Statistical Yearbook* (1994–2010).

According to Table 4.2, the trade combination degree between China and India presents an annually-increasing tendency. Moreover, from 2001, the combination degree nearly reached 1, and then arrived at 1.4 in 2008, which means that the trade relationship between China and India is very close. Although, their trade combination degree decreased from 2008 to 2010, the value was still bigger than 1 during that period. Therefore, the financial crisis did not cause a very strong impact on their trade relationship. With the increase of bilateral trade volume, their combination degree continues to rise yearly, which means that their combination degree is continuously strengthened. This illustrates that the two countries have areas of potential cooperation in economics and trade.

Good tendency for China-India's bilateral investment development

In recent years, the bilateral investment between China and India has been escalating and the investment field has been continuously broadened. China mainly invests in the fields of electronics, communications, light industry, and so on in India, while India's investment in China mainly involves the fields of metallurgy, electric appliances, medicine, printing ink, and so on. India's investment in China has accumulated over USD300 million since 2006. In 2009, China attracted up to USD55.2 million of direct investment from Indian businessmen. In 2010, this figure slightly decreased but still reached USD49.31million. On the other hand, the direct investment from China to India showed a tendency to increase. In 2003, China's direct investment leftover in India was only USD0.96 million. But this number reached USD479.8 million in 2010. In the perspective of China's direct investment flow in India, it was only USD0.15 million in 2003. But it reached USD101.88 million in 2008. Due to the impact of the global financial crisis, there even appeared negative growth in 2009, but the direct investment flow recovered to USD47.61 million in 2010.

Table 4.3 China's direct investment flow and leftover in India (2003–2010)

Unit: USD100 million

Year	2003	2004	2005	2006	2007	2008	2009	2010
Flow	15	35	1,116	561	2,202	10,188	–2,488	4,761
Leftover	96	455	1,426	2,583	12,014	22,202	22,127	47,980

Besides, the mutual investment between Chinese and Indian enterprises is also very impressive. Many large IT companies, such as Tata Consultancy Service, Infosys Technologies Limited, Wipro, Satyam Computer Services Ltd., and HCT Technologies have all set up their research centers in China and gradually increased the number of Chinese employees. At the same time, Chinese enterprises are very active in a "go global" strategy. For example, Huawei, TCL, Haier, ZTE Corporation, Dongfang Electric Company Limited, and the like are all taking part in the bidding for relative Foundational Engineering actively and these companies succeeded in taking on some major infrastructure projects in India, which mainly focused on electric stations, telecommunications, and subways. India has become one of the most important overseas contract project markets for China.[4]

For the above reasons, with a very close trade relationship, China and India both have a certain dependence on each other's economy and share common strategic interests. Therefore, it is rational to cooperate with each other. What's more, after the establishment of China-India Free Trade, both sides will broaden their openness and hence bring out the "trade-created" effect and scale economy effect as well as benefits in their economic development. Consequently, in terms of economic meaning, it is feasible to establish a free trade zone between China and India, and both sides will benefit from it.

Progress in China-India Establishing FTA

Both China and India are developing countries and located nearby with good geo-advantage. Moreover, in recent years, their economic cooperation has presented a rapid developing tendency. But, because of the influence from various factors, their trade cooperation still remains at a low level, which does not match the two countries' economic developing scale and speed. Therefore, the higher trade cooperation between China and India in the form of the establishment of the free trade zone is requested.

The establishment of the China-India free trade zone is necessary to implement a win-win situation

The establishment of the China-India free trade zone is needed to promote China and India's global competitive strength

China and India are the fastest developing big economies at present. Since the rise of China and India will exert an outstanding influence on the world economy, the question whether they choose to compete or cooperate has become a focus for the other countries in the world. Since the 1980s–1990s, China and India have performed reform successively and gained better effects in order to foster their economic development and enhance their economic strength. Since China initiated its reform and opening up policy in 1978, its economic annual growth rate always reached nearly 10% (1979–2008), and India's economic annual growth also reached 6.7% after it carried out its opening up policy.

As for the proportion of the import and export volume of China and India to the import and export volume of the world, both countries' trade shows a certain developing rate. According to the "Growth Rate of the Major Economies in the World during 1990 to 2007" by the statistics from the United Nations Statistics Agency, China's growth rate was 13.34% while India's was 7.63%, both ranking at the top of the list.[5] Besides, from the statistics of ITS2011 published by the World Trade Organization (WTO), China's goods trade export volume accounted for 5.9% of the world export volume in 2003 and then 10.6% in 2010. During the same period, India's proportion increased to 1.5% from 0.8%. Meanwhile, the proportion of China's goods trade import volume accounting for world import volume rose from 5.4% in 2003 to 9.3% in 2010, and India's from 0.9% to 2.2% during the same period.

Table 4.4 Growth rate of the major economies in the world (1990–2007)

Country	China	India	Germany	Japan	The U.S.	Brazil	Russia
Growth rate	13.34%	7.63%	3.96%	2.21%	5.27%	6.12%	4.92%

Source: United Nations Statistical Office.

It can be seen that both China's and India's economies have comparatively good developing potentials. If the FTA can be established, it will definitely promote further development in both countries' economies. The completed China-India FTA will involve 2.5 billion people, an area of over 12 million square kilometers, domestic total output value of more than USD6 trillion and a foreign trade volume of more than USD3 trillion, which will be significant to the regional economies. Such a large scale market will bring the two countries to a new economic growth point, effectively improving their abilities in international competition. Since 2008, the financial crisis has had different impacts on countries all over the world. It also lets countries realize the importance of international cooperation. After the completion of the China-India FTA, it not only can deepen economic relations between the two countries, but also can improve the two countries' influence on the world economy, and strengthen the ability to co-resist international risk.

The establishment of China-India FTA is significant in fostering Asian integration

India first took part in international economic integration in 1968, and participated in three preferential trade arrangements and agreements before the 1990s. Nowadays, nine agreements that India participated in have taken effect, and another 11 are being negotiated and studied.[6] China took part in international economic integration later than India. China has accelerated the pace of regional economic cooperation after entering the Asia-Pacific Economic Cooperation (APEC) in 1991. Till now, China has signed 11 economic integration agreements, and is negotiating six free trade agreements and studying on the FTA with Japan, Korea, and India.

On a general survey of the regional trade agreements both countries took part in, China and India share common strategic interests. In terms of the chosen cooperation countries, both China and India place great emphasis on the cooperation with the other surrounding countries in Asia, such as the Association of Southeast Asian Nations (ASEAN) nations, Japan, Korea, Pakistan, Singapore, and other countries. The cooperation with surrounding countries is beneficial for creating a safe international environment for economic development. Also, both countries pay attention to cooperation with developing countries, especially with Latin American and African countries, such as Chile and Perú. It is easier to find their common interests in the cooperation with developing countries, which enhances the international influence of the developing countries and helps them pursue more interests in the world. Therefore, China and India have the same strategic interests in joining in international economic integration, especially in promoting Asian economic integration which is beneficial for Asia's economic reconstruction and development. In today's world, in Europe, the European Union (EU) keeps expanding; in America, there is the North American Free Trade Area, while Asia is in a state of disunity. China-India cooperation is for the purpose of promoting the regional cooperation and integration in Asia.

If the establishment of "10+3" and the South Asian Association for Regional Cooperation (SAARC) are the first steps to implement Asia integration, then the establishment of a China-India FTA is an essential second step to foster Asia's integration.[7] As the biggest and fastest developing countries, the cooperation between China and India exercises special importance for Asia. A report on the China-India FTA by the World Bank pointed out that "In terms of preferential trade, the SAARC aims at an Asian trade zone, and its best breakthrough point is the China-India free trade zone, because these two countries are growing up with their big scale and Chinese goods possess global competitive power. India's trade is facing fewer challenges than the SAARC free trade zone. And China-India will provide the best perspective to finally set up the Asian free trade zone."[8] Consequently, the establishment of the China-India free trade zone can effectively foster the cooperation between South Asia and East Asia and, at the same time, exert strategic meaning in implementing Asian integration earlier.

Progress of establishing the China-India free trade zone

Both sides negotiated establishing a free trade zone and achieved an agreement

In May 2001, China joined in the *Bangkok Agreement* whose members include China, India, Korea, Bangladesh, Sri Lanka, and Laos. Later, it was renamed the *Asia-Pacific Trade Agreement* in 2005, which was the first regional trade arrangement China took part in. After Indian Prime Minister Vajpayee visited China in 2003, both sides set up a joint research group to study the complementary potential in their trade cooperation. In October of 2003, leaders of China and India met in Bali and exchanged views on the question of how to establish the China-India free trade zone. In 2004, China proposed a new plan to comprehensively promote the trade relationship between China and India and to establish the China-India free trade zone before 2015. On March 23, 2005, both sides finished the joint research report, pointing out the limitations for the development of bilateral goods trade including customs procedures, certification standards, supervision, quota restrictions, multilateral problems in bilateral agreement, and trade remedy. It suggested that the new measures meant to improve the bilateral trade environment be issued as soon as possible, and joint research on establishing China-India free trade zone should be performed.

Both sides decided to form regional trade and arrange a joint research group, and made a detailed study on feasibility and benefits of the establishment of China-India FTA. In April 2005, Premier Wen Jiabao and Indian Prime Minister Manmohan Singh signed *The People's Republic of China and The Republic of India Joint Statement*, in which the two countries agreed to establish "peace and prosperity" through a "strategic partnership." Premier Wen Jiabao's visit further promoted the development of Sino-Indian relations, the establishment of a free trade area had been gradually added to the agenda. On March 16, 2006, China and India decided to officially start a joint feasibility research study on China-India regional trade arrangement. By January of 2007, this joint research group had already held three meetings, achieving agreements on the background and necessity of establishing FTA, the present situation of goods trade, service trade, and investment content. In October 2007, regional trade arrangement joint group announced completion of the FTA joint research report, pointing out that the two countries should reduce trade and investment barriers, realize a mutual benefit "win-win" situation and foster Asia economic integration by establishing the FTA.

During this period, China and India signed the *Bilateral Investment Promotion and Protection Agreements* (BIPA), which were considered essential measures in establishing the FTA. It offered both sides the investment position of most-favored-nation and permitted investment and capital remittance. In May 2010, when Indian President Pratibha Patil visited China, the two countries exchanged their views on further developing the strategic partnership. The two parties reached a broad consensus and pushed for bilateral cooperation. The agreements they made on the establishment of FTA laid a good foundation for accomplishing the building of the China-India FTA. In December 2010, The Chinese Premier Wen Jiabao visited India, and greatly promoted bilateral trade cooperation. Both parties emphasized in the *Joint Statement* that, on the one hand, they should avoid trade friction with each other. On the other hand, they should resist trade protectionism. Premier Wen Jiabao outlined the preparation of opening a new platform for the goods imported from India, in order to solve a serious balance problem in China-India trade relations. They also signed a protocol worth USD16 billion, involving financial, infrastructure, energy, telecommunications, and pharmaceuticals to solve India's trade deficit problem.

Both parties gradually cooperate further in broader ways

The large consumer market in China attracts keen investment interests of Indian enterprises. Many large-scale Indian IT companies have set up research and development centers in China, making full use of the cheap talent in China. On the basis of China's location advantage, Indian companies take China as a "springboard" to expand their business to Japan, Korea, Russia, and Central Asia. Besides, they also invest actively in the departments of automobile, hotel, steel, and telecommunications. The investment of Chinese companies in India begins in India but expands out to Sri Lanka, Bangladesh, and Nepal. From this perspective, the win-win situation will bring out greater financial benefits for the establishment of the China-India FTA.

As big energy consumers, the cooperation fields between China and India have always been focused on gasoline and oil. In January 2006, when Petroleum and Natural Gas Minister of India Aiyar visited China, the two countries signed the memorandum on "Strengthening the Oil and Gas Cooperation" which made the bilateral cooperation content more extensive. Of course, with the continuous further cooperation, China and India do not cooperate only on gasoline and oil but also on wind power generation, solar energy, nuclear power, and biomass.[9] According to the news report, in the future, India will invest USD1 trillion in domestic manufacturing and infrastructure, which provides a great possibility for Chinese companies and financial institutions to enter the Indian market.[10]

But, after India has made the FTA with ASEAN and Japan, China and India still have not started FTA negotiations. There are lots of difficulties to be overcome.

Difficulties and Challenges in Establishing China-India FTA

Although the China-India trade relationship has made great progress, there are still plenty of difficulties in establishing China-India FTA. As the present Chinese ambassador to India Zhang Yan recently said, "the China-India relationship is very fragile. It is easy to be harmed and hard to be restored." The main reasons are as follows.

Historical problems

The problems left over by history include the South Tibet boundary dispute, and the Tibet issues. The boundary dispute between China and India which was derived from the British colonial rule in India has a long history. And the two countries have had serious disagreements in the demarcation of the border for a long time. China divides the boundary based on the historical fact formed by the China-India boundary, while having inherited the political heritage from Britain, India tries to hold the "McMahon Line" they impose on China. This will be certain to result in the bad influence on the development of China-India relations and make the boundary issue inextricable.

On the other hand, the China-India boundary dispute is closely connected with the Tibet issue. For one thing, the Indian government had to admit that Tibet is an autonomous region in China. On the other, a certain number of people in India's ruling class still consider Tibet as a key region having an impact on the safety of India. They think "Tibet should be treated as a buffer zone between India and China to avoid the threat from China." The former cabinet minister of India, and expert on China issues, Subra Manyam once said that the Indian government carried a "fuzzy policy" in the issues of Tibet and the Dalai Lama, which damaged their confidence with each other, and went against the development of trade relations between these two countries.[11] What's more, India was beaten badly in the India-China War in 1962 and then lost its privileges in Tibet, both events left great traumas in Indian people's minds and so they still hold a grudge. Therefore, the boundary dispute and Tibet issue both probably impact the factors in their relations and become the barriers to establishing the FTA.

Geopolitical collision

There is a comparatively complicated China-India competition complex, considering China as its main geopolitical and economic competitor. The relations, such as the sensitive triangular relationship among China, India, and Pakistan, and the complicated triangular relationship among China, India, and the U.S., will place great influence on bilateral relations. India and Pakistan have been rivaling each other since the Partition of India. Although their relationship was alleviated for a time, their bilateral political relationship was very intricate due to their disagreements in the aspects of territory, nations, and religion. The crucial reason for their conflict is the ownership problem of Kashmir. Wars have begun several times for this, causing political instability in these countries. In recent years, under the active appeal from the international community and the mediation efforts of the United Nations, both India and Pakistan have shown the willingness to solve their disputes peacefully. But since the ownership problem of Kashmir has not been solved, with a fragile base, the reconciliation between India and Pakistan is only symbolic. Once there is a new problem emerging, it will result in certain changes in their relationship. Under the circumstances of China-India's unstable relationship, the China-Pakistan relationship stands the historical trial and presents an "all-weather" friendly cooperative relationship. China and Pakistan support each other and cooperate with each other in the fields of politics, economy, diplomacy, and national defense. For instance, Pakistan supported China in regaining its legal seat in the United Nations and China offered military and economic aid. However, the friendly relationship between China and Pakistan makes India full of doubts, which has a negative influence on China-India relations, to a certain extent. China was in a dilemma regarding India-Pakistan relations. China could not give up the friendly relationship with Pakistan for the sake of the China-India relationship, but at the same time, it still wants to maintain cooperation with India. This complicated relationship among China, India, and Pakistan brings uncertainties for China-India's economic cooperation. Moreover, India even considers China's developing friendly relationship with countries surrounding India as a strategy aimed at surrounding India. As a result, India intends to fight against China with the help of the U.S. and counterbalance China by the conflicts with its surrounding countries. For example, India holds an active attitude in establishing the FTA with the ASEAN, Japan, Australia, Korea, and America, but a passive attitude towards China.

Conflicts in practical interests

Those conflicts include trade friction and market competition. In China-India trade, there is a big trade deficit in India, and India refuses to admit China's position in the market economy, which leads to continuous frictions between these two countries. At the present, because China's trade surplus to India reaches up to USD20 billion, India takes trade remedy measures to China frequently. Since the WTO was set up on January 1, 1995, India has been the biggest beneficiary in anti-dumping duty. According to the statistics, India had conducted 98 anti-dumping investigations against Chinese goods from 1994 to the end of July 2006, accounting for 47.3 % of the anti-dumping investigations against Chinese goods in the world.[12] From January to July of 2009, among the total 45 anti-dumping investigations from 17 countries against China, the number of investments from India accounted for 21. India takes the elimination of the trade deficit as one of the preconditions to establish the FTA, while China takes the admission of its position in the market economy as one of the prerequisites to establish the FTA.

Because of the existence of trade deficits, Indian industries hold doubts in establishing the China-India FTA, with the worries of the strike from their Chinese counterpart caused by an open market. The Associated Chambers of Commerce and Industry of India warned that the Indian government should be cautious before signing the FTA with China. Because the Customs tariff in India is much higher than it is in China, the implement of free tariffs will inevitably lead to the surging of Chinese goods. This chamber suggested the government should not sign FTA with China in a rush, but first sign a preferential trade agreement to reduce the tariff gradually for five years to protect domestic industry. Worrying about the bilateral trade being more unbalanced, Indian industries hold strong antipathy against the establishment of China-India FTA. Besides, there is great competition between the goods and energy needs from both countries. Even though the cooperation between two countries can decrease their competition, these interest conflicts still exist, which makes it easy for India to implement a "China Suboptimal" strategy which intends to marginalize China.

Defects in mathematical model

Economists usually apply two mathematical models to analyze FTA's economic effects: One is the "partial equilibrium model" focusing on calculating the economic effects in specified fields, mainly speculating on the basis of statistical data. The other is the common equilibrium model, inspecting the impact of reducing or eliminating tariff on the national economy. According to the research results of the mathematical models, the scholars of both countries think that China will gain more benefits from China-India FTA, while on the contrary, India's interests will even suffer a great loss. But in terms of facts, there are serious limitations in both models, because they ignore the variability of the current state. Economies keep changing, which involve lots of uncertainties and unexpected policy changes. Therefore, the model results do not necessarily reflect the economic results brought by China-India FTA. Taking the establishment of China-ASEAN FTA for example, many economists believe it brings out political interests instead of economic ones. However, after the launch of China-ASEAN FTA, the bilateral trade relationship develops very rapidly. Their bilateral trade volume reached USD292.776 billion in 2010, an increase of 3.7 times that in 2003 (USD78.252 billion). Practice proves the uncertainty of the results from mathematical models.

For the above reasons, apart from the political and cultural factors, it is feasible to establish the FTA between China and India. But China-India trade relations are restricted by the factors of the China-India boundary dispute, the Tibet problem, the relationship between China, India, and Pakistan, and between China, the U.S., and India, which all become the barriers to establishing the China-India FTA. Hence, there is a long way to go to establish the FTA between China and India, which will last for a long time.

Measures and Solutions to Accelerating the Establishment of the Bilateral FTA

Although there are plenty of difficulties in establishing the China-India FTA, it is not completely impossible. Both countries should improve the following aspects and then enhance their cooperation.

1. Completing political and military communication and cooperation system and setting up political mutual trust. The lack of political mutual trust is the basic reason why it is hard to develop their strategic-partnership substantively, as well as the essential barrier in establishing and developing the FTA. The mistrust between China and India will bring out lots of barriers for their economic cooperation. In order to establish FTA gradually, the two countries should strengthen their mutual trust, overcome cognitive barriers and reinforce their communication and intercommunion, trying to find the common points in cognition and then solve the boundary conflict. Therefore, it is necessary to launch a regular meeting and Prime Minister hotlines, the communication and cooperation system between the leaders of these two countries together with the communication between the youth in these two countries. Besides, these two countries should start from enhancing their trade relations, strengthen friendly negotiations, reduce the unnecessary trade remedy and restrictive measures, and eliminate the frictions through dialogue and discussion.

2. Promote economic and trade cooperation and balanced trade development between the two countries. Despite the fact that China and India are both developing countries, their economies have developed quite differently due to differences in political systems, opening up mode, religion, and culture. Therefore, they can complement each other concerning economics. As the Global Factory, China has formed the structure of a national economy which features manufacturing and exports, whereas India is renowned as the "Global Office," due to its high proportion in the third industry relying on technology to form the national economical structure focusing on the service industry and domestic demand. What China is good at is what India is deficient in, like producing clothing and mechanical goods; vice versa, what China lacks is what India is proud of, like manufacturing chips and software. Therefore, there will be tremendous economic benefits if the two countries work together. As to the trade deficit between China and India, both sides should share common knowledge. Rather than pursuing a balance of trade surplus deliberately, China is committed to expanding the consumer demand and hoping that the Indian enterprises open up the market and export more products to China. Plus, the two nations could cooperate in the field of information technology, environmental protection, infrastructure, and agricultural development.

3. Adjusting the nationalist sentiment rationally and abating abnormal competitiveness between the two countries. Both sides should respect the public's feelings towards their motherland but within limits and avoid inciting nationalism on border conflicts. The Indian media often spreads rumors that China will invade India, or that China poses a great military threat to India, and so on, and these exert a negative influence on the healthy links between the two nations. Both countries should build a win-win situation instead of being hostile to each other. The late Chinese leader Deng Xiaoping once said that Asia will not be reckoned rich if China and India are still poor. Both nations have shouldered the responsibility of reviving Asia and should be happy about each other's development. Actually, China and India have greater cooperative potential in service trade and economic trade, such as finance, insurance, transportation. The further cooperation in marine issues, aviation, tourism, and international exhibition will surely promote development on both sides.

4. Handling sensitive problems with caution to maintain the stability of the two countries. The fact is that India is very sensitive towards China's strengthening infrastructure and economy in Tibet, and this is beneficial to the

economic communication between the two nations. They could consult each other on connecting border transportation facilities to contribute to the economy and trade. At the same time, as China is highly sensitive to the problem of the Dalai Lama and the Taiwan issue, India should stop supporting the Dalai Lama and contacting Taiwan, thus the two countries might be able to trust each other in the future and build the free trade area successfully, in the hopes of promoting the healthy development of a strategic partnership between the two nations.

5. Completing bilateral cooperation system and leading to the FTA. Because there are plenty of barriers in establishing the FTA in order to implement this goal, it can be started based on several factors: On the one hand, China and India can have an open cooperation first, build a comparatively easy cooperation framework, and choose several important fields to cooperate in. For instance, to achieve agreements, enhance cooperation and improve the trade environment in solving the problems of tariff and non-tariff barriers (NTB), the uniform rules of origin, customs data, approval standards, inspection and quarantine measures, and currency exchange. After a long period of honing, both parties will gradually move to establish the FTA. On the other hand, both countries should make use of the Asia-Pacific Trade Agreement and the system of "the BRIC summit" [BRIC — Brazil, Russia, India And China] to strengthen their relationship. Both, as members of the Asia-Pacific Trade Agreement, can foster the multilateral trade liberalization with this agreement. At the same time, the cooperation and negotiation among China, India, Russia, Pakistan, and South Africa will be useful in reducing the disputes and finding out new common interests to foster China-India bilateral cooperation.

In summary, it is possible to establish the FTA between China and India. But due to the large number of influential factors, it will be hard to implement in a short time. The establishment of the China-India FTA requires the efforts of both sides to eliminate various factors to finally achieve the agreement. Therefore, it will take a long time to finally implement the China-India FTA.

Notes

1. Lin Shiyan 林世炎, "China-India bilateral economic and trade cooperation" 中國與印度雙邊經貿合作發展：問題及對策, *Heilongjiang Foreign Economic Relations and Trade* 黑龍江對外經貿, 5 (2010):28–30.
2. "India's Goods Trade and China-India Bilateral Trade in 2010," http://countryreport.mofcom.gov.cn/record/qikanlist.asp?qikanid=3492&title=2010 年印度貨物貿易及中印雙邊貿易概況.
3. Tan Zhong 譚中, "Wen Jiabao's visit to India fostering the development of China-India partnership" 溫家寶訪印促進中印夥伴關係發展, *Lianhe Zaobao* 聯合早報 (Dec. 20, 2010).
4. Hua Biyun 華碧雲, "Economic cooperation between China and India benefiting the two countries" 中印經濟合作惠及兩國人民, *China Report* 中國報導, 4 (2010):42–45.
5. Liu Anan 劉阿男, "The comparison and analysis of China and India opening up mode" 中印對外開放模式的比較與分析, *Journal of Liaoning Economic Management Cadre Institute* 遼寧經濟管理幹部學院學報, 4 (2009):39–41.
6. Gu Liubao 顧六寶, and Yang Hongling 楊宏玲, "The practice and strategic intention of China and India in their participation in international economy integration" 中印參與國際經濟一體化的實踐及戰略意圖探析, *Journal of Hebei University* 河北大學學報, 6 (2009):50–54.
7. Huang Liming 黃莉敏, "Study of relevant questions on China-India FTA" 中印自由貿易區相關問題研究, *Commercial Culture and Social Fabric* 商業文化·社會經緯, 2 (2008):183–184.
8. Refer to Hua Biyun, 2010.
9. Ibid.
10. Refer to Tan Zhong, 2010.
11. Wei Ling 衛靈, *Study of Sino-Indian Relations after the Cold War* 冷戰後中印關係研究 (Beijing: University of Political Science and Law Press, 2008).
12. Jairam Ramesh, *Making Sense of CHINDIA: Reflections on China and India* 理解 CHINDIA: 關於中國與印度的思考, trans. Caifeng 蔡楓, and Dong Fangfeng 董方峰 (Yinchuan: Ningxia People's Publishing House, 2006).

5 Chapter

The Rise of India and Its Pursuit of Great Power Status

Chen Fenglin

Abstract

Since its independence in 1947, India has been gradually marching toward the rank of the major developing countries through the unrelenting efforts of its leaders over several generations. As the first post-war leader of India, Jawaharlal Nehru expressly stated in his book *The Discovery of India* that India shall rise to become an "extraordinarily impressive" major power. Examination of India's several decades of historical development indicates that this target has already constituted India's fundamental pursuit. Since the 1990s, India has advanced its pace of liberalization, marketization, and internationalization, rising to be one power to be reckoned with by the international community among the major powers in the region. In the course of its future development, the rise of India may have a profound impact on South Asian and Sino-Indian relations and can thus be regarded as one of the most important developments of the 21st century.

Amidst the rise of the Eastern powers as a whole, the rise of India, along with its constant pursuit of the status of a great power, has undoubtedly become one of the most remarkable subjects of interest. In the past 20 to 30 years. The endless emergence of books and conferences on India's development and foreign policies at home and abroad underlined the fact that international attention on India is only rising. Since the 1990s, India has indeed demonstrated extraordinary influence in the international arena. Not only has it unveiled a more liberal political system, but it has also realized rapid and sustained economic growth, with especially outstanding achievements in the field of high technology. With a population of 1.1 billion, India is creating a new chapter of history of the East across an expanse of 2.98 million square kilometers. According to Angus Maddison's statistics, 52% of global GDP in the year 1820 originated from Asia, of which China contributed 29% while India accounted for 16%.[1] After succumbing to British colonial rule in the modern era, India had long been slighted as an insignificant country. But just like the phoenix which rises from the flames and resurrects in Nirvana, India has stood out from many other developing countries in the post-war decades and has been exerting increasingly critical influences. From today's perspective, examining the rise of India, and the possible influence and impact of its rise on the Asian regional order, is an indispensable task in all aspects.

Ideological and Cultural Foundation of India's Rise

The rise of India is underpinned by an enduring and profound historical and cultural foundation. Spanning thousands of years, India's culture has been one of the world's most influential cultural systems for a sustained period of time, with its influence scattered in China, Southeast Asia, and the surrounding countries. The profundity and variety of its achievements are exceptional in the world, with the nation demonstrating extraordinary vitality even up to the present day. Perhaps because of this, the economy of India today has momentum backed up by robust support. Some scholars have pointed out, "Across its more than 4,000 years of history, each generation of India has left the future generation with a legacy, albeit only bit by bit...No country has such a long and interminable culture like India."[2] In addition to providing a solid ideological and cultural foundation and forming the national-psychological basis for the rise of India now, its rich cultural heritage also fills the Indian people with confidence and a sense of superiority towards the future of their country. The history of India evolves from the past and inherits the recognition of its people towards their country. "As long as civilization exists, the country has never been stagnant and has been steadily developing instead. India's civilization dates back 4,000 years, with each historical period leaving an important legacy for today."[3]

In its long history of evolution, Indian society has undergone a number of major changes. Nevertheless, the heavy historical heritage that has remained in people's hearts has not been altered. Successive leaders in the post-war period have expressed their deep admiration for Indian history which has continued to inspire their infinite yearning towards India's glorious history and its great power status. This type of psychological structure is mutually adaptable with the socioeconomic development of India, which not only has a profound impact on the mentality and ideological character of its people but also affects their actions once established. The Indian people are full of hope for the future of their country and believe that India is full of vibrancy and capable of restoring its historical status as a great power in the near future. As Mira Kamdar in *Planet India* remarks, "A positive and optimistic mood has swept across the entire nation and ignited the imagination of India."[4] With its rapid economic development since the 1990s, India's domestic policy has been aimed towards becoming a major world power. From national psychology, cultural renaissance, speeches of state leaders to relational games among the major powers, none of these aspects have fallen short of highlighting the rapid pace at which India is stepping onto the world stage. Their reported remark that "40 years from now, India is going to redefine the positioning of the West on the world stage," underlines their full confidence as much as their fiery ambition.

The historical and cultural foundation of the rise of India must be related to specific individuals in order to elucidate the influence of Indian culture on today's landscape. In this regard, Jawaharlal Nehru, who served as Indian Prime Minister in the post-war period, is undoubtedly an outstanding representative. Nehru embodied an ingenious fusion of Indian national traditions and Western culture, retaining the cultural essence of the East and West to a considerable extent. This undoubtedly constituted the ideological basis of his nationalism, democracy, and his target of advancing India as a great power. Leaders who grew up in the background of Indian history and culture have developed a sense of identification with, and inheritance towards, their own country's culture. Rather than annihilating the memory of the Indian people for their own history, the long-term impact of British colonial rule has, on the contrary, ignited their pursuit and longing for national independence, the tradition of which has also been inherited by its subsequent successors. From the perspective of social form, Britain conquered India and altered the course of its development, but it failed to completely conquer and annihilate the Indian culture. Despite different views held towards the ideological and cultural foundation of the rise of India, we still believe that the Indian people have derived a certain strength from their own history, which bears witness to India's culture as a living dynamic system and one that has been rejuvenated with a new form of life thanks to several decades of economic growth in the post-war period. Today, India has embarked on a path towards a market economy and political democratization, opened its doors to the world, positioned itself at the converging point of Eastern and Western civilizations, and created history for realizing its new revitalization. In comparison, the development of India is less remarkable than that of China, especially in terms of social infrastructure and social mobilization. Regardless of how the international community views India, it has indeed emerged as a regional major power in South Asia with pervasive influence on the international order and relations of major powers, and the country has risen to become an international new power given its myriad contributions in culture and technology.

The rise and development of any country is not founded on an empty basis, nor does it emerge from nowhere, but it is closely linked to a certain social system, the level of productivity and people's thinking. On the level of ideological thinking, the religious thinking and characteristic national culture of India as a strand of rational intellectual thinking persistently comes into play every now and then by influencing people's values, ways of thinking, religious beliefs, customs, mentality, etc. Religious culture is deeply embedded in people's hearts in India and this invariably creates order. A long historical and cultural tradition has long been regarded as the country's fountain of wealth and resources. Reportedly in his New Year's address in 2003, Indian Prime Minister Atal Bihari Vajpayee drew reference to a prose passage by the renowned Indian philosopher Shami Bibekānondo, "The same India, despite having endured the onslaught of several centuries, a hundred foreign invasions and a hundred gigantic changes of its customs and traditions, always stands dauntingly on the same piece of land, exhibiting eternal vigor and indelible vitality and outweighing any rock in the world in hardness. Its vitality and soul embody the same essence, with no beginning and end but eternal immortality."[5] One must know that India achieved development after it cast off British colonial rule in the post-war era, which underlies the great significance of political independence. In a certain sense, the fact that Vajpayee took great pride in the glorious history and culture of his country reflects the cultural consciousness of the Indian people, but some have also commented that, "Throughout the 20th century, India still held onto self-conceit and a sense of historical and cultural pride — the type of pride that Indian people manage to maintain by reminiscing over the past days of prosperity."[6] To exaggerate a little, one may say that they may even have been infected with the chronic illness of Indian cultural superiority.

With respect to the target of realizing India's rise, Jawaharlal Nehru provided a clear vision in *The Discovery of India* towards which India has been aiming to advance in the past decades. The effective means of achieving this goal is through leveraging its advantages in terms of domestic political and economic resources to establish a more complete industrial system. Otherwise it cannot secure a place amid international competition. In view of the prominent status that major countries take up amid general competition in the field of international relations, Nehru put forward the theory of Indian centralism. In his opinion, for such a major Eastern country like India, it is imperative to achieve political and economic independence as well as rapid development, so that it can be ranked among the world's major powers and restore its past status as a major power that was once deprived of power by the West. He wrote, "In the future, the Asia-Pacific region will replace the Atlantic to become the world's major hub. Although India is not directly an Asia-Pacific country, it will inevitably play an instrumental role in the region. In the Indian Ocean region, from Southeast Asia to Central

Asia, India will ultimately become a center of economic and political activities.[7] Among all the post-war Asian leaders, Nehru may have been the first person to formulate such an extraordinary conception of the future political and economic prospect of one's country. This is related to the international influence of India in the early post-war period. Shortly after the Asian-African Conference in 1955, the notion of becoming Asia's leader began to germinate in Nehru's mind, prompting him to alienate China, build up closer ties with the U.S. and attempt to obtain the support of the U.S. towards his dream of advancing India to be Asia's leader. In addition to putting forward the goal of lifting India to become a great power, he also identified the disadvantageous position of weaker countries in international relations by stating that "Small nation-states are destined to perish. While they may linger on as a culturally autonomous region, it is impossible for them to become an independent political unit."[8] Perhaps Nehru stressed the urgency of the rise of India in order to highlight the severe conditions of small countries with respect to international relations. Nevertheless, a leader's keen sense of crisis, urgency, and grand ambitions is rendered very evidently. While the Eastern and Western countries were engaged in the confrontation of two major camps, almost all countries were subject to this type of unequal pattern of international relations, leaving India to confront an unprecedented choice regarding its diplomatic policy.

Marketization of India's Economy and Technology and Its Achievements in Internationalization

In conjunction with its policy of democratization and opening up of systems, India has sped up its pace of marketization and internationalization with respect to economic and technological development and has fast become a classical example of the rise of Eastern powers since the 1990s. Contributing to India's economic development was the better basis laid down during the pre-war era of British rule. Rich land resources, adequate labor force, and a superior geographic location constituted the favorable conditions for socioeconomic development. According to the statistics of the League of Nations, during the 25-year period from 1913 just prior to the outbreak of World War I to the beginning of World War II, India's industrial growth increased by 139.7% and the world's total industrial output value over the same period increased by 82.7%, among which the United States grew by 43.0%, Germany by 49.3%, and Canada by 61.8%.[9] This was a remarkable achievement. Fortunately, while almost all countries in East Asia and Southeast Asia became the battlefield of World War II, India was spared the disastrous damage of war and all the industries during the British rule were able to be preserved in their entirety. The sectors of textiles, steel, sugar refining, transportation, mining, dock construction as well as school education demonstrated different degrees of development, forming a basis of material culture for social development in post-war India. The Indian society has long been marked by a paradoxical phenomenon. As Nehru remarked, "India is not an impoverished country. It possesses all the rich resources that can make a country prosperous, but its people are destitute. Its cultural structure endows it with noble heritage and its civilization carries immense potential power."[10] The British preoccupied themselves with colonial exploitation and plundering in India. On the other hand, these infrastructures have been preserved after the end of British colonial rule. Reportedly, Britain became India's debtor after the end of World War II, with London's Bank of England in possession of India's huge deposits which would later become the main source of foreign currency exchange for India's first Five-Year Plan.[11]

Since the War, India's economic development and social progress were characterized by a gradual process of development. During the period between World War II and the 1980s, India's economic development was relatively slow, with the national per capita income growth rate generally at around 1.2% and basically running at a low level. The scanty growth of the Indian economy in the 1980s can be largely explained by changes to its domestic regime. The main efforts of the government leaders at the time were primarily targeted at maintaining social stability, thus leaving them with barely sufficient time to ponder over economic issues. Despite its reform attempts, the variety of domestic problems nevertheless stalled the progress of the reforms. Tremendous traditional inertia such as that arising from deep-rooted moral values and customs also translated into resistance against modernization. Compared with China in the same period, India clearly lagged behind in its pace of reform, and if its pressing domestic livelihood issues are not resolved, various types of political crises may be triggered and result in turmoil again. Therefore, accelerating and advancing economic reform has become a top priority for the Indian government.

In July 1991, the Indian government advanced reform on a full scale, which was focused on the industrial, commercial, and foreign trade sectors and aimed to realize marketization and liberalization, and to keep up with the pace of world economic globalization. Measures such as reducing national intervention in economic activities, encouraging the establishment of emerging industries, and opening up commodity prices in an appropriate manner injected vitality into the national social and economic landscape. Through practice, India's economic reform policies were shown to be effective. After the East-West Cold War confrontation came to an end in the 1990s, India promptly adjusted its foreign policy, with the aim of leveraging major transformation in the general situation to accelerate its own development and undertaking economic relations with the United States, European Union, Japan, China, Russia, and other countries with an open attitude. The policy adjustment allowed India to turn this into an opportunity for entering the international market and for lifting its level of participation in the international economy further. In the first half of the 1990s, India's average annual economic growth rate exceeded 6%, demonstrating a relatively higher economic growth among all developing countries. Judging from all types of indicators, India's reform in the 1990s had already identified a path of development suited to its national conditions and characteristics. In terms of economic and technological internationalization and marketization in particular, its economy was on a par with international standards, advancing the progress of lifting India's status as a major power and turning its dream of becoming a powerful country into a reality. The process of India's rise has given shape to the "Indian mode" which encompasses its national substance and characteristics, forming a new perspective of development and enriching the theory and practice of modernization of the Eastern countries.

Economic reform in the 1990s strengthened the basis of India's target as a major power and corresponded with the illustrious blueprint designed by its founding leader Jawaharlal Nehru. India exhibited vigorous economic growth in the 1990s. Except for registering an annual GDP growth rate at 1.43% in specific years, it consistently achieved a substantial growth rate in the majority of years, with the GDP growth rate at 9.4% in 2006 and 9.62% in 2007.[12] This indicates that India's economy has entered a period of rapid growth and concomitantly induced profound transformation in other areas of the society. Jawaharlal Nehru once stated in the 1950s, "India possesses a variety of resources, plus the wisdom, technology as well as the capability of rapidly advancing ahead...On the basis of its progress in scientific theories and scientific applications, it is able to catapult itself into a great industrial nation."[13] Following its entry into the 21st century, India's target of rising to be a major power is even clearer. The industries heavily invested and supported by the state generally pertain to highly technological and high value-added industries, such as computers, biological engineering, electronics, and information technology, aerospace, and nuclear technology. This has helped India secure a place in international competition. Nandan Nilekani remarked, "The success of factory industry prompted the entire Indian business community to develop an awareness of the almost unique strength and position that India occupies in the international economy. In the global market...its current capital, labor, and industry and other economic factors are very suitable for the country to participate in competition in the global marketplace."[14] Since the 1990s, the one basic objective underlying India's economic reforms was internationalization and openness, only with these could its reforms be aligned with its vision of becoming a major power and could the enterprise long dreamed of by its successive leaders be realized. In other areas, India has also achieved comprehensive development with respect to its national economic and social development goals. Despite the variety of problems persisting in India's socioeconomic development, we have already borne witness to its share of the world's GDP and advancement into the rank of the most promising "BRIC" countries (i.e., Brazil, Russia, India And China), which justifies the saying that India is the world's fourth largest power in terms of its share of the world's GDP. According to Angus Maddison's statistics, India's GDP accounted for 5% of the total world economic value in 1998, second to the U.S. which took up 21.9%, 11.5% of Mainland China, and 7.7% of Japan.[15] In practice, India has already become a new world economy and a vast market. Today's international competition boils down to a competition of overall national strength, which in turn determines the future prospect of a country. Judging from its technological strength, India has already advanced into the rank of the world's major powers with respect to space technology and nuclear technology. It has also demonstrated outstanding achievements in nurturing technological talents. With up to 3.4 million technological practitioners, India ranks at the world's forefront.[16]

Historically, the Indus Valley is an important region for human civilization. The re-emergence of the Eastern countries, including India, in the post-war period has altered the standard used by the canon of Western modernization towards the Eastern societies and challenged the world system theory, the attachment theory, and the classic modernization theory. Classical Western modernization theories are no longer able to explain the reality of unprecedented gigantic changes in India, China, and other countries. For instance, the world system theory postulates that the capitalist world economy is established according to different divisions of labor to give rise to three distinct regions, each undertaking three different roles: The periphery areas (that is, backward countries) supply cheap labor, markets, and raw materials to the core areas (that is, developed countries), channeling profits from the periphery areas to the core areas in terms of the distribution of benefits. Evidently, explaining the current social changes in the Eastern countries by means of this theoretical approach is unfeasible, since the rise of India, China, and the Association of Southeast Asian Nations (ASEAN) countries cannot be explained both in theory and in practice by classical theories belonging to the traditional Western canon. Conclusions can be drawn only through the concrete experience of the Eastern countries. The author believes that the process of world economic development is an ever-competitive process. In the era of agricultural economy in general, the rise of a country and the demise of another country entail a relatively long duration, often taking decades or even centuries; in entering the era of industrial civilization, competition among countries and regions, as well as their rise and fall, is notably more vigorous than before, and their development is also marked by an extremely uneven and unstable pattern. The downfall of a center is soon superseded by the rise of another economic center, evolving alternately and interchangeably.[17] The re-emergence of the Eastern countries corresponds with the general trend and general law of the development of world history.

The Diplomacy of India as a Rising Major Power

India's diplomacy is underpinned by its profound historical and cultural heritage which exhibits clear and consistent direction and plays an influential role in international relations both in South Asia and the Asia-Pacific region. During the reign of Nehru, India pursued the "Non-Aligned" policy and strove to maintain more unity and coordination with Asian, African, and Latin American countries. India's aim was to reduce political interference from the West and promote the nation's involvement in international affairs while striving for a peaceful international environment for its national development. It can be said that the Non-Aligned Movement advocated by India and other countries lifted India's international influence to an unprecedentedly high level, until in the 1960s when India adopted a hard-line stance towards its foreign policy and manifested the tendency of regional hegemony in its approach to Sino-Indian relations and India-Pakistan relations, which led to the Sino-Indian War in 1962 over the border conflict. After the outbreak of the Sino-Indian war, India sought support and accepted substantial military and economic aid from the Soviet Union. This action by India was in practice equivalent to relinquishing the policy of non-alliance with any country which it had pursued and carried a far-reaching impact on its foreign policy. Nehru played a groundbreaking role in the formulation and practice of India's foreign policy and the subsequent foreign policies were largely a continuation and evolving of Nehru's foreign policy.[18] In the 1970s, in order to compete with the United States for world hegemony, the Soviet Union extended its reach southward to the Indian Ocean under the guise of ensuring "freedom of navigation on the high seas" and this supported the doctrine of India's regional hegemony, reinforcing the ties between India and the Soviet Union. The Soviet Union saw the superior geostrategic value of India as a converging point for transportation between the East and West. In the later Indira Gandhi and Rajiv Gandhi eras, despite the different international landscape, the basic direction of their foreign policy still largely pertained to the diplomatic strategy of the regionalism of a major power.

Indira Gandhi and Rajiv Gandhi were successors to Nehru's foreign policy. India's aspiring status as a major power during the Nehru era suffered setbacks due to the Sino-Indian War, which also challenged its international status. Indira Gandhi undertook to revive the dream of advancing India as a major power, continuing to implement the pro-Soviet policy with respect to its foreign policy. The 1970s marked the period of close ties between India and the Soviet Union. "The Soviet Union rolled out significant and large-scale military assistance programs which enabled it to exert influence on the largest and most promising country in the region in terms of naval development."[19] Compared with his forefather, Jawaharlal Nehru, Indira Gandhi's foreign policy was rooted in realism, which also presented an option for altering any unfavorable international position. Long-term wars of aggression launched by the U.S. in Indochina not only undermined America's national strength but also weakened its influence in South Asia, providing an opportunity to the Soviet Union to strengthen its relations with India; Following the war launched by India against Pakistan, conflict between the two nations intensified, eventually leading to closer ties between Pakistan and China. In August 1971, India and the Soviet Union signed the *Treaty of Peace, Amity and Cooperation*, which specified that "both parties undertake not to provide any assistance to any third party involved in a conflict with the other party, and in case one party is attacked and is under the threat of attack, both parties shall immediately undertake mutual negotiation." In essence, the treaty obviously pertained to a military alliance, causing extremely tense relations among countries in South Asia. With the support of the Soviet Union, India took an even tougher stance in international affairs in the South Asian subcontinent, triggering discontent and anxiety among the neighboring countries following the outbreak of the India-Pakistan war. The foreign policy approach to regional affairs pursued by India was an embodiment of strength and an awareness of reality which isolated the country in the South Asian region. Data showed that from 1955 to 1971, economic assistance provided by the Soviet Union to India amounted to 10,312,500,000 rubles, which was mainly applied in the construction projects within India's heavy industry and military industry. The assistance was extremely important to India and played an instrumental role during the subsequent Indo-Pakistan war.

Since the 1970s, India has accelerated the process of military modernization. With the assistance of the Soviet Union, its military production capacity has greatly improved. During this period, the Soviet Union's military strength was basically on a par with that of the United States, with its number of intercontinental ballistic missiles surpassing even the number the U.S. had; in terms of naval strength, the Soviet Union developed an ocean-going navy, extending its power to the Mediterranean Sea, West Africa, the Indian Ocean, and the Indo-China region, competing for hegemony in Asia with the United States. The foreign policy of "great power chauvinism" pursued by India in the South Asia region corresponded with the Soviet Union's "Asian collective security system" needs, turning the country into an ally of the Soviet Union in South Asia. Despite discrepancies in their social systems and ideologies, geo-strategic interests became their shared choice. The assistance of the Soviet Union became a double-edged sword. As an Indian official pointed out, "As part of its global strategy, the Soviet military aid diplomacy encompassed the double roles of defense and aggression...The defensive character of the Soviet military aid diplomacy was clearly manifested in its relations with India."[20]

In the 1980s, India's diplomacy was faced with a new situation. As confrontation between the Soviet Union and the United States subsided, the Soviet Union adopted a defensive stance globally, obliging the country to implement strategic contraction and mark the end of dependency on the Soviet Union. Rajiv Gandhi clearly discerned that the significant changes in the international landscape would bestow India with greater room to exercise its influence, and, in particular, accord it more room to maneuver among the three major powers represented by the United States, China, and the Soviet Union. This signaled his attempt to alter India's marginal position caused by earlier over-reliance on the Soviet Union. In the eyes of the Indian leaders, given the Soviet Union's implementation of a strategic contraction strategy and China's rapid rise, it was imperative for India to seek a strategic balance among the three major powers represented by China, the United States, and the Soviet Union, thus giving shape to the traditional style of Indian diplomacy. Therefore, in promoting domestic economic reform, India adjusted its approach to relations between major powers, which in principle gave rise to its liaison and interaction with the major powers. Nevertheless, it must be pointed out that India injected more momentum into nuclear power development in the 1980s. In Rajiv Gandhi's view, possessing the same strength of nuclear weapons as the other major powers was a necessary condition for entering the rank of major powers and for securing India's dominant position in the South Asian subcontinent.

In the early 1990s, with the end of the Cold War, the United States accorded more attention to its domestic economy and employment. On the other hand, Russia was also temporarily incapable of exerting influence in the South Asian region. To a certain extent, with the diminishing pressure from the major powers on South Asia, the international situation was advantageous to India establishing its dominant position in South Asia and the Indian Ocean. India had been striving to exert its role as a major power in South Asia and the Indian Ocean region and strengthen its participation in international affairs. Such efforts have been marking the pervasive presence of Indian people in international organizations and international activities. India's recent proposition for becoming a permanent member of the United Nations Security Council only figured as one of a series of diplomatic activities that lent proof to its efforts in strengthening its target of attaining great power status. India adopted a strategic stance in its relations with Russia and made use of Russia to balance its current great power relations, in the hope that international relations will not be dominated by a particular state. In terms of its relations with the United States, India has already regarded the United States as a key focus. The key focus of India's foreign policy experienced a historical shift from the Soviet Union to the United States, which was dictated by the changing international situation and reflected the essence of India's diplomatic realism. Complicated international political realities emerging in Southeast Asia and the South China Sea imparted a few more factors of China into the U.S.-India relations. Moreover, issues concerning cooperation in East Asia also induced the United States to incline towards drawing India into standing on its side, reflecting at the same time that U.S.-India relations were on a course of reinforcement. The frequent U.S.-Indian joint military exercises in recent years particularly shed light on the active role of India on the world's stage. Meanwhile, India has been actively participating in issues concerning East Asia cooperation and the South China Sea in order to play an international role commensurate with its great power status. We believe that if India's participation in affairs concerning the East Asia region can bring lasting peace, stability, and development to the harmonious region, there lies a right path for its foreign policy.

Comments

Since the implementation of a comprehensive reform and forward leap in the 1990s, India has already advanced into the rank of major powers. Whether in terms of GDP or overall national strength, India is on a course of unprecedented development and the nation is situated in an era considered to be of rapid development. An open economic system together with political democratization showcase the vitality of the Indian society, and its hope to be accepted by the international community and so play a role in the international system. Like China, India rose in line with, and in response to, a variety of complex domestic and international situations, changing the basic trend of East-West relations. Playing a role in the future international system, and creating peace, stability, and development in Asia, are the shared missions of China and India.

In an absolute sense, if India realizes its rise in a peaceful manner, actively fulfills its role as a major power in the international society, liaises with other countries to form a stakeholder body, it can be accepted by the international community as a world power. In 2005, Indian Prime Minister Manmohan Singh remarked to Chinese Premier Wen Jiabao who was then on a visit to New Delhi, "If India and China join hands, the world order can be changed." The vastness of the international landscape accords sufficient capacity to accommodate the development and rise of India and confers India with adequate time and space. The rise of India and its pursuit of great power status reveal a number of regularities: First, scientific and technological progress is the fundamental pillar of a country's rise. Without exception, almost all emerging countries take scientific and technological progress as a fundamental pillar of external competition and advancement into the rank of great powers. Second, economic strength forms the material basis for a country's rise. Whether in recent or modern times, economic strength is the material basis and premise for realizing a country's rise. Third, institutional innovation is a direct force contributing to a country's rise. Institutional innovation not only pertains to innovation of the political system, but also to ideas, concepts, policies, and other aspects. Institutional innovation induces a fundamental shift in the social, political, and economic systems as well as their modes of operation, placing institutional factors, economic factors, and technological factors in a mutually promoting and mutually propelling dynamic.

Fourth, the process of the rise of a country is, in essence, a process of participation in international competition. Since a modern society is a universally connected system, its development has fundamentally changed the survival state of the country, forging tighter cooperation and ties among countries. Participating in international competition and division of labor in a peaceful manner brings peace, stability, and development to the international order. Otherwise, it will lead to international confrontations, conflicts, and wars.

Notes

1. Giovanni, Arrighi, and Hamashita, Takeshi, et al., *The Resurgence of East Asia: 500, 150 and 50 Year Perspectives* 東亞的復興：以 500 年、150 年和 50 年為視角 (Beijing: Social Sciences Documentation Publishing House, 2006), 96–97.
2. Basham, A. L., ed., *Cultural History of India* 印度文化史 (Beijing: The Commercial Press, 1999), 2.
3. Refer to Basham, A.L., 1999, p.6.
4. Kamdar, Mira, *Planet India: How the Rapid Development is Transforming the World* 印度星球：快速發展給世界帶來的影響 (Beijing: SDX Joint Publishing Company, 2009), 11.
5. Wu Yongnian 吳永年 , Zhao Gancheng 趙干城 , and Ma Ying 馬嬰 , Introduction to *A New Theory of Indian Diplomacy in the 21st century* 21 世 紀 印 度 外 交 新 論 (Shanghai: Shanghai Translation Publishing House, 2004), 3.
6. Nilekani, Nandan, *Imagining India: The Ideas of A Renewed Nation* 與世界同步：印度的困頓與崛起 , trans. Xu Xiaoli 許效禮 , and Wang Xianggang 王祥鋼 (Beijing: CITIC Publishing House, 2011), 95.
7. Nehru, Jawaharlal, *The Discovery of India* 印 度 的 發 現 , trans. Qi Wen 齊 文 (Beijing: World Knowledge Press, 1956), 712.
8. Ibid.
9. Sun Peijun 孫培鈞 , and Liu Chuangyuan 劉創源 , eds., *Study on the Economic Development Strategy of South Asian Countries* 南亞國家經濟發展戰略研究 (Beijing: Peking University Press, 1990), 15.
10. Refer to Nehru, Jawaharlal, 1956, p.698.
11. Refer to Sun Peijun, and Liu Chuangyuan, 1990, p.16.
12. Zhang Liqun 張力群 , *Study on India's Economic Growth* 印度經濟增長研究 (Nanjing: Southeast University Press, 2009): 87–88.
13. Refer to Nehru, Jawaharlal, 1956, p.698–699.
14. Refer to Nilekani, Nandan, 2011, p.97–98.
15. Maddison, Angus, *The World Economy: A Millennial Perspective* 世 界 經 濟 千 年 史 , trans. Wu Xiaoying 伍曉鷹 , and Ye Xiaofei 葉曉斐 (Beijing: Peking University Press, 2003), 121.
16. Lin Chengjie 林承節 , ed., *The Development Path of India's Modernization* 印度現代化的發展道路 (Beijing: Peking University Press, 2001), 119.
17. Chen Fenglin 陳奉林 , "Examining the history of the east Asian economic circle" 對東亞經濟圈的歷史考察 , *World History* 世界歷史 , 3 (2009):48.
18. Sun Jinzhong 孫晉忠 , "On the theory and practice of India's regional foreign policy" 試論印度地區外交政策的理論與實踐 , *Development of the Eastern Diplomatic History* 東方外交史之發展 , eds. Chen Fenglin 陳奉林 , and Wei Chuxiong 魏楚雄 (Macau: Macau University Press, 2009), 397.
19. Cottrell, A. J., and Burrell, R. M., eds., *The Indian Ocean: Its Political, Economic and Military Importance* 印度洋：在政治、經濟、軍事上的重要性 (Shanghai: Shanghai People's Publishing House, 1976), 467.
20. Charlie. P. R., "Review of India-Soviet military cooperation" 印 蘇 軍 事 合 作 回 顧 , *The strategic situation of South Asia* 南亞戰略態勢 (Beijing: Current Affairs Press, 1986), 60–61.

6

Chapter

China-India Cooperation in the Neighborhood: Opportunities and Challenges

Li Li

In the current era, China cooperates with India mainly on three levels: Global, regional, and bilateral. At the global level, China and India have the same appeals on the governance of the global economy as well as a similar position on many global issues such as climate change, energy, and the World Trade Organization (WTO) negotiations since both nations are developing and newly-rising great powers. Based on their common ground, they cooperate smoothly and continuously. At the bilateral level, they both cooperate and compete with each other. While competing with each other due to the border conflicts, they cooperate mainly on economy and trade. Because it is difficult to deal with the border conflicts in a short time, they will continue to promote their economic cooperation on the condition that they both make efforts to guarantee that their borderland is safe and sound. Compared to the definite perspective in cooperation at the global and bilateral levels, their regional cooperation seems most uncertain and controversial. The mainstream opinions in Western and Indian academia are relatively pessimistic: Along with China and India rising simultaneously, the interests and influences of these two nations will interweave in the expanding process, which will lead to unavoidable collisions or even conflicts. For example, China's economic and diplomatic expansions in South Asia and the Indian Ocean are considered an erosion of India's sphere of influence,[1] whereas the advancement of China-Africa cooperation and India-Africa cooperation side-by-side is interpreted as a competition over Africa between them.[2] Although it is not so pessimistic in Chinese academia, there are still many people bearing a grudge against India's "Look East Policy" with the worry that the intervention from India would widen the rift between China and some Southeast and Northeast Asian countries.[3] Therefore, the author of this paper will focus on the cooperation and competition between China and India in their neighborhood and their actual influences on the China-India relationship.

The so-called "China-India neighborhood" refers to China, India, and the neighboring region, which can be described as the following three layers. The first layer is the China-India shared neighborhood, namely the areas both China and India border on, which refers, strictly speaking, to South Asia and Myanmar. But since India faces Thailand, Malaysia, Singapore, Indonesia, and so on across the sea, Southeast Asia is classified together with South Asia as the China-India shared neighborhood out of convenience. The second layer is the surrounding area of China (i.e. Northeast Asia, Russia, and Central Asia) and that of India (i.e. the Indian Ocean). The third layer is the China-India extended neighborhood which mainly refers to East Asia and Africa. Hence, on the basis of the classification mentioned above, this paper consists of four parts. In first part, the author discusses the China-India cooperation and competition in South Asia and Southeast Asia. In the second part, the author elaborates on India's administration on the surrounding area of China as well as China's strategy for the Indian Ocean, and their effects on the China-India relationship. In the third part, the author discusses the opportunities and challenges on China-India cooperation in East Asia and Africa. In the last part, the author makes a summary on the above analysis.

Cooperation and Competition between China and India in South Asia and Southeast Asia

From the geopolitical perspective, South Asia is always considered as belonging to the orbit of India, while Southeast Asia belongs to that of China. However, due to the rapid rise of China and India at the same time, the connection between China and South Asia becomes increasingly close and India's existence is continuously enhanced in Southeast Asia.

In South Asia, the all-weather friendship between China and Pakistan is being consolidated. China's support for Sri Lanka in wiping out the Liberation Tigers of Tamil Eelam (LTTE) and its construction of Hambantota has taken their relationship to a record high. The need for China is increasing in Nepal after the Maoists returned to the mainstream on the political stage in the post-civil-war era. China has become Bengal's biggest trading partner. The international community, including Afghanistan and the U.S., expects China to play a more active role in the reconciliation among Afghan ethnics and their reconstruction. Over 100,000 Chinese people visited the Maldives in 2010, and China has become the biggest source country of visitors to the Maldives.[4] The negotiation between China and Bhutan on the border issue progresses smoothly because both sides expressed a strong desire to establish diplomatic relations, and China has been accepted as an observer country of the South Asian Association for Regional Cooperation (SAARC).

In Southeast Asia, under the "Look East Policy," the relationship between India and the Southeast Asian countries has been enhanced in every aspect. Economically, the India-ASEAN Free Trade Agreement (IAFTA) made a substantive breakthrough. Besides, India signed the Bilateral Free Trade Agreement with Thailand, Singapore, and other countries. On January 1, 2010, the IAFTA came into effect and, moreover, their negotiation on the free trade of service and investment is still in process. In military affairs, India has signed the Bilateral Defense Cooperation Agreement with Vietnam, Singapore, Indonesia, Malaysia, Cambodia, and the like, mainly involving training of manpower, joint military exercises, and maritime security cooperation. What's more, the biennial Milan exercise and annual Malabar exercise have been the important platforms for India to perform military communication and cooperation with ASEAN as well as the U.S., Australia, Japan, and other countries. In political affairs, India continuously exchanges top-level visits with the ASEAN countries. Meanwhile, the connection between India and ASEAN has become closer. India became the all-round Dialogue Partner with ASEAN in 1995, joined in the ASEAN Region Forum (ARF) in 1996, built up the "10+1" mechanism with ASEAN in 2002, and became one of the founder states of the East Asia Summit (EAS) in 2005.

In fact, both China's expansion in South Asia and India's aggressiveness in Southeast Asia are the natural manifestation and outcome of the rise of these two countries, instead of the sole subjective design from one side to weaken or guard against the other. Nevertheless, Western media and academia tend to interpret the relationships of China-South Asia and India-ASEAN from the perspective of a China-India rivalry. Each side cautiously surveys the other from its own sphere of influence inside China and India. The main reasons for misunderstandings and misinterpretations of this kind lie in the following three aspects that are the key barriers to carrying out cooperation between them.

First, the border issue between China and India has gone so far that many people still believe the relationship between them is of competition or even rivalry. Only two years ago, China criticized the India-U.S. nuclear deal, India allowed the Dalai Lama to visit the southern part of Tibet (India calls it Arunachal Pradesh), and India deployed more troops to the China-India boundary and the Chinese government issued a separate visa to the citizens in Indian-controlled Kashmir. Those ugly spectacles between the two countries once caused a halt in their military communication, and the Indian military even proposed the "Two Line Battle" (fighting against Pakistan and China at the same time) again.[5] Due to the circumstances that the China-India border dispute could not have any breakthrough in a short time, and the fact that there are still uncertainties in the China-India relationship, China's influence in South Asia and India's availability in Southeast Asia do bring about an objective diversionary situation with each other. In this case, the subjective intent that they are rivaling each other is likely to be exaggerated.

Second, the contradictions and conflicts between China and India due to some of their neighbors are difficult to solve. In South Asia, the Indian-Pakistani rivalry is chronic, whereas China and Pakistan are all-weather friends. Therefore, the triangle of the China-India-Pakistan relationship is the top problem that needs to be solved in the realm of China-India cooperation in South Asia. In Southeast Asia, China has conflicts with Vietnam, The Philippines, and Indonesia on South China Sea issues. Meanwhile, India enhances its military cooperation with those countries, and even plans to explore the oil and gas fields where China has disputes with Vietnam which definitely raises the alert and dissatisfaction from China.[6]

Finally, the shared neighboring countries have fuelled the China-India competition. All the neighbor countries of China and India are of small and medium size. Only a kind of balanced policy can serve their best interests in surviving on the margins of these two big global powers. As for the small South Asian countries, they have overall dependence on India, and that dependence is increasing along with the rapid growth of India. In order to keep their self-independence, these South Asian countries prefer to strengthen their relationship with China that would never take an advantage to bully weak countries, nor interfere with the internal affairs of other countries. For the Southeast Asian countries, against the backdrop of being closely bound with China in economic affairs, it seems that they could let China make concessions on territory issues only with the help of external force. And India is considered to be a good choice.

Then, is there any room for China and India to cooperate in their shared neighborhood? And how large would be the room for such cooperation? The question is whether the barriers mentioned above could be broken down. First, even though it is difficult to solve the China-India border disputes in a short time, it would not affect the cooperation between China and India on the issues in South Asia, Southeast Asia, and even in other fields. Early in 1988, China and India established two main principles, i.e. "not letting the border issue affect the cooperation in other fields" and "keeping the border peaceful and safe before the border disputes are solved." At present, both China and India need a favorable and stable environment to focus on their domestic development. On one hand, both countries will continue to deal with the border issue according to the two main principles mentioned above. The leaders from China and India agreed to foster "The China-India Border Affairs Consultation and Coordination Mechanism" in April of 2011, which reiterated such principles. On the other hand, the stability of the shared neighborhood is also of common appeal to both China and India. Therefore, in those countries with unstable political situations — such as Afghanistan, Nepal, and Myanmar — the desire and room for cooperation between China and India is far greater than competition and rivalry, considering stability a principle of overriding importance. Although their interests are not the same and each governs its country in its own way, a virtual cooperation will take shape due to their similarities in policy goals. Just like in wiping out the LTTE and then ending the long-lasting civil war in Sri Lanka, both Chinese and Indian governments gave essential support to the Sri Lankan government. Besides, they are still the two biggest foreign aid countries in Sri Lanka's reconstruction.

Second, there is a way out of the conflicts between China and India concerning their neighbor countries. The dispute on the South China Sea between China and some other Southeast Asian countries is not irreconcilable, and China shall not change its policy to settle the territorial disputes by seeking peaceful settlement. Also, the India-Pakistan contradictions show signs of conciliation. Because Pakistan's possession of nuclear weapons and the civil war launched by the terrorists are testing the Pakistan government's ability to govern, a "failed" Pakistan is not in accord with India's interests. Hence, in February 2011, India agreed to restart the peace process with Pakistan. When Bombay was attacked by terrorists in July 2011, India did not target Pakistan for that for the first time. Actually, considering the concerns and the feelings of their counterparts, China and India are soft-pedaling on their cooperation with those countries and are sensitive to them in order to avoid provoking more conflicts. Finally, as for the small countries' attitudes and practices to keep a balance between them, what China and India have to do is to ensure their independence as well as to indicate that the cooperation between China and India surpasses the competition without forcing them to choose either side. Therefore, the small countries' close association with both China and India at the same time should not lead to negative influence. Instead, this will create more chances for their cooperation. For example, China and India built the energy pipeline in Myanmar together.[7] In fact, China and India have shown a great promise for cooperation in their shared neighborhood in the construction of infrastructure and hydraulic engineering.

Cooperation and Competition between China and India in Central Asia and the Indian Ocean

Besides the shared neighborhood, India has developed its cooperation rapidly with other neighbors of China such as Japan, Korea, Mongolia, and the Central Asian countries. The India-Russia relationship has lasted for many years with a solid foundation, especially in the areas of military and energy cooperation. Meanwhile, the China-Russia strategic cooperative partnership is developing stably and deepening. The China-Russia-India trilateral dialogue has featured its own mechanism, and these three countries cooperate well in the BRICS (Brazil, Russia, India, China, and South Africa) framework. It is obvious that the development of the India-Russia relationship does not affect the China-Russia one, and the trilateral cooperation is moving forward steadily instead. In fact, Northeast Asia has already become a part of India's "Look East Policy." However, what China worries about most is the tendency of the India-Japan relationship because it shows a heavy flavor in strategic cooperation. In 2007, the initial strategic dialogue among India, the U.S., Japan, and Australia was aimed at China, which aroused strong opposition from China.[8] Later, Australia and India withdrew from it in succession, and then the Dialogue stopped. But on December 19, 2011, the U.S., India, and Japan held their first trilateral official dialogue in Washington, D. C. Although they tried to play down their directness against China by not mentioning "China" in the brief joint statement, coping with a rising China was the unspoken reality. The key to avoiding the suspicion and jealousy between China and India is that India should remove the fuzziness of its "Look East Policy" and prove that the policy is not a tool to deter China. In general, India's influence on China due to the development of its relationship with Japan, Korea, and Mongolia has much in common with the situation in Southeast Asia, which, therefore, is not reiterated here. The cooperation and competition between China and India in Central Asia will be emphasized in the following section.

Former senior officials in Indian Foreign Affairs Rajiv Sikri pointed out that India has three interests in Central Asia, i.e. to promote the stability and secularization of Central Asia, fight against terrorism, separatism and fundamentalism, cut off their influence in Pakistan and Afghanistan, and prevent the Domino Effect; to establish a firm footing in Central China and prevent it from being controlled by the big country antagonistic to India, and to protect India's energy and economy interests in Central Asia.[9] Based on the analysis of some Chinese scholars, China has similar interests in Central Asia. First, China shall eliminate the threats from "Three Evil Forces" (separatism, terrorism, and religious extremism) on the stability of its borderlands. Second, China shall ensure its friendship with Central Asian countries, prevent the U.S. from turning Central Asia into a front for a fight with China, and protect the peaceful environment in West China. Third, it shall exploit the affluent oil and gas resources and potential consumer market in Central Asia. Finally, maintaining the stability of Central Asia is essential to protecting the continental bridge connecting West China with West Asia and Europe.[10] It can be seen that China and India share the same interests from cracking down on the "three evil forces," maintaining the stability of Central Asia, to exploring the oil and gas resources as well as having economic and trade cooperation with Central Asia.

But behind all these shared interests, China and India have different opinions in Central Asia due to their cognitional gap. First, China mainly guards against the U.S. in this region while India mainly guards against China there. Second, both China and India are very aggressive in Central Asia's energy and market, which leads to unavoidable competition between them. For instance, India Oil and Gas Corporation competed with the Chinese company in outbidding Kazakhstan Gas Corporation. Then, the Chinese company won and China-India competition was exaggerated.[11] Finally, India has become active in the Shanghai Cooperation Organization (SCO) in the past two years instead of being passive as before. But China is unable to show any open support about it out of consideration of the balance between India and Pakistan and the worry of decreasing the effectiveness of the SCO in the wake of the India-Pakistan conflict. This has also aroused suspicion and dissatisfaction from India. Nevertheless, the disagreements mentioned above still stem from the lack of mutual trust rather than a real conflict of interest.[12] In fact, after several rounds of face-to-face competitive bidding in overseas energy projects, both China and India have realized that such competitions only cause failure on both sides, or on either side. Otherwise, they would have to bid at an extremely high cost. Hence, since 2006, the two countries have tried to turn their competition to cooperation in the energy field, and their gas and oil companies started to explore a joint bid via the third country.[13] China and India are still negotiating on India's joining in the SCO. In June of 2011, the SCO's Kazakhstan Summit made new terms of accession, indicating that India's joining in the SCO would be placed onto the agenda soon.

After the Chinese Navy was appointed to the Gulf of Aden to fight against the pirates and the Chinese government helped to build Gwadar Harbour in Pakistan, Hambantota Harbour in Sri Lanka, and Kyaukpyu Harbour in Myanmar in the Indian Ocean, the saying of China's carrying out "the string of pearls strategy" toward India is rather popular in the West and India.[14] At the same time, India sped up the construction and introduction of aircraft carriers and submarines, which made some Chinese people worry that India might make use of its geographic advantages to threaten the security of China's seaward passage and force China to make concessions on the border issue.[15] Moreover, the enhancement of strategic cooperation between the U.S. and India also increased the possibility of their joint force in deterring China in the Indian Ocean.

Nevertheless, all the sayings about the fighting or conflict over the Indian Ocean are actually nothing but fancies or guesses, far away from the actual situation. Actually, the following important factors will decrease the possibility of the extreme situation. First of all, the core purpose of China's Indian Ocean strategy is to protect the security of its seaward passage rather than aim at India. Second, China's construction of harbors in the Indian Ocean focuses more on finding the substitute passage for importing energy in order to get out of the Malacca Swamp instead of surrounding India. Third, the Chinese Navy always focuses on the Pacific Ocean. As a result, the Chinese Navy shall not challenge the Indian Navy in the Indian Ocean in either geographic advantages or military power. On the contrary, it is the U.S. that has a power similar to India in the Indian Ocean, which means that there would be rivalry rather than cooperation between the U.S. and India there. Finally, the Indian Ocean is a boundless ocean, so there is no single country that can dominate it exclusively. However, the solution to non-traditional security problems such as pirates, smuggling, and maritime terrorism requires international cooperation. And China, India, and the countries involved have the same interests in maintaining maritime security. The U.S. and other Western countries welcome the Chinese Navy to escort them in the Gulf of Aden, and the Chinese and Indian Navies have agreed to hold a joint anti-pirate maneuver in the Gulf of Aden while exchanging their views on maritime security,[16] which means that China and India will have a promising future in their cooperation in the Indian Ocean as long as they can get rid of the Cold War mentality.

Cooperation and Competition between China and India in West Asia and Africa

Generally speaking, China and India have maintained good political relations with West Asian and African countries since the 1950s thanks to their acceptance of the theory of the Third World and having the same interests and demands as developing countries. Particularly, over the last 10 or 20 years, with the rapid economic development in China and India, their economic link with West Asian and African countries has been increasing obviously with an expanding influence.

With energy security as the core issue, India has carried forward economic and trade cooperation with the Middle East, especially the Gulf States, in West

Asia. India's foreign dependency rate of oil reaches up to 70%. Two thirds of its imported oil comes from the Middle East, among which Saudi Arabia accounts for 20%, Iran for 17%, and Kuwait for 11%. The trade between India and the Gulf States is also prosperous. India's trade volume with the United Arab Emirates (UAE) reaches up to.USD43.4 billion, with Saudi Arabia up to USD21 billion, and with Kuwait up to USD10.5 billion. Besides, the Gulf States have attracted 4.5 million overseas Indians (mainly Indian laborers), and their overseas remittance reached up to USD50 billion in India in 2010.[17] Similarly, China also has significant interests of strategic economy in West Asia. China's foreign dependency rate of crude oil has reached 55%, 5% higher than the security boundary recognized internationally. At present, half of the crude oil imported to China comes from the Persian Gulf, which plays a decisive role in China's energy security. Among all the countries supplying China crude oil, Saudi Arabia ranks top, accounting for 1/5 of the total. Meanwhile, it also functions as China's biggest trade partner in that region, and their trade volume reached USD43.2 billion in 2010. Iran is China's third biggest crude oil supplier (accounting for approximate 11%) with its trade volume with China reaching USD29.4 billion. Moreover, West Asia is China's important project contractor and cooperation market of labor service. In 2007, their contractual volume recorded USD10.12 billion.[18]

In Africa, China and India are developing side-by-side as well. In 2010, compared to the China-Africa trade volume of USD126.9 billion,[19] the India-Africa one was USD40 billion.[20] India's aggregate investment in Africa had reached USD50 billion[21] and that of China USD32.3 billion.[22] China and India are both important donor countries in Africa. In 2009, China promised to offer Africa loans of USD10 billion on favorable terms over the next three years.[23] In 2011, India promised to offer Africa loans of USD5.4 billion on favorable terms over the next five years.[24] Africa's cooperation with China and India has been so institutionalized that there are China-Africa Cooperation and India-Africa Forums.

Because of the spontaneous expansion of interests and influence of both China and India in West Asia and Africa, together with the rapid increase in demand for energy and resources, some scholars and politicians who believe that "the fight between the dragon and the elephant is unavoidable" focus on West Asia and Africa against the background of potential China-India border disputes. This leads to the prevailing saying in recent years that China-India competition is inevitable in these areas, especially in Africa, which turns out to be a wrong prediction full of subjective suppositions. The author of this paper has found the following factors that illustrate the opportunities for China-India cooperation rather than challenges. First, there is vast territory with abundant resources in over a dozen West Asian countries and more than 50 African countries for both China and India to develop together. As a matter of fact, in the past decade, Africa has benefited mainly from the expansion of trade and investment carried out by China and India there. Second, China and India have complementary advantages in their cooperation with West Asia and Africa, respectively. For instance, due to the support and promotion from the Chinese government, China's economic activities always boast a high efficiency and significant scale. On the contrary, most Indian companies there are private ones with flexibility and affinity. On the other hand, China's financial power is slightly better than that of India, but India precedes China in such soft strengths as language and number of overseas Indians (several million of them). Therefore, there is neither a winner nor a loser between China and India in West Asia and Africa. If they can concentrate on finding mutual support from each other, their cooperation will be increasing dramatically. Third, as mentioned above, in energy and resources fields, China and India have realized that "cooperation can help them achieve their mutual benefits, but rivals will do harm to both sides." So it is unlikely that they would start cutthroat competition. As a matter of fact, they have cooperated smoothly in the energy field in Sudan.[25] Finally, despite the differences in political system, China and India have significant similarities in their political principles in handling their relations with West Asia and Africa as developing countries, without diverging on the ideology, interfering with the internal affairs of other countries and even resisting those major powers getting involved in the internal affairs of other countries. On a careful observation of the way that China and India dealt with the Darfur conflict in Sudan, Mugabe's government of Zimbabwe, the Libya crisis, and the Iran nuclear issue, it is easy to notice that, quite differently from the Western countries, China and India share a very similar position.

Conclusion

Overall, the common interests of China and India outweigh their conflicts even though they are not the same in various shared neighborhoods. No matter the neighborhood, their expansion in interests and influence stem from their own desires for development instead of holding back each other or treating each other as the enemy. The cooperation between China and India at the regional level shows a great flexibility. The regional cooperation is expected to be the bright spot in the future, helping to increase mutual trust and lay a foundation for the solution of border disputes on the condition that both sides regard their differences as normal. The two countries shall focus on their complementary fields in order to expand room for their cooperation instead of bringing the border issue into the triangular relationship among China, India, and another neighbor.

Notes

1. "India and China: A Himalayan Rivalry," *The Economist*, Aug. 19, 2010, http://www.economist.com/node/16843717.
2. "The Indians are coming: India is vying for raw materials and more in Africa," *The Economist*, Apr. 28, 2008, http://www.economist.com/node/11117571.
3. Bai Ling 白玲, "India's look east policy and its influence on China" 印度的東向政策及其對中國的影響, *Consumer Guide* 消費導刊, no. 8 (2009), http://www.bianjibu.net/guanlixue/gonggongguanli/5708.html;

   Liu Xiaojuan 劉曉娟, and Zhang Jian 張建, "Non-economic factors resulting inIndia's look east policy" 印度東向政策形成中的非經濟因素, *South Asian Studies* 南亞研究季刊, no. 4 (2006):98–101.
4. "China becomes the largest source country of Maldives" 中國成為馬爾地夫最大客源國, *Xinhuanet*, May 11, 2011, http://news.xinhuanet.com/travel/2011-05/11/c_121405773.htm.
5. Rajat Pandit, "Army reworks war doctrine for Pakistan and China," *The Times of India*, Dec. 30, 2009, http://articles.timesofindia.indiatimes.com/2009-12-30/india/28104699_1_war-doctrine-new-doctrine-entire-western-front.
6. "Editorial: India-Vietnam oil exploration deal must be stopped," *Global Times*, Oct. 14, 2011, http://english.peopledaily.com.cn/90780/7617302.html.
7. "Two Indian companies permitted to take shares in Sino-Myanmar natural gas pipeline" 印度兩公司獲准入股中緬天然氣管道, *Petroleum Business* 石油商報 (Feb. 25, 2010), http://www.pbnews.com.cn/system/2010/02/25/001278069.shtml.
8. Siddharth Varadarajan, "Four-power meeting drew Chinese demarche," *The Hindu*, Jun. 14, 2007, http://hindu.com/2007/06/14/stories/2007061410501500.htm.
9. Rajiv Sikri, "Beyond oil and gas: India's interest in central Asia," *Global Envision*, Jul. 11, 2007, http://www.globalenvision.org/library/23/1683.
10. Liu Fenghua 柳豐華, "China in central Asia: Its policy evolution" 中國在中亞：政策的演變, *Studies on Russia, Central Asia and East Europe* 俄羅斯中亞東歐研究, no. 6 (2007):63–72.
11. "China and India: A rage for oil," *Bloomberg*, Sep. 5, 2005, http://www.businessweek.com/magazine/content/05_36/b3949086_mz015.htm.
12. Sachin Parashar, "India keen on SCO membership but China may play spoilsport," *The Times of India*, Jun. 9, 2010, http://articles.timesofindia.indiatimes.com/2010-06-09/india/28294120_1_sco-india-and-pakistan-relevant-countries.
13. Li Li, *Perception Change and the Transformation of China-India Relations* (New Delhi: KW Publishers, 2009), 161.
14. Gurpreet S. Khurana, "China's 'string of pearls' in the Indian Ocean and its security implications," *Strategic Analysis* 32, no. 1 (Jan. 2008):32.
15. Ishaan Tharoor, "The coming China-India conflict: Is war inevitable?" *Time*, Mar. 23, 2010, http://www.time.com/time/world/article/0,8599,1974028,00.html.
16. Rong Ying, "China-India relations: New starting point and new framework," *CIIS website*, Aug. 10, 2011, http://www.ciis.org.cn/english/2011-08/10/content_4395790.htm.
17. See the column of "Foreign Relations" of the website of the Indian Ministry of Foreign Affairs for its bilateral relations with the Gulf States: http://www.mea.gov.in/mystart.php?id=2001&pg=a.
18. See the column of "Countries and Organizations" of the website of the Chinese Ministry of Foreign Affairs for its bilateral relations with the Gulf States: http://www.fmprc.gov.cn/chn/pds/gjhdq/gj/yz/.
19. "Chinese-African trade volume reaching USD126.9 in 2010" 2010年中非貿易額達1269億美元,

Phoenix.net, May 13, 2011, http://finance.ifeng.com/roll/20110513/4015815.shtml.

20. "India, Africa target USD70 billion trade by 2015," *Rediff*, Mar. 28, 2011, http://www.rediff.com/business/report/india-africa-target-usd-70-bn-trade-by-2015/20110328.htm.
21. "India on a road to rediscover Africa," *Rediff*, May 21, 2011, http://www.rediff.com/news/column/column-india-on-a-road-to-rediscover-africa/20110521.htm.
22. "China's total of investment in Africa reaching USD32.3 billion by the end of August" 中國對非洲投資總額8月末達323億美元, *Sina Finance*, Oct. 9, 2010, http://finance.sina.com.cn/roll/20101009/12288751292.shtml.
23. "China will offer Africa a Loan of USD10 billion with exempting a portion of debts" 我國將向非洲提供100億美元貸款，免除部分債務, *China News Agency*, Nov. 8, 2009, http://news.sina.com.cn/c/2009-11-08/171819002040.shtml.
24. Refer to "India on a road to rediscover Africa," *Rediff*, May 21, 2011.
25. Yejoo Kim, "Chinese and Indian cooperation in Africa: The case of Sudan" (Oct. 17, 2011), http://www.consultancyafrica.com/index.php?option=com_content&view=article&id=869:chinese-and-indian-cooperation-in-africa-the-case-of-sudan&catid=58:asia-dimension-discussion-papers&Itemid=264.

7
Chapter

Areas of Convergence and Divergence in India-China Relations

Rajeswari Pillai Rajagopalan

India-China relations have had several ups and downs in bilateral relations, with more downs than ups in recent years. In fact, the two countries are currently enjoying one of the better times in their bilateral ties and this is essentially in the economic realm. The economic ties between India and China have gone up from USD4 billion a decade ago to over USD60 billion in 2010. This upward movement in the economic sphere has not reflected positively in the politico-strategic dynamics of the bilateral ties. This paper will attempt to identify some of the factors that contribute to the strains in the politico-strategic ties while identifying four or five potential areas for cooperation in the security-strategic domain that can reduce some of the trust deficit issues that in a sense characterize the bilateral relationship. Addressing this core issue remains important even while there are improvements in the bilateral economic and commercial interactions. A few issues that can be explored for cooperation include: Military-to-military ties; Sea Lines of Communication (SLOC) and maritime security; United Nations' peace-keeping operations; reconstruction and rehabilitation following natural disasters and calamities. Despite the limiting factors, these are a few areas in which both India and China have already begun cooperation and some of them are potential areas for cooperation as well.

India's ascendancy as a major power has called for fresh debate on how China engages this nation. Recent years have witnessed several ups and downs in the bilateral relations, with ups almost entirely concentrated in the economic realm. However, the strengthened economic relations have not reflected positive trends in the politico-strategic ties between the two sides. While the economic interaction between the two sides may have reached great heights, this cannot eliminate the growing suspicion on the strategic front. A National Bureau of Asian Research study recently argued, "Economic interdependence is hardly a 'silver bullet' guaranteed to pacify interstate conflicts. Though it may constrain the conflict escalation processes, interdependence also generates serious economic frictions that can easily offset or overwhelm its conflict-suppressing effects."[1] Meanwhile, there have been several studies arguing that economic traction between the two sides has several positive spin-off effects on India-China relations.[2] I would argue that commerce has only a limited role to play in a country's strategic game plan. Nevertheless, it provides a good cushion to build on ties in other areas. Trade and commerce, however, do not alter the realities on the strategic front. In fact, China has been increasingly testing India's dominance in its own backyard.[3] Despite South Asian Association For Regional Cooperation (SAARC) being India's creation, Beijing is much more active today in the organization than India is.[4]

Beijing's presence in South Asian countries, solidified through increasing trade and investment measures, has reduced India to a big geographical entity with not much influence.[5] China's proactive approach towards South Asia appears to be a result of its own deepening relationship with South Asian countries as well as fulfilling its objective to emerge as a kind of "guardian" to all the South Asian countries. Second, it seems an aftereffect of the U.S.-China Joint Statement in November 2009 for the two countries to jointly manage South Asia.

The "hot-cold" nature of their relationship is seen in several issues, ranging from border tensions, and the changing policy on Jammu and Kashmir, to the China-Pakistan equation, to tensions in the Indian Ocean region. Nevertheless, it is the emerging Asian strategic framework that may be the issue hindering bilateral ties.

In conclusion, it is suggested that the two countries explore new avenues of cooperation in the politico-security arena that might smooth out some of the trust deficit issues that have been crucial in fomenting closer relations between New Delhi and Beijing. While one cannot make predictions about India-China relations with any certainty, the state of these relationships will impact significantly on the emerging Asian security architecture.

This paper will examine some of the factors shaping India-China relations while analysing the trends for the future. These include market access issues; India's rising profile and China's Pakistan policy; Beijing's changing policy on Jammu and Kashmir; military imbalance and competition; border and territorial issues; and conflicting approaches towards the emerging Asian security architecture.

Background

India-China relations have gone from one of the end of the spectrum to the other. Nehru's "Hindi-Chini bhai bhai" relations soon gave way to war in 1962, and acrimonious ties following India's nuclear tests in 1998. However, the relationship has subsequently improved with the two countries enjoying one of the best phases in the history of their bilateral relations.

The following section will deal with some of the issues that have been hampering the bilateral ties, and also identify areas for potential cooperation.

India's Rising Profile and China's Pakistan Policy

While India has never been categorised as a threat or a challenge by China in any of their documents or statements, the reality is that India has figured as a major factor in their policies since the early years. India not being listed as a challenge could be a deliberate omission on the part of the Chinese. The Chinese do have concerns about India and its role, particularly with regard to Tibet, among other issues. The very fact that the Dalai Lama has taken refuge in India is a cause of concern for China.

Chinese wariness about India is not entirely new. India has always figured in China's strategic calculus; this may have become more pronounced in the last decade or so. China's balance of power approach, despite the rhetoric of Panchsheel Principles, has not been reassuring. For instance, the China-Pakistan relationship is a classic case. By helping Pakistan on nuclear and missile technology issues, Beijing kept up a constant conflict with New Delhi and, to a great extent, achieved the objective of preventing India from rising fast as China's peer competitor. China-Pakistan nuclear cooperation has also altered the strategic framework in the Indian subcontinent. Besides, Pakistan's cross-border terrorism and several military engagements have had a debilitating effect on India's economy, thus creating a huge gap between India and China. For that matter, China's strong ties with other South Asian countries has also a similar objective — to contain India's rise and influence even within South Asia by strengthening Beijing's strategic relations with "India-wary" countries. Thus, Beijing has made significant inroads into India's own backyard through cross-border economic and strategic penetration into Bangladesh, Nepal, Pakistan, Sri Lanka, and the Maldives. Therefore, China's geostrategic objectives, its military security concerns vis-a-vis India, along with unresolved border and territorial issues, and the need to safeguard what is considered as its "soft strategic underbelly" — Tibet and Xinjiang — drive much of China's South Asia policy.[6]

Of all the countries in South Asia, Pakistan has interests that correspond with Chinese ones — of defeating, rather that containing, India. Besides, Pakistan is paranoid about India wanting to undo the partition, whereas China remains suspicious of India's hidden agenda in Tibet. In fact, it is their interests vis-a-vis India that have survived and thrived in the China-Pakistan partnership. Thus, from China's perspective, India's preoccupation with the subcontinent's security concerns seriously undermines India's sense of being equal to China in the overall power ladder. China believes that if the one-million strong Indian army remains engaged with Pakistan on its western front while fighting various insurgencies within the country, it will not stir up problems for China on the Tibet front.

Thus, China does view India as a "future strategic competitor" that would join any anti-China grouping in the future. Mohan Malik brings to the fore an internal study undertaken in 2005 that recommended that China undertake measures to keep its current strategic leverage in terms of territory, P-5 membership, and being in the "Nuclear Club" while holding onto diplomatic advantages through its special relationship particularly with India's neighbouring countries and also maintain its economic lead over India.[7] India's role and stand on Tibet may also be irksome to the Chinese leadership.

Beijing is also wary of India's "Look East" policy, and the strengthening of New Delhi's ties with Japan, Vietnam, and the Association of Southeast Asian Nations (ASEAN) countries. Beijing feels that India's diplomacy in Southeast Asia could potentially hamper China-ASEAN ties as well as reduce Beijing's manoeuvring space in Asia.

Market Access Issues

India-China economic relations have been on an upward swing, with the bilateral trade crossing USD60 billion and this is expected to reach USD100 billion in the next few years. Despite the increasing economic traction, India has been faced with a peculiar problem of Chinese market access. Chinese markets have remained closed to India in three critical areas: IT sector, pharmaceuticals, and agricultural produce. India is reported to have raised the issue with China repeatedly although there has been no progress and the market access continues to be an issue for India.

Strangely, Indian companies that function out of China work for foreign companies or multinational corporations that are based in China but not necessarily service the Chinese companies — state-owned or otherwise. Therefore, India's IT sector — particularly the software sector that has penetrated the global market — remains shut off in China.

Second, India's pharmaceutical sector established itself in certain niche areas, and it is one which has cracked the global market but still remains outside of the Chinese market. India has a sizeable Research and Development (R&D) and technological base in the area of pharmaceuticals and it has produced a variety of cheap and effective drugs for a number of diseases including AIDS. However, India has not been allowed to operate in the Chinese market. An often-cited reason is the lengthy licensing process which takes up to three years and, even after this process is over, it is not certain if the company gets market access. A second issue that has been halting the Indian companies is again one related to time — the longer time to have its commercial infrastructure put in place. Lastly, the apparent difficulty to compete with Chinese companies on account of cost remains an issue. More importantly, it has been reported that the licensing process that involves passing on information, such as drug composition, has led to problems for India. It has been suggested that Chinese companies have been given the Indian drug formula and composition and afterwards the Chinese companies produce the drug under their own brand name.

Beijing's Changing Policy on Jammu and Kashmir

China's policy on Jammu and Kashmir has undergone significant change in the last few decades. Beijing had followed a policy of neutrality in the 1980s and 1990s, although this approach has changed to more of an active and partisan role today. China's policy on Jammu and Kashmir today, a mix of aggressiveness and determination, questions India's territorial integrity. The new approach is seen as a reflection of the rising politico, economic, and military might of the nation. This policy may also be a result of the fact that the U.S. is on a relative decline and there are new power centers making their marks, including India and China. The Obama Administration's approach towards China, particularly in its first year, contributed to newfound confidence in China even though the policy was a mix of appeasement (given the economic crisis and the fact that China was buying U.S. treasury bonds). Of particular significance is the U.S.-China joint statement of November 2009 in which the two countries agreed to jointly manage South Asia. All of these actions have made China a much more significant player in Asia, even at the cost of India. China's newfound confidence is also reflected in its behaviour towards other neighbors and the U.S. The number of maritime issues between the navy of China's People's Liberation Army and the U.S. Navy, and conflicts involving Vietnam and Indonesia, and India on the land border, are reflective of China's growing power and its willingness to flex its muscles.

China, in fact, follows a policy of a double standard in regional conflicts. On the one hand, China is extremely sensitive to the South China Sea issue where it does not want any external intervention; however, the Chinese policy on Jammu and Kashmir today is one of intervention. While the issuance of stapled visas may not be directly linked to the changed policy on Jammu and Kashmir, China has begun to make serious assertions that the Indian-controlled part of Kashmir is a disputed territory.

Military Imbalance and Competition

In the India-China context, there is a clear disparity and military imbalance based upon the forces, equipment, or the military infrastructure. In the last few years, the infrastructural developments that China has undertaken in the Tibet Autonomous Region (TAR), as well as on the India-China border, provide the potential for the People's Liberation Army (PLA) to mobilise forces and equipment in a much shorter span of time. It would enable China to mobilise large forces by train and by road onto Indian borders. Earlier, this exercise not only took a long time but also was impossible during periods of snow. The expressways and the new rail line into Tibet have changed the scenario totally. It is believed that China has about 160,000 troops in Tibet, and with improved infrastructure, it will be able to amass another 100,000 troops from the central reserve in a span of six weeks. Indian military planners have also noted that China has vastly improved its air force capability in the region, with multiple air bases and forward airstrips near the border. The PLA Air Force is also believed to have improved its command and control structures, as was evident from an air battle drill staged on March 30, 2008. China can also deploy heavy-lift planes in Tibet, though they may not be able to land and take-off fully loaded because of altitude restrictions. Besides the positioning of intermediate range ballistic missiles, such as the DF-4 and DF-21 in Tibet, it is reported that they could also deploy DF-31 ICBMs at bases such as Delingha. This may mean that even a limited conflict between India and China would have the potential to spiral out of control to become a dangerous nuclear flashpoint.

After years of reports of China upgrading its combat capabilities in Tibet, New Delhi has finally begun to react. The Indian government's decision on June 8, 2009 to deploy two additional army divisions and two air force squadrons near its border with China sparked new tensions between the two countries, with Beijing reiterating yet again that a large stretch of the state of Arunachal Pradesh belongs to them. With this new deployment in Assam, India's troop strength in the region will cross more than 100,000. Meanwhile, the Indian Air Force has deployed two squadrons of advanced Sukhoi-30 MKI aircraft in Tezpur, Assam. Though only four fighters are deployed now, there are plans to increase this to its full complement in a gradual manner. Additionally, India has acquired three Airborne Warning and Control Systems (AWACS), which also potentially have uses on the eastern border. In addition, India is also undertaking upgrading of airstrips and advanced landing stations along the northeast, including at Tezpur (Assam), Chabua (Assam), Jorhat (Assam), Panagarh (West Bengal), and Purnea (Bihar). If the AWACS are deployed to the northeast, it could be significant as it is a potent force multiplier capable of monitoring the movement and activities of troops and aircraft on the Chinese side. The state of Arunachal Pradesh is also planning to raise a 5,000-strong force, comprised of the local populace, to supplement Indian Army efforts during a crisis. This is being modeled on Ladakh Scouts that proved useful during the 1999 Kargil War with Pakistan. The Indian moves have clearly irked the Beijing leadership as reflected in several editorials in the PLA mouthpiece *People's Daily*. One editorial said, "China won't make any compromises in its border disputes with India." The question is whether this anger stops with these editorials or whether they translate into a more serious problem on the border.

Despite such rhetoric, China may not be in a mood to engage in a border conflict with India, as it would affect the growth trajectory of China quite adversely. Second, while Beijing may like to intensify its pressure on India, it recognizes that India is not the same country it defeated in 1962. India's upgraded military capabilities, specifically air power if used in combat, will significantly alter the outcome of a conflict.

Border and Territorial Issues

Chinese claims on Arunachal Pradesh are linked to sovereignty, territorial integrity, and the respective status of India and China in the emerging Asian security and strategic framework, as argued by several China scholars. This issue goes back to the early days of independence of both countries, and indeed our legacy of the colonial times. The dispute revolves around uncertainties of where the colonial borders lay where British India met Tibet. Though there is probably no single correct interpretation of the border, the newly independent and highly nationalistic leaderships of both countries were unwilling to give way to each other's claims.

Despite the fact that the two countries have remained engaged since 1981 on the border issues, there has been no progress and this illustrates the complexity of the issue as well as the inflexible approach taken by the two countries in finding a mutually acceptable solution. The baggage of history has added complexity to the already vexing issue between the two sides. The Indian leadership, particularly the military leadership, has not forgotten the 1962 war and it continues to be a psychological issue factoring in as it deals with China.

It is to be recognized that India-China border issues are only a symptom of the larger problem in the India-China equation; it has a dampening effect on the overall bilateral relations as well as India's own territorial integrity issues. The border negotiations have been done through several different channels over the years. There was a big push by successive Indian Prime Ministers, and various other efforts in channels like the Special Representatives talks, however, there has been no progress on the demarcation or the delineation of the Line of Actual Control (LAC) on the ground or on military maps. The LAC has become a matter of perception; the Indian side has a perceived one, and the Indian military and border police patrol up to that perceived LAC whereas the Chinese have a different perception of where the LAC is and they patrol up to their perceived LAC. The overlapping area commonly called the "no-man's land," or the red zone, has witnessed several patrol face-offs in recent years. Despite the ambiguities, it has to be acknowledged that there has been no incident of firing since the last major incident at Nathu La in 1967 except for a serious stand-off incident at Sumdorong Chu Valley in 1987. However, in the absence of a demarcated LAC, the potential for conflict due to misperceptions is high. These limited conflicts spiraling out of control cannot be discounted, particularly with Beijing deploying tactical nuclear weapons close to the border areas. President Wen Jiabao's recent assertion that we should leave the border issue for the future generation means that China is not interested in settling the border issue in the near future.

As explained, the history and unsettled boundary issues, as well as their respective roles in the emerging Asian strategic framework, have created severe constraints in the working out of a good partnership between India and China. The mutual trust deficit between the two sides hampers implementation of any number of confidence-building measures that have been instituted by the two sides. Agreements and protocols were signed in 1993, 1996, 2003, and 2005 including: *Political Parameters and Guiding Principles for the Settlement of the India-China Boundary Question, Agreement on Confidence Building Measures in the Military Field Along the LAC,* and *Modalities for the Implementation of Confidence Building Measures in the Military Field Along the LAC.* As long as these confidence-building measures are based on distances on the map, it is unlikely that they will be implementable. For instance, on the issue of the deployment of troops and heavy weapons as given in Article 3 of the 1996 Agreement, this cannot be implemented as these have to do with distances from the LAC. Therefore, unless and until the LAC is demarcated and delineated, these measures are meaningless.

Lastly, China has also been trying to use the "Sikkim card" as a bargaining tool for its larger claim on the state of Arunachal Pradesh and, more particularly, Tawang. In August 2007, the Chinese demanded that India remove two bunkers on the Sino-Indian border close to the tri-junction of Sikkim, Bhutan, and Tibet, raising doubts about China's earlier acceptance that Sikkim is part of India. Similarly, in May 2008, China began to make fresh claims on Sikkim, otherwise a peaceful sector on the LAC. There have been repeated protests by China about troop movement in Sikkim, or when Indian leaders visit the area. Sikkim was an otherwise settled issue between India and China; in 2003, during Prime Minister Vajpayee's visit, China had agreed that Sikkim was a part of India and, in reciprocity, India agreed that Tibet was a part of China. However, China's repeated protests on the Sikkim issue raise doubts about China's commitments in this regard. The Chinese assertion in this regard has been where Sikkim has been introduced as an agenda item in the boundary talks between the two countries.

China is essentially trying to twist India's arm in order to have leverage on the boundary issue. For instance, the Chinese border incursions have been increasing. While most of the intrusions took place in Ladakh and Arunachal Pradesh, border incursions into Sikkim have also gone up significantly. While the numbers may not be critical, this still demonstrates the changed Chinese attitude towards India. The Chinese incursions are also getting deeper into Indian territory than before. Nevertheless, the Indian establishment continues to maintain that these are minor issues and that India and China as responsible powers will not stumble into a military clash.

The Chinese are firmly convinced that increasing rhetoric along with increased incursions on the eastern sector will pressure India to agree to major compromises on the border and territorial issue. China also believes that it should be in no hurry to resolve the border issue with India.

Conflicting Approaches towards the Emerging Asian Security Architecture

After several centuries, we are now witnessing the simultaneous rise of three major powers in Asia. While both India and China recognise their inevitable roles in shaping the Asian security order, they do differ radically on the kind of Asian layout for the future. India has continued to work at an inclusive approach as opposed to using the Chinese exclusivist approach which appears directed against India, U.S., and Japan. Beijing has continued to believe that its peaceful rise and emergence as a dominant power in Asia is only an assumption of its rightful place in the region and, in fact, a return to the old, but natural, order for the region. India may not be willing to see an Asia dominated by any one power.

China is increasingly trying to test India's dominance in its own backyard.

For instance, China's increasing foray into the Indian Ocean region, allegedly to secure its own energy supplies and ensure energy security, has upped the ante in New Delhi. China has been seeking to build alternate energy transportation and trade routes, anticipating problems on the Malacca Strait at some point in the future. However, given the kind of China wariness that exists in New Delhi, China's expanding influence and presence in India's neighborhood has clearly upped the ante within the establishment as well as outside.

India's rising profile is repeatedly questioned by China within the bilateral and multilateral formats. More recently China objected to a loan proposal by the Asian Development Bank because part of the loan would be used for a hydropower project in Arunachal Pradesh, which China claims as its own. China had also opposed the Nuclear Supplier Group (NSG) waiver to India in 2008 for international nuclear commerce with India and has objected repeatedly to Indian proposals to add the names of Pakistan-based terrorists to the United Nations' terrorist watch list. Beijing is also critical of India's potential membership into some of the technology export control regimes, of which the NSG appears to be the most difficult to gain entry to. China has already made its position clear that it will not support a country-specific exemption to India for its membership. This is an area in which China could score a point if it decides to build criteria for India's membership. Chinese actions, therefore, raise suspicions in Delhi mainly for two reasons. One, factors like history and unsettled boundary and territorial issues will continue to hinder any prospect of India and China forging closer meaningful ties in the foreseeable future. The baggage of history continues to be a strong factor in India-China ties. The history and unsettled boundary issues, as well as their respective roles in the emerging Asian strategic framework, have created severe constraints in working out a good partnership between India and China. The trust deficit between New Delhi and Beijing is not something that is going to change dramatically in the next few years. Therefore, the border issue appears to be only a symptom of the larger problem that exists between India and China; it is India's increasing role and influence, which is the crux of the issue.

Future Trends

Looking at the complexity of issues involved in India-China relations, one cannot expect major changes in the near future. Despite the economic traction between the two sides, some of the tensions and the potential for conflict on the politico-strategic front are likely to remain unless certain measures for cooperation are identified in the security arena. These could include strengthening of the military-to-military exercises, and joint exercises to respond to natural disasters. India's long-term experience with peacekeeping operations could be another area for cooperation. The two sides have to make a conscious effort to reduce the trust deficit gap that characterises the relationship. For instance, if China were to take steps to find ways to enable India's membership into some of the technology export control regimes, it would have a far-reaching impact on future ties. China should, in fact, take the lead in setting new criteria that will enable India's membership in the NSG and other relevant forums.

Notes

1. William R. Thompson and David P. Rapkin, "Will economic interdependence encourage China's and India's peaceful ascent?" *Strategic Asia 2006–2007: Trade, Interdependence and Security* (Washington, D.C.: National Bureau of Asian Research), http://www.nbr.org/publications/strategic_asia/pdf/Preview/SA06/SA06_China_India_Rise_preview.pdf.
2. For example, Christopher J. Rusko and Karthika Sasikumar, "India and China: From trade to peace," *Asian Perspective*, vol. 31, no. 4 (2007), http://www.asianperspective.org/articles/v31n4-d.pdf.
3. The increasing number of intrusions / transgressions on the India-China border, even in the sectors that were otherwise peaceful; the Chinese Ambassador in India stating that the entire State of Arunachal Pradesh belongs to China; China's issuance of stapled visas to people from Jammu and Kashmir; denial of visa to General B.S. Jaswal, Commander, Northern Command; China gaining de facto control of Gilgit-Baltistan region, are instances of China trying to test India on the politico-strategic front.
4. While one can say that India has been laid back, and even apathetic to its own neighbors, China's argument that it is simply engaged in practical diplomacy may be farfetched.
5. China is clearly taking important steps to solidify its relationship with SAARC as a whole, in addition to having excellent relations with each of the member countries. At the 2010 SAARC Summit, Beijing proposed an assistance of USD300,000 to the SAARC Development Fund. At the 2011 SAARC Summit, China demanded that it be included in the SAARC as a Dialogue Partner.
6. J. Mohan Malik, "South Asia in China's foreign relations," *Pacifica Review*, vol. 13, no. 1 (Feb. 2001), http://sga.myweb.uga.edu/readings/sa_in_chinas_fr.pdf.
7. Mohan Malik, "India-China competition revealed in ongoing border disputes," *PINR Report* (Oct. 09, 2007), http://www.pinr.com/report.php?ac=view_printable&report_id=695&language_id=1.

   The study, undertaken on the behest of Chinese leadership's "Foreign Affairs Cell," had incorporated inputs from China's South Asia specialists like Cheng Ruisheng, Ma Jiali, Sun Shihai, among others.

Chapter 8

India-China Cooperation: Some Elements for Building Scenarios

Kishan S. Rana

It is a paradox that, in modern times, after India and China's liberation from colonial rulers, our two countries have found it difficult to forge a sustained and cooperative relationship in stark contrast to our shared inheritance of over two millennia that essentially consisted of productive exchanges, friendship, and harmony. Political, social, and economic transformation of our times, plus technological transformation summed up in the word "globalization," has shrunk distance and geography. The heartlands of our two large states are more proximate to one another, to the point where the Himalayas and the buffer of sparsely populated intermediate regions no longer separate Beijing and Delhi. Much as we may wish to hark back to history, objective factors place us in more direct, multifarious confabulation than ever before, on bilateral, regional, and global issues. Legacy remains important, but we have to find a new paradigm to forge the past and the present into a balanced, productive mutual relationship.

This paper looks at prospects for the future, including the elements that might go into building alternate scenarios of the future of India-China relations. Of course, bilateral ties would also be molded by changes in the global environment, and that limits the utility of such an exercise. But the bilateral perspective bears examination, because it identifies the factors that are relevant. The paper ends with some policy recommendations.

A Comparison

China and India are both on high economic growth trajectories, thanks to the thoroughgoing reforms that commenced in China in 1978, and in India in 1991. In 2010, China overtook Japan as the world's second biggest economy. In purchasing power parity (PPP) terms, India is on track to become the world's third biggest economy in the next several years. Coinciding with this, other major Asian economies, including Indonesia and South Korea, and several Association of Southeast Asian Nations (ASEAN) states, are also forging ahead, contributing to what is characterized as an "Asian Century." The weight that emerging powers, especially those in Asia, exercise in world affairs is now acknowledged as never before, be it in the operation of G-20, or in the gatherings of scholars in the West, where a major refrain is their need to better connect with the BRICS (Brazil, Russia, India, China, and South Africa) and with the constituent individual countries and regions.

Seen in a historical perspective of the situation as it existed some centuries back, before the arrival of colonialism, some see this as no more than a restoration of the primacy that Asia enjoyed in the world economy, with China and India as the two leading global economies, each contributing to about a quarter of world GDP right up to the 15th century.

Extrapolation of trends in economic growth is hazardous because this assumes constancy in the factors that are current at a particular time, and overlooks the unpredictable. With this caveat, on present evidence, both China and India can look forward to steady growth, despite turbulence in the global economy that has flowed from a persisting crisis in the U.S., and in Europe that commenced in 2008, and was exported to the rest of the world. What will surely be affected is their pace of growth; on present evidence it seems that the figures of annual GDP that rise 10% or more may not be replicated in the near future.

Consider for a moment an unusual prediction that appeared in *Foreign Policy* over a year back:

> In 2040, the Chinese economy will reach USD123 trillion, or nearly three times the economic output of the entire globe in 2000. China's per capita income will hit USD85,000, more than double the forecast for the European Union, and also much higher than that of India and Japan. In other words, the average Chinese megacity dweller will be living twice as well as the average Frenchman when China goes from a poor country in 2000 to a superrich country in 2040. Although it will not have overtaken the United States in per capita wealth, according to my forecasts, China's share of global GDP — 40% — will dwarf that of the United States (14%) and the European Union (5%) 30 years from now. This is what economic hegemony will look like.[1]

Is this credible? Arvind Subramainan, author of *Eclipse: Living in the Shadow of China's Economic Dominance* (2011), has written in a similar vein; he estimates that by 2030, China's per capita GDP in PPP terms will be half that of the United States.[2] Exponential projections such as this one recall the sarcastic John Kenneth Galbraith comment: "The only purpose of economic forecasting is to make astrology look respectable."

The problem with long-term forecasts is that there are too many variables. The velocity and volatility of change — the more so in our globalized world — should lead us to closely examine possible caveats. One such caveat is the demography trend: We do know that the moment of China's "demography dividend" has passed. China is set to be the world's only country that will confront a rising "dependency ratio" (the proportion of those of working age in relation to dependents). Strange as it may sound, China runs the risk of running out of labor, which may affect productivity and growth. A bigger issue is environment space. Taking GDP from today's USD12 trillion to USD123 trillion, as Fogel postulates, will require environmental resources that the country simply does not have any longer, be it fresh water, or pollution-absorbing capacity, or even arable land space. True, China is attempting to shift some of its resource mobilization activities aboard, notably to Africa, with massive investments lined up across the entire continent. But the extent to which this might work is finite, and may hinge on an even greater range of variables.

At the same time, the positive elements that contribute to China's GDP growth are many. These include: Its high rate of domestic savings; high investment in infrastructure, and the sizable stock that has already been built up; huge investments in education and the formation of human capital and skills, which is vital for long-term growth; tightly organized development of the science and technology capacity and in Research and Development (R&D) that leads to innovation; a sprit of entrepreneurship among the people. We should add to this the substantive Chinese work in recent years in environmental management and the development of renewable energy options.[3]

If we compare India and China, it is India that is still the relatively less known entity in terms of its socioeconomic growth and potential. India's economic reforms began in 1991, forced by necessity in the wake of a severe economic crisis. It was Prime Minister P.V. Narasimha Rao who, on winning an election in July 1991, had the vision and courage to convert that crisis into an opportunity, to embark on the "unthinkable": Opening up an economy that had become increasingly statist and over-regulated.[4] Since then, successive governments in New Delhi have deepened the process of liberalization, dismantling excessive controls. At the same time, prudence has marked national finance macro-management, including the retention of controls on the flow of international capital, which has helped the country to safeguard itself from external events such as the Asian crisis of 1997–1998, and the 2008 global economic recession that was triggered by the housing and bank crisis in the U.S. Gradual disinvestment in public sector enterprises has been another feature of this economic policy, which has also produced beneficial consequences on these mainly state-owned enterprises, in that many among them have improved their operational efficiency, competitiveness, and transparency. Much more remains to be done.

In the late 1990's India was called a "stealth economy" because it was growing at a good pace but that fact was not widely recognized.[5] Today, that sobriquet no longer applies. India now receives high appreciation for the potential it offers both in terms of domestic socioeconomic growth, as well as its external capacity as a global partner. Another key feature is that some Indian states have forged ahead at a high pace, setting competitive standards for the states that have lagged behind. For instance, Gujarat, Haryana, Karnataka, and Maharashtra have been the pace-setters; that has produced a demonstration effect that has rubbed off on other Indian states, including Bihar, Odisha, and Uttar Pradesh, often seen as the laggards. Such regional growth disparity is almost universal among developing states, and becomes a serious issue when it persists; this is one more area in which the experience of India and China is mutually relevant.

May I digress a little and speak of India's strong and weak points in the current phase of the development process? The strengths include:

GDP growth of about 8% in the past seven years. Notwithstanding the vicissitudes in the world economy of the past three years, this growth has been an unprecedented phenomenon for the country. But there are clear signs now that the pace of growth is slowing down.

The domestic savings rate is around 36%. The high rate of investments is primarily based on domestic resources. The role of foreign direct investment (FDI) is relatively small but important.

- High growth in exports, during the current financial year 2011–2012 (April to March) have been running at about 52%, taking the estimate for the year to USD300 billion, which would represent a 30% jump over the previous year. But it is not clear how far the growth can be sustained in a difficult external environment.
- Buoyant inward and outward foreign direct investment is again reflecting strong entrepreneurship, and a high level of business confidence. An example of a stark difference in India-China business profiles: Family-owned enterprises valued over USD50 million account for 67% of India's total, the highest in Asia; the comparable figure in China is just 13%.[6] In contrast, the share of state-owned enterprises (SOEs), which India calls public sector enterprises (PSUs), is very much higher in China than India.

The Indian negatives are no less daunting, though many of these are also in a state of transition.

- While the size of the below-poverty line population has declined, about 30% are still in this vulnerable category despite a reduction in the overall figure since 1991. Massive social programs and targeted subsidies, part of an inclusive growth strategy, are making headway and further reductions are expected.

- The 2010 decennial census has shown that the rate of illiteracy has declined from about 32% in 2000, to just over 20%. But education, at the primary level, and vocational training remain major weaknesses, now being addressed through new national initiatives by the government, and also by a vigorous voluntary sector and NGOs.[7]
- The figures of malnutrition, infant mortality, and childbirth mortality remain much too high, even while they have improved significantly in the past 15 years. Healthcare and nutrition remain major challenges.
- India's tax-to-GDP ratio is one of the lowest for a comparable country, barely over 10%. In advanced countries, this figure is more than 15%. That means that the tax base is insufficient for all the publicly funded projects.[8] But a silver lining is that this is set to rise significantly when in the next year the direct tax code is revised and a general sales tax goes into effect.[9]

Overall, the Indian glass is much more than half-full, and with each passing year, it gets fuller.

Nature of Power and the Democracy Argument

In a recent address, Shivshankar Menon, India's National Security Advisor, analyzed India's self-image and its conception of power.[10] He said:

> We must always therefore be conscious of the difference between weight, influence, and power. Power is the ability to create and sustain outcomes. Weight we have, our influence is growing, but our power remains to grow and should first be used for our domestic transformation.
>
> History is replete with examples of rising powers who prematurely thought that their time had come, who mistook influence and weight for real power. Their rise, as that of Wilhelmine Germany or militarist Japan, was cut short prematurely.

India's central quest is, and must remain for a long time to come, the eradication of poverty and rectification of all the other health, education, and social inadequacies that afflict a quarter and more of the population. Creating an external environment that facilitates and contributes to this objective is the overriding responsibility for India, not the abstractions of power or global status.

India has consistently been cool to the Western thesis of democracy's triumphalism, which gained new momentum after the end of the Cold War. India has been a reluctant participant in Western-driven institutions such as the Forum of Democracy. On the face of it, this seems inconsistent with India's faith in its own democratic credentials, but the explanation is simple: Few Indians see democracy as an "exportable" commodity, much less as a form of governance that can be sponsored in, or pushed onto, any country from outside. There is no dearth of examples that prove that "one person, one vote," and the formal process of elections are insufficient to produce democracy; Africa has shown how in several countries, leaders that have lost at the ballot box have been reluctant to quit, and have been able to negotiate compromises that effectively negate the results of the elections, or prolong the agony of their people through engineered civil unrest. It is apparent that without strong institutions, the methods of democracy cannot deliver results or produce sustainable good governance.

What counts in the final analysis is not the shape of the democratic process or the forms of constitutional arrangements that different countries deploy to suit their own genius and political environment, but the delivery of accountable governance, in which ordinary citizens feel ownership. People need to give expression to their free choice, including their demands for a change of government when an existing regime loses the confidence of its people.

In Asia, India has been reserved towards efforts by some countries to produce a grouping of democracies which appear to be designed to indirectly target China; my impression is that India has paid little heed to calls by Australia, for instance, to create such a cluster of Asian democracies. This response has been a simple expression of a calculation that Asia needs inclusive actions that build and sustain commonalities, not new formulas that contribute to mutual division.

Is Indian democracy a Western import? Most Indians would argue that we have made it our own, in our adaptation of democratic methods. It seems to fit well with our ancient tradition of tolerance and management of the multiple pluralities that are the hallmark of India, be it in terms of religion, language, ethnicity, modes of life, and all the forms of cultural expression that are divergent and yet make up a great national mosaic, which permits us to proclaim that we find "unity in diversity." Democracy becomes for us the political expression of all these diversities, the mode of governance that enables us to harmonize, with all our imperfections, the pushes and pulls of an Indian way of life.

It seems to me that where India needs to act is in terms of looking more closely at its democratic experience, not to show that this is superior to any other system, but to study closely its working, and highlight its special features. We also need to work to strengthen our institutions, to contain and eradicate corruption, as part of an ongoing dynamic to improve domestic governance. In Egypt and elsewhere, India has shared its rich experience with the democratic process, and the organization of elections, in the harsh conditions of a developing country with limited resources.

What India powerfully demonstrates is that development is consistent with upholding democratic values. The Indian pattern of economic governance involves both a strong regulatory role for the state, and free markets in which entrepreneurship is given a strong and autonomous role; this is a pragmatic policy. In contrast, authoritarian regimes often can and do move faster than countries like India, where building internal consensus in favor of new policy involves time, persuasion, and compromise.[11] We in India believe that the consensus we eventually manage to build is stronger, and more durable, than an imposed decision. This is perhaps of potential relevance to other countries, but it is not for us to preach this. Does this amount to a "New Delhi consensus" or an Indian model for economic growth? This is an interesting thought, even if more hard evidence is needed to advance such a claim.

Scenario Elements for the Future

Building full scenarios that attempt to anticipate future developments is more complex than one might imagine. Presenting several "cases" or alternatives would be one way to focus our minds, and might graphically overcome complexities; this is feasible only by using a simplified and summarized format. Let me attempt a soft start at this by sketching the elements that could go into developing such alternate scenarios. I add that some of what follows is also partly prescriptive, and I make no apology for blending analysis with some personal suggestions.

First, let us consider the foreign policy profile of each country. Some fear that a resurgent and powerful China will practice hegemony; statements from Beijing in the past year on the South China Seas, and on relations with neighbors such as Vietnam, have hinted at this. Yet, in its actions, China has mainly been prudent, be it at the United Nations Security Council or bilaterally in relations with different partners. Countries located on China's periphery or in its extended neighborhood have observed the extraordinary transformation that has taken place since the launch of reforms in 1978 with a mixture of admiration and apprehension. The question that persists for them: Will China sustain the status quo, and equilibrium, working for stability, acting with prudence, taking into accounts the interests of other states? Or might it pursue a revisionist agenda, seeking a transformation in the regional and global order? It is for China to address this in a convincing manner.

What of India's profile? India's self-perception is of a benign state, seeking cooperative relations with all. But India's neighborhood ties in South Asia, marked especially by long-drawn problems with Pakistan, have fallen short of this ideal, and some Indian actions have been viewed with suspicion by its smaller neighbors. With each country, cooperation in the economic and transport arena, and in the exploitation of river resources, has remained blocked for long. At the same time, we should note that in the past year the atmosphere in all these bilateral and regional ties has undergone marked improvement; new avenues of cooperation with Bangladesh, Nepal, and Sri Lanka have opened up, marking a transformation in each of these relationships. Several positive developments have taken place in India-Pakistan relations, including Islamabad's belated decision in November 2011 to give Most Favored Nation (MFN) commercial treatment to India.[12] The 17th South Asian Association for Regional Cooperation (SAARC) summit held in the Maldives in mid-November 2011 produced positive results. But the South Asia regional group has a long way to go, to remove its sobriquet as the world's least integrated region.[13] India has to build on these developments, and press forward with reinforcing credible and mutually productive relationships throughout its neighborhood.

Second, the direct India-China relationship is complex, but largely positive. Our leaders have maintained a steady flow of summit exchanges, marked by deep mutual understanding. The range and intensity of a mutually beneficial official dialogue also reflects this. Yet, our unresolved border dispute casts a heavy shadow, and affects public perceptions.

Trade exchanges have flourished, with two-way trade in 2010–2011 at a remarkable USD63.09 billion; barely 10 years earlier, the volume was USD3 billion. In these exchanges, India has an unfavorable bilateral imbalance of USD23.86 billion.[14] This imbalance has become a cause for concern, the more so as it has persisted and grown over several years. Indian exporters find that the "guidance" provided by China's state system in relation to such economic exchanges does as yet not favor action that would correct this imbalance, be it in pharmaceuticals and chemicals or in relation to software. Equally, improved marketing by Indian companies is also needed; the Indian Commerce Ministry has drawn up plans to double Indian exports to China over the next three years, especially by promoting value added exports.[15] Achieving this will require far-sighted and mutually supportive actions by both countries.

The volume of India-China investment is relatively small, but it is growing. The obstacles to be overcome include the building of greater mutual trust, and surmounting, in some cases, concerns over security. But in some instances, the economic logic of shared interests between the two growing economies is driving new investments, and that is all for the better.

The range of potential areas of bilateral cooperation possible between China and India has simply not been comprehensively prospected. Be it in agricultural research, education policy, or environment management, or indeed in virtually any developmental field that one can name. Many of the circumstances that confront the two countries are similar, as are the challenges. We need contacts that are much deeper and more extensive, to give new life to mutually beneficial cooperative exchange. This is also a matter of developing stronger mutual trust, which should create the virtuous circles that would take such direct exchanges to a much higher level.

Another key element in the bilateral relationship is the existing modest level of contact and exchanges among non-state actors, especially institutional and people-to-people levels, when measured against the potential. Think-tanks, research agencies, and a broad range of institutions of India and China simply do not know each other sufficiently; in practice each contact that is established leads to mutual realization that we can profit mutually from such cooperation. In the past two or three years, these exchanges have grown. Yet, much more remains to be done.

In 2010, about 500,000 visitors traveled from the one country to the other, as tourists and on business, but this is an unbalanced flow; it consists of about 400,000 Indians to China, but only 100,000 Chinese in the reverse direction. For some years now, India has been on the China's approved list of tourist destinations, but the lack of infrastructure, including a sufficient number of Chinese-speaking guides in India, is cited as a reason for this modest inflow, at a time when the volume of overseas travel by Chinese has expanded dramatically. More sustained promotional efforts are needed on both sides. Such people-to-people exchanges, including study tours by people in different walks of life, especially youth, are required.

About 9,000 Indian students study in China, the vast majority of them pursuing medical studies on a self-financed basis. In the reverse direction, about 1,500 to 2,000 Chinese students come to India, mainly self-financed; the majority comes for management studies, involving short stays of about one semester. There exists the potential for a much greater exchange of students. The number of scholarships that each country offers to the other should also undergo expansion. Furthermore, several thousand Indians now live and work in Shanghai and

Beijing, and also in Guangzhou. Perhaps half that number now resides and works in India.

A significant area of concern to both sides should be the persisting misunderstanding and exaggerated reporting in the media on both sides. This features in the statements by our leaders and senior officials. We sometimes overlook a basic asymmetry in the character of the media in India and China. Other than Doordarshan and All India Radio, the official broadcast agencies that are now totally overwhelmed by the hundreds of private TV and radio channels, the Indian government has no control over the broadcasters; the print media are totally out of government control. This is in sharp contrast with the situation in China, where virtually nothing of a political nature can be published in the print media without conforming to official guidelines. Furthermore, the government runs all of China's broadcast media, TV, and radio. Is it credible that China cannot rein in its media, as and when it wishes? Does this not mean that unlike the situation in the Indian press, a hostile editorial in *People's Daily* or *China Daily* carries implied official acquiescence?

The media dissonance fuels and sharpens antipathy among the huge tribe of Internet commentators of the two countries, the netizens that are so adept with social media. It is hard to judge the volume of comments in each country about the other country; is the intensity of hostile comments more extensive in the case of China than India? Regardless of whether this is true or not, we need, for sure, much greater mutual understanding, self-restraint, and even empathy by netizens in both our countries. In both countries, recent surveys of public perceptions have shown a decline in the numbers of citizens that view the other country in a positive light, so that timely action is needed.

Expanded exchanges between journalists and media personalities are essential, as is a need for reportage that is balanced and analytical. The few programs that already exist in this field need to be strengthened and expanded.

Third, we might consider the prognosis for economic growth of India and China, over a limited time span, of the next five or seven years, perhaps even to horizon 2020 — beyond that we may be too much in a speculative environment. We should look at several possible options, perhaps via sets of high, medium, and low cases. This is a task for skilled economists to undertake, to develop comparative perspectives. Might it be possible for Indian and Chinese think-tanks to collaborate on developing such a prognosis? Is it possible to consider such a proposal?

We might also try and anticipate how each country would cope with a possible slump in GDP growth, say to 5% or less, even if this seems hard to imagine at present. India has enjoyed 8% growth over the past seven years, but this has not been the situation for the entire 20 years of its reform era; the late 1990s saw a much slower pace of growth. One might speculate that India may be better placed to deal with a slowdown than China, much as this would be unwelcome in both countries. This should be worth further examination.

Fourth, we should analyze the dynamics of demographic change in India and China. Broadly speaking, if we consider the evolution of population, in its composition and growth, as a process, China is ahead of India in what virtually all countries have experienced, by way of a demography transition. This is captured well in a telling statistic: The population median age in China is 35.5 years, while the figure for India is 28.2 years.[16]

As noted above, China's phase of "demography dividend" ended in 2010, and it confronts a sharply rising dependency ratio — the proportion between those of working age and those that are dependents. India, in contrast has just entered its demography dividend phase, which is estimated to last till 2035, when it too will confront a rise in its dependency ratio. And as seen above, it remains to be seen if India will be able use its population advantage well, in terms of training and finding work opportunities for the bulge in the working population. A long-term projection of demography trends suggests a comparatively favorable position for India, in comparison with that of China. This entire subject needs closer examination.

Fifth, both countries are major global seekers and consumers of resources, be they minerals or hydrocarbons, or agricultural products. Further economic growth makes inevitable an accentuation of this trend. Will this accentuate mutual competition? Possibly, but some elements of cooperation can also emerge in this process. India and China have worked jointly on hydrocarbon acquisition projects in the past. For instance, in Africa our nations are perceived as locked in tight competition, even if the reality is that the continent has potential that is large enough for both states to pursue their own distinctive ways of developing cooperation. And the scale of operations of each is not the same in any case. Here too, it is possible to manage the competition, and wherever feasible, to search out new forms of collaboration.

Sixth, we might consider the kind of thesis advanced by economist Joseph Stieglitz, that the critical element in growth is not capital formation or factor productivity, as postulated by classical economists, but whether a knowledge society is created, where learning and innovation dominate.[17] Stieglitz further argues that for this to take place on a sustained basis, the society needs to be open, democratic, and inclusive. He also makes it clear that he is not talking about the ballot box, but a society in which ideas are openly debated, a sprit of inquiry dominates, and all sections of the country feel a sense of ownership in the process of governance. He also advocates a comparatively low level of income inequality, and a balance in the process of economic decision-making, between open markets, and a liberal economy, and the guiding role of the state.

The situation regarding income inequalities in both countries, and the degree to which growth has been inclusive should be considered. This has important potential implications for the future. China's Gini coefficient has risen in recent years and was 0.47 in 2010.[18] In the May 12, 2010 edition of *China Daily* it was reported: " 'The Gini coefficient in China has been continuously rising after it reached the alarming 0.4 level 10 years ago,' Chang Xiuze, a researcher with the academy of microeconomic research under the National Development and Reform Commission, was quoted as saying in the Economic Information Daily."[19] The Gini figure for India is 0.38; the level of inequality has been rising, though not as sharply as in China. The contrasting trend that might mitigate this situation in that both India and China saw a rise in the middle class, and of course, an easing of the incidence of poverty. But we cannot wait for this. Domestic economic and social policy in both countries needs to take into account an urgent need to address inequality.

Seventh, in some ways the economic growth challenge is much sharper for India than China. Noted Swiss economist and analyst Professor Claude Smadja captured this well in a recent speech in New Delhi when he observed that for the past four years, "economic growth in India has been on autopilot, as no significant reform has taken place during this time."[20] Smadja added that this has been good enough for growth that is averaging around 7.5% per year, but this is much below the potential of what can be achieved. That is the issue: Unlike China, India handicaps itself by performing sub-optimally. One example: A McKinsey study estimated some years back that amending India's antiquated property and land management laws would add about one to one-and-half percent to GDP growth, but little has action has been taken.

Smadja offered a telling statistic. Between 2010 and 2020, the U.S. share of global output is likely to fall from 27% to 18%; Europe, currently 23%, may also fall from 23% to 18%; China's share is currently 16% and this is expected to go up to 24%. India is currently at 5.7% and this will go up to 8%; in effect, in 2020 as in 2010, India's figure will be one-third that of China. India simply cannot afford to dawdle at its current pace, where it does not valorize all its assets, and take its development to the best trajectory that is possible. In essence, India needs to give a real push to its reform agenda. This can be done only if reform is not treated as a political football between the ruling coalition and the opposition political parties.[21]

In sharp contrast, China is perceived to have mobilized its resources in a far more efficacious manner, so clearly visible in the consistently high level of growth it has achieved over a 30-year period, averaging 10% per annum. The world has not seen such a remarkable transformation. This does not minimize the challenge that it faces in sustaining this scorching pace in a complex global environment.

Final Thoughts

If one were to compile a wish list of the things that India and China might do to expand mutually beneficial cooperation, and to work together as locomotives of growth, for themselves and for the global economy, the following points would feature in such a list:

- We need much more intensive, multi-layered dialogue among official agencies and among non-state actors, covering bilateral, regional, and global issues. This should cover the inter-governmental Track One, and also engage the varied stakeholders that come under the broad rubric of Track Two. Often it is the non-state actors that are especially innovative in building networks that share experiences and expand mutual knowledge; they need encouragement and support. Such exchanges are essential to improved understanding, and to build on our shared interests. They will also contribute to trust building.
- Our mutual goal should be to deepen mutual cooperation. Of course, along with the opportunities for collaboration, there also exist elements of mutual competition and contestation. The challenge in managing this set of contradictions will lie in strengthening the positives, while containing, coping with and, where possible, reversing the negatives. We must, each of us, ensure that worst-case scenarios do not become self-fulfilling prophecies. That would not serve either country, or our neighbors and the world community.
- Let us consider the political architecture in Asia. We need a pan-Asian, inclusive structure for political cooperation, which does not exist at present. The ASEAN Plus Three (APT) mechanism, which was established in 1997, consists of the 10 ASEAN states, plus China, Japan, and South Korea, but it leaves out India. It happens to be the only effective pan-Asian organization,

and has under it over 50 groups and entities that meet on a regular basis. It is in this sense a complete and diversified regional entity. The East Asia Summit (EAS), which met for the first time in 2005, consisted of the 13 APT countries, plus Australia, India, and New Zealand. At the meeting held at Bali in November 2011, EAS was expanded to include the United States and Russia. This 18-member grouping is diffuse in membership, and remains limited to a single annual summit encounter, with no subsidiary activities. One method might be to widen APT to bring in India, but that seems to run against Beijing's opposition. Ultimately, expansion of ATP is a matter for all the members of that group to consider. The central issue: A pan-Asian group without India would be incomplete.

- A different and unconnected approach is for China, India, and Japan to institute their own regular consultation process, perhaps making a soft start with a Track Two process of exchanges between think-tanks. If that works, and produces meaningful results, the three countries could consider expanding that to a parallel track for intergovernmental dialogue. That was precisely the step-by-step method used with the China-India-Russia Trilateral, which started as a forum of think-tanks and then expanded to annual ministerial meetings and, subsequently, exchanges at summit levels.

At heart, the challenge for India and China is to rebuild mutual trust. Is that possible? Surely, this task should preoccupy our thinkers, scholars, and activists. We are not the only countries in the world that face a situation where antipathy and mutual doubt about one another constrict action on mutually beneficial cooperation. History and the experiences of others provide ideas for feasible, practical action. Should we not embark on a mutually agreed program of "trust building measures," perhaps a corollary to programs of "confidence building measures" that countries undertake in post-conflict situations? Can we treat this as one of the recommendations to come from our conference?

I hope these reflections contribute to our dialogue at this conference. May I end by offering my warm congratulations to the China-India Fortune Foundation for sponsoring this first Academic Summit on China-India Cooperation meeting? I hope our conversation in this forum leads to deeper mutual exchanges. Thank you.

Notes

1. Robert Fogel, *Foreign Policy* (Jan.–Feb. 2010), http://www.foreignpolicy.com/articles/2010/01/04/123000000000000?page=0,1 (accessed Feb. 24, 2010).
2. *Business Standard* (Oct. 26, 2011).
3. A BBC TV program broadcast in the second week of November 2011 postulated that by 2020, 15% of electric power in China would be generated by renewable sources; its work in exploiting solar power has been remarkable.
4. We should also acknowledge that Indira Gandhi on her return to power in 1980, and Rajiv Gandhi (1984–1989), initiated the first of the changes in economic management; these actions were hesitant and limited.
5. This phrase was coined by Rajat Gupta, then head of McKinsey, the global consulting enterprise.
6. "Bloomberg Credit Suisse report," *Business Standard* (Nov. 4, 2011).

   In much of Asia, the figure is over 58%, except in Taiwan where the figure is 35%.
7. For instance, billionaire entrepreneur Aziz Premji is to set up two model primary schools in each of India's 640 districts. A number of other private foundations, NGOs, and volunteer groups are doing well in improving the quality and number of such schools.
8. The total number of income tax payers, even now, is barely 34 million, in a population of more than a billion.
9. Minhaz Merchant, "How to keep India shining," *Times of India* (Nov. 2, 2011).
10. 16th Prem Bhatia Memorial Lecture, New Delhi, Aug. 11, 2011.
11. An example is the debate over several years in the late 1990s that preceded the opening of the general and life insurance sectors to foreign investment, at a time when this was reserved exclusively for state enterprises. That decision has led to a reinvigoration of this sector, and today all sections in India accept this move to privatization as obvious and logical.
12. Under WTO rules, member-states are obliged to extend MFN treatment to one another. And this action was, in fact, delayed by Pakistan for 17 years. India steadfastly refused to take this case to the WTO, preferring to avoid adding one more issue to a contentious relationship.
13. Different entities, including the World Bank and *The Economist* have used this phrase. On the plus side, India cut the list of sensitive items for the least developed countries (LDCs) in South Asia from 480 tariff lines to just 25, announcing that zero tariffs would be applied to all the newly exempted items, with immediate effect; the main beneficiaries would be Bangladesh, Nepal, and Sri Lanka (*Business Standard*, Nov. 12, 2011).
14. Indian trade figures is from *Business Standard*, Nov. 8, 2011.

    A target of USD100 billion has been set for 2015. Going by the past record, this level is likely to be achieved much sooner.
15. *Business Standard*, Nov. 8, 2011.
16. *The Economic Times*, Nov. 25, 2011.

    Other comparable figures: Brazil: 29.3; the U.S.: 36.9; Japan: 44.8.
17. Joseph Stieglitz presented these arguments in a lecture in New Delhi on Nov. 4, 2011.
18. The Gini coefficient is on a scale of 0 (perfect equality) to 1 (complete inequality). It is the accepted measure to track the degree of income equality in a society.
19. Chen Jia, "China's wealth divide past warning level," *China Daily* (Nov. 07, 2011), http://www.chinadaily.com.cn/china/2010-05/12/content_9837073.htm.
20. Claude Smadja spoke at a public lecture organized by Aspen India at New Delhi on Nov. 8, 2011.

21. An example: In late November 2011, the government announced its decision, pending for almost a decade, on opening up retail trade for foreign investments, which would permit the entry of major global retailers. BJP in 2004 had proposed this very policy, but it now leads vehement opposition against this move in the name of protecting domestic small retailers. But it is silent on the jobs the move would create, and add to the income of farmers, modernize the retail chain, and serve ordinary consumers.

9

Chapter

India-China Cooperation: Exploring Areas of Cooperation

Srikanth Kondapalli

Abstract

India and China have been posting near double digit economic growth rates in recent years, although they are troubled by differences related to unresolved territorial disputes, security concerns on Kashmir, terrorism, Tibet, the Indian Ocean region, etc., and the role of third countries such as Pakistan, the United States, and others in the bilateral equations. As rational actors, the leaders of India and China have explored and initiated broad-based cooperation in multilateral fields (i.e., coordination in the areas of international and regional security and economic institutions and in climate change proposals, energy security, etc.), and bilateral issues such as economic and trade relations, low level joint military operations between the army, navy, and air forces, and the like. It is argued in this paper that as the overall national strategies of India and China coincide (i. e., with their focus on economic development and domestic issues), and as the global strategic situation has been exhibiting flux with no single country able to dominate events, India and China have initiated measures to cooperate with each other in mutually beneficial arenas. Despite mutual security concerns and a low level of strategic trust, these two countries are expected to further enhance and expand cooperation in different arenas in the near future.

Background

With the reformulation of India-China relations from the 1988 "cooperative and constructive" security strategy to the April 2005 (reiterated in November 2006) "strategic partnership and cooperation" agreement, bilateral cooperation between these two countries is expected to expand from the regional to global arena to encompass several areas unexplored before. For sure, this is not the first time that India-China cooperation has exhibited a larger canvas, with such experiments dating back to the 1940s and 1950s. Specifically, the cooperation at the Bandung conference, support to Afro-Asian anti-colonialism efforts and the like are notable. Yet, India-China cooperation in the current phase is qualitatively different from that of the previous period in several respects. The inexorable ground realities of today are unfolding chances for several possibilities of greater cooperation between the two countries than in the days of yore. Today, India-China cooperation is exhibited in bilateral and multilateral fields and it encompasses a number of issues ranging from energy, environment, trade, investments, counter-terrorism, etc. As India and China configure their national strategies in the direction of enhancing sustainable economic development, such areas of cooperation between the two are bound to increase in the future.

In 2010, India and China celebrated the 60th anniversary of the establishment of diplomatic relations. High-level mutual visits, an agenda for cooperation in a number of areas, burgeoning trade and investment, and multilateral cooperation marked the positive direction in bilateral relations even as some core national interests continued to bog down relations between the two countries. In the last week of September 2011, India and China concluded a "highly productive and successful" strategic economic dialogue at Beijing, as the agreed minutes of the meeting indicated. Proposed during Premier Wen Jiabao's visit to New Delhi in December 2010, the dialogue process came against the backdrop of the global meltdown, the Euro zone crisis, and the scaling down of the economic growth rates by India and China.

India and China kept up the momentum of high level communications between the two leaderships by a number of mutual visits. After President Patil's visit to China (the third such visit from India while two Chinese presidents have visited India so far), Politburo standing committee member and internal security czar Zhou Yongkang visited India in November 2010 and Indian External Affairs Ministers visited Wuhan to attend the India-Russia-China trilateral the same month, and Premier Wen Jiabao visited New Delhi in December 2010. Previously, both premiers met at Hanoi in October. Premier Wen's visit to India had yielded tangible results for both China and India in a number of areas, including enhancing trade, investments, cooperation in green technologies, etc. Other topics included the introduction of the Chinese language into high school education in India which indicates the relative victory of Chinese diplomacy and helps to spread Chinese soft power in India — specifically as no Indian language is to be taught in any Chinese schools reciprocally. Also the Joint Communiqué of the two Premiers indicated that bilateral trade is expected to increase to more than USD100 billion in the next five years from the estimated USD60 billion in 2010. The proposal for annual meetings not only between the foreign ministers but also at the President / Prime Minister level and the operationalization of a hotline from November 2010 should bridge the communication gap between the two nuclear powers in Asia. Frequent "strategic level communications" are necessary to remove any misperceptions between the two rising powers of Asia. In this context, despite certain Chinese reservations, four strategic dialogues were conducted between the two sides, the last one in late 2010 at the foreign secretary level which provided scope for discussing confidence building measures even in the nuclear field. Overall, nevertheless, while premier level contacts were maintained, medium-level contacts need to be also strengthened. For instance, despite calling for annual discussions between the foreign ministers, the Chinese foreign minister missed the India visit in 2011. Also, President Hu Jintao and Vice President Xi Jinping could not make it to Delhi in 2011, although Hu is expected to attend the BRICS (Brazil, Russia, India, China, and South Africa) meeting to be held in Delhi in the first part of 2012. Likewise, the 15th round of border talks between the Special Representatives has been postponed due to the Dalai Lama addressing the valedictory meeting of the International Buddhist Convention held at Delhi in November, almost coinciding with the proposed talks. Nevertheless, the annual defense dialogue between the two countries was held with the visit of General Ma Xiaotian to Delhi in December 2011.

On April 14, 2011, during the BRICS meeting at Sanya, both India and China launched the "Year of India-China Exchange." Nearly half a million people visit both sides every year and this indicates an increase from the previous year's figures. More than 9,000 Indian students are studying in China, mainly in the medical sciences, in comparison to nearly 2,100 Chinese students in India, mainly in the information technology field. On February 2, 2002 the China Eastern Airlines Co. Ltd. stated that it will fly between Shanghai and Delhi twice a week with a stopover at Beijing from the end of March 2002. In 2011, about 40 direct flights a week are flying between the two countries. The 100-member youth delegations have made uninterrupted visits every year on both sides since 2006.

Multilateral Cooperation

As multilateralism has become a major phenomenon in the post-Cold War era, India-China cooperation is gradually being expressed in these institutions. Both expressed the view that cooperation and coordination is needed in the United Nations (UN) and the World Trade Organization (WTO) on energy and environmental issues. Commonalities between the two include respect to the UN Charter and non-violability of individual sovereign states, non-intervention, peaceful resolution of disputes, just economic order, etc. While India became an observer in the Shanghai Cooperation Organisation (SCO) at the Astana Summit in 2005 and a member in the East Asian Summit (EAS) at Cebu in January 2007, China became an observer at the 14th summit of South Asian Association for Regional Cooperation (SAARC) in April 2007. However, these entries are not without hiccups, with China being either lukewarm or even hostile to the Indian entry into SCO or EAS, while India wanted China to first sign a bilateral memorandum of understanding (MOU) with the South Asian countries before contemplating to join the SAARC. Nevertheless, the format of multilateral interactions between India and China are increasing in the wider area. This is partly due to the November 2006 India-China joint declaration that called for "close cooperation" between the two in the Asian region.

Cooperation at the G-20

India and China have joined the economic integration process in the last two decades. The G-20 mechanism provides an arena for these countries to expand trade, investments, and technology acquisitions. The Pittsburgh Summit designated G-20 as the premier forum for international economic cooperation. Following this was the Toronto summit of G-20 countries held from June 26 to 27, 2010, and then this was followed by the meetings in Hokkaido, Seoul, and Cannes. These meetings focused on ways to overcome the sluggish global economy, primarily affected by the global financial crisis. These meetings emphasized reducing fiscal deficits of advanced economies by 2013 and long-term debt-related issues by 2016. The G-20 reiterated the need for reform of the financial institutions and the maintenance of seniority positions in these institutions based on merit, and opposed tariff barriers for free trade and investments. However, differences also emerged at the G-20 meetings. The two largest exporting countries, China and Germany, were asked by the United States to stimulate domestic demand so as to give impetus to global trade. While France and Germany wanted to impose global bank levies, several others in the G-20, including India, were reluctant. India became the rotating chair of the G-20 in 2002 and so is not new in its interactions and preparations regarding the organizational work or the policies to be pursued. Indian concerns at the G-20 can be broadly stated as no roll-back on the stimulus packages (announced in the aftermath of the global financial crisis), maintaining global economic growth momentum by curbing trade protectionism, and reform of the international financial institutions. As a rotating chair of the G-20 in 2005, China is also not new to this global financial mechanism. India and China had worked closely in this mechanism from the beginning, although some subtle differences between the two exist. For instance, at the bilateral and multilateral level, India had been insisting that China should move towards market economy status with non-discriminatory practices. Given the huge trade imbalance between the two — with China earning more than USD21 billion in 2010 trade with India — this issue had become a major issue in bilateral relations. China was opposed to raising the issue of Renminbi convertibility and so this issue was not raised at the Summit, despite some Western countries' concern in this regard. Since bilateral trade as such is not huge (about USD61 billion but expected to rise to USD100 billion in 2015), the Renminbi convertibility has not yet become a major flashpoint in India-China relations.

India and China have identical views regarding the G-20 mechanism and both have coordinated and cooperated on a number of issues. For instance, in the aftermath of the global financial crisis, both India and China opposed protectionist tendencies in the Western countries as these were detrimental to the sustainable and balanced growth of these as well as other developing countries. Indian PM Manmohan Singh attended the 7th Asia-Europe Meeting (ASEM) meeting at Beijing in October 2008, and called against protectionism. Likewise in the Doha Rounds, both countries voiced concerns about any tariff barriers. Both countries also argued for the reform and reorganization of the Bretton Woods institutions. While the Toronto G-20 Summit called for enhancing national bank savings rates, India and China had already exhibited high rates in this regard.

Climate change

Indian and Chinese coordination on the climate change proposals attracted global attention recently, although both now account for a significant proportion of global pollution levels. While the U.S. is the largest emitter of pollution, China had become the second largest and India the fourth. Even though India's emissions currently — and it plans to reduce these by 2020 by about 20% — are far below the U.S., or even Chinese, emissions, there had been some forward momentum at Copenhagen. For instance, Indian CO_2 emissions are calculated to be about 30% of those of China. Overall, it had been calculated that the total CO_2 emissions for all these countries are estimated at about 1.1, 5.1, 5.8, and 27.1 billion tons, respectively, for India, China, the U.S., and the global averages and their per capita emissions are estimated at 1, 3.8, 19.6, and 4.2 tons in that order. It is also estimated that China is to produce about 6.5 billion tons (with another estimate mentioning 9 billion tons) of emissions soon. China had stated that it will reduce emissions by about 40% by 2020.

To tackle these issues internationally, the Kyoto Protocol of 1997 suggested that the developed countries reduce their greenhouse gas emissions by 40% by 2020 from the 1990 levels. The U.S. had rejected this proposal as it does not include the action plan for the developing countries. India and China had advocated the provisions of the Kyoto Protocol by arguing that the per capita emissions from the developing countries were far less than those of the developed countries. Besides, for generating sustainable economic growth rates and development, the developing countries are dependent on coal and other resources and adopting clean-fuels has an exorbitant cost. Both India and China had coordinated such positions in the international marketplace, such as at the Bali Summit meeting and at the Copenhagen conference in December 2009. On October 21, 2009, both signed a joint plan for cutting greenhouse emissions, emphasising the role of the UN and the Kyoto Protocol. At Copenhagen, it became clear that China was isolated by the U.S. and European partners who suggested that as China is rising to be the second largest economy, it needs to take the lead in cutting down its emissions. This was not acceptable to China. The final accord, which is non-binding, was signed between the U.S. and BASIC countries (Brazil, South Africa, India, and China). In the lead-up to this accord, Chinese Premier Wen Jiabao called up his Indian counterpart to coordinate positions at Copenhagen. Later, Indian environmental minister Jairam Ramesh during his visit to Beijing in early May 2010 suggested that India bail out China at the Copenhagen meeting on climate change issues. He said: "At the Copenhagen talks, the Chinese in their heart of hearts know we saved them from isolation…Given our English skills and our more 'cussedness' in negotiating skills, we bailed the Chinese out of many difficult situations. The Chinese know India was absolutely essential to the fact that China did not get isolated at Copenhagen."

Counter-terrorism

Another arena for coordination and cooperation by India and China is in the area of counter-terrorism. The national challenge identified by both countries remains terrorism. The specific words used are for India "cross-border terrorism" and for China on how to counter the "three evils" (extremism, separatism, and splittism). Both support the UN Security Council Resolutions 1267, 1373, and 1540 and condemn all forms of terrorism. Both are concerned about developments in Afghanistan and are in touch with this issue. This is significant as the U.S. President announced that the International Security Assistance Force troops will be withdrawn by July 2011, while Afghan President Karzai suggested in July that his country is prepared for foreign troop withdrawal in 2014. During the visit of the Indian National Security Advisor Shivshankar Menon to Beijing in June 2010, the issue of stability in Afghanistan, ethnic reconciliation, and the extraction of minerals were discussed, although the factor of Pakistan may impinge on such plans. Subsequently, in the bilateral declaration of the two premiers in December 2010, India and China expressed the view that they will work for the reconstruction of Afghanistan.

Both countries are involved in a structured counter-terrorism dialogue, besides foreign office consultations, a strategic dialogue between the Indian Foreign Secretary and the Vice Foreign Minister of China, annual defense dialogue, and cooperation on science and technology. Towards counter-terrorism cooperation, joint army operations were conducted in 2007 and 2008 but discontinued in 2009 due to bilateral differences as well as the issuance of stapled visas to Kashmiri residents in India.

Bilateral economic and trade cooperation

In the bilateral arena, trade is one of the major booming areas of cooperation between India and China. The bilateral economic relations of India and China are carried out through the traditional border trade and the more recent trade through ports. Though border trade existed between the two countries for centuries, it came to a standstill after the 1962 war, only to resume in the 1990s. In 1954, when India recognized Chinese sovereignty over Tibet, a trade agreement was also signed between the two countries for eight years. However, following the onset of a chill in bilateral relations from the late 1950s, this trade treaty was not ratified, which drastically affected the economies of the traditional border trade posts. Following the first visit of Indian pilgrims through the Indo-Tibetan side after 22 years in 1981, Chinese officials expressed their hope that the Tibetan border town of Taklakot would become a thriving border trade post in the region. During the path-breaking visit of Rajiv Gandhi to Beijing in December 1988, India and China agreed to set up a joint group to cooperate on economic, trade, and science and technology issues. During Premier Li Peng's visit to New Delhi in December 1991, an agreement between the two countries on the resumption of border trade was signed. Subsequently in the 1993 Joint Working Group meeting it was decided that border trade points in Himachal Pradesh (Namgya) and Tibet (Zhuba) are to be opened. By 1996, trade across both these passes amounted to about INR85 lakhs (USD8.5 million), in 1998 to INR51.7 lakhs (USD5.1 million), in 1999 to INR63.9 lakhs. With the agreement in 2003 on the opening up of the Nathu La in Sikkim with Changgu as the trading port and Renqinggang of Tibet to border trade, such figures are expected to go up. It is estimated that overall border trade amounts to about USD100 million, though, according to some, the illegal border trade may be as much as USD1 billion. Dumchile, for instance, is a smuggler's haven in the western sector. In mid-2000, India suggested that more border trade points should be opened on both sides. It is estimated that nearly 12 border trade points are to be opened up in the bordering areas.

Overall bilateral trade, however, was not affected due to problems in political relations (after May 1998 nuclear tests and the stapled visas issue). That the bilateral economic relations are headed for a more systematic and comprehensive relationship is indicated by the joint declaration between the two premiers on January 14, 2008 which signalled that they welcomed the conclusion of a feasibility study, set up by both in April 2005, on a possible "high quality" Regional Trade Agreement (RTA), provided such an arrangement is "mutually advantageous." China became India's largest trading partner. While bilateral trade was about USD200 million in the early 1990s, USD3 billion by 2001, and about USD5 billion by 2002, it increased in 2010, however, to more than USD61 billion, although the Indian side lost as much as USD22 billion in the unfavorable balance of payments position. Indeed, this issue had become one of the main points of discussion between the two visiting leaders, with India arguing that China should move towards a full-fledged market economy and that the Indian companies — specifically pharmaceuticals and information technology-related — should have non-discriminatory treatment in the Chinese market. This is yet to be realized.

On the positive side, however, several India and Chinese companies have also expanded their business operations. More than 200 Indian companies have invested in China, while Huawei and ZTS have major stakes in the Indian telecom sector. In mid-1999, Huawei Technologies of China started investing in the Indian software city of Bangalore. According to its chief operating officer in India, Jack Lu, it invested about USD8 million initially and this increased to about USD30 million in 2001 to expand its software development center. Overall, the Chinese companies' involvement in the Indian manufacturing sector, specifically power and telecommunications, is expected to increase to a significant proportion of the Indian economy in the near future. Indian software giant Infosys had acquired land in Shanghai for its commercial operations and Tata's Jaguar and Land Rover witnessed a 70% jump in sales in China in 2010 as compared to the previous year. Mahindra as well carved out niche areas in the China tractor market. The role of the Indian IT software companies in China is noteworthy. From 1997, there was an expansion in this field when the National Institute of Information Technology established about 30 training centers in China, mostly concentrated in Shanghai and other places. It had established about 100 training centers across China by the end of 2002. Similarly, another Indian IT giant, Aptech, collaborated with the Beijing University that is adjacent to the Chinese IT center in the Zhongguancun area, for training personnel. In 2001, the Satyam Computer Service Ltd established its office at Shanghai Pudong Software Park. Other Indian giants like TCS, Wipro, Infosys, etc., are being invited by China to fill this gap and expand their operations.

The Chinese Ambassador to India, Zhang Yan, on the eve of Premier Wen's visit to Delhi, reiterated the long-held view of the Chinese that India should sign a free trade area (FTA) agreement. Although India is in the process of signing FTAs with a number of countries, it has so far been reluctant to do the same with China. Overall, today, these FTAs have proliferated to nearly 200 such regional / bilateral agreements encompassing more than half of global trade. China has concluded, or is in discussions, to set up FTAs with about 30 countries including the Association of Southeast Asian Nations (ASEAN) countries in 2002, and Chile and Pakistan in 2006.

While China is widely known to have exerted pressure on India for an FTA, the latter is wary of jumping into the fray as the proposal is fraught with long-term consequences not only impacting the domestic economic sectors but also the larger strategic landscape of Asia and beyond. As a large country, with more than a billion population (exhibiting a younger profile) and posting near double-digit economic growth rate figures, along with mature service and software sectors, India needs to study carefully such proposals. Indeed, India currently has concluded FTAs with six countries (with Sri Lanka in 1998 and ASEAN in 2010) and six preferential trade agreements. India has also signed higher level Comprehensive Economic Partnership (CEPA) Agreements with South Korea, Japan, and is involved in FTA discussions with the European Union, Taiwan, and possibly in the future with the United States.

The India-China differences on FTA have several dimensions. First, reportedly opposed by the Mumbai Club, the indigenous producers are wary about competition from the Chinese goods not only in their influx into the Indian market (thereby displacing indigenous products) but also in posing stiff competition in other global markets. Despite relative opening up of the Chinese economy from 1978, but reinforced from the southern tour of Deng Xiaoping in 1992, this section argued that Chinese products are heavily subsidized, costing procedures not fully compatible with free market mechanism, RMB currency convertibility issues, and a weak system of the rule of law. While these are common global complaints against China, in the Indian context, other issues such as high transportation costs (in terms of land routes between the two countries complicated further by Chinese intransigence in solving the border dispute) and insurance rates have added fuel to the fire in stalling FTA proposals with China. Indeed, the Federation of Indian Chamber of Commerce and Industry was lukewarm to the idea of a FTA arrangement with China while the Shanghai Chamber of Commerce is widely believed to be exerting pressure on the Chinese leadership to explore more business opportunities with India.

Second, while the Indian side had called for pan-Asian FTA (by Prime Minister Manmohan Singh at the second East Asian Summit in Cebu in January 2007), the Chinese side, along with South Korea and some ASEAN countries, opposed this idea. Indian proposals were backed by Australia, New Zealand, Malaysia, and Indonesia. It appeared that India was concerned about the uninterrupted Chinese inroads into central, south, and southeast Asia through infrastructure projects and the effect this could have on the marginalization of India. A pan-Asian FTA could avoid such pitfalls as there could be a better, level-playing field. In this scenario, the "rules of origin" principle could stall the Chinese influx of cheaper goods into the Indian market. In this context, the American retailer Walmart, and the French Carrefour, which predominantly dish out cheap Chinese products, were reportedly blocked by the Indian government to protect Indian industry, specifically small and medium enterprises, and the retail sector. The current stiff opposition in the Indian parliament and outside to the FDI entry into the retail sector is another case in point.

Third, India-China economic relations, while on the upswing in bilateral trade figures, have not provided for much comfort to the Indian side. With the negative balance of trade position to India and in favor of China (to the tune of about USD22.2 billion in 2010), the trade basket is confined to predominantly raw materials or low-end products, along with more Indian investments in China as compared to less Chinese investments in India, drastic measures were called for but with no way ahead to redress such phenomena. Meanwhile, Indian anti-dumping duties on Chinese products are increasing while China for the first time imposed duties on Indian chemical dyes. This could lead to further friction between the two sides. Again, border trade (estimated to be above USD100 million) is miniscule when compared to the overall bilateral trade (above USD60 billion in 2010). In this context, border trade through Shipki La, Lipulekh, and Nathu La has not shown substantial increases. The 2006 agreement to open Demchok is also unlikely to radically change this situation, even though no major progress was achieved in opening this trade post. Indeed, as the Chinese violated the 2006 understanding on trading "local" products and attempted to export electronic and other goods produced elsewhere into mainland China, these were swiftly sent back. As mentioned above, the dragging border dispute also implies that both sides could not set up custom houses for regulating trade in the border areas.

In the meantime, China is exploring an alternate route: Disbursing cheap loans to the Indian firms. For instance, China Development Bank, ICBC, etc., has announced a USD10 billion in loans to Anil Ambani's Reliance industries, mainly in the power sector, with orders for equipment for nearly 30,000 megawatts. Indeed, the power sector is an emerging field in the India-China context, with demand for equipment for nearly 80,000 megawatt projects worth USD50 billion being ordered from the Chinese companies like Shanghai Electric Corporation, Dong Fang, Harbin, SEPCO Electric Power, etc. Cashing in on the Indian power demand, the Chinese banks are offering cheaper credit, but mainly in RMB loans. Such a move, although demanded by some Indian companies, has two long-term consequences: One, major Indian companies in this sector, like BHEL, Larsen & Toubro, and Thermax, are likely to be adversely affected. Additionally, there are also complaints about the poor quality of equipment supplied by the Chinese side. Others also cite the project delays such as in the 80 kilometer road construction project in the Theog-Kotkhai-Hatkoti-Rohru region of Himachal Pradesh by the Chinese company Longjian Road & Bridge Ltd Co. which began work in 2008 and was supposed to be completed by 2011 and which has now been postponed by at least two more years.

Another infrastructure project, reportedly explored at the first strategic economic dialogue, is the development of high-speed railways. China indeed made rapid strides in high-speed railways, although this came at a high cost which was reflected in the multi-billion dollar scandal involving Minister Liu Zhijun, a protégé of Jiang Zemin, and the architect of high-speed railways, who was dismissed in February 2011 on charges of corruption. The Shandong (2008) and Wenzhou (2011) train crashes have also called into question such projects. During Premier Wen's visit to Delhi in 2010 a proposal was made to sell Chinese high-speed railways to India, but in vain. India is said to be exploring the possibilities of cooperating with the Chinese or Japanese firms in this sector.

Conclusions

India-China cooperation is exhibited on selective issues: Economic, energy, maritime, environmental, and other related issues. But some other areas are bound to reveal several surprises. While bilateral cooperation is exhibited in economic and trade relations, and multilateral cooperation in the coordinated responses of India and China on a number of issues, issues like political trust, permanent peace and security in international issues, are expected to take a long time to fructify between these two Asian countries. Given these realities of interactions between India and China, it is safe to suggest that the step-by-step approach and gradual progress could be achieved between the two in areas mentioned above, while attempts should be made to expand the envelope of cooperation.

First, India is looking for positive assurances from China on a number of issues — market access, investment flows, anti-dumping, etc. — given the wide trade imbalance (of more than USD22.2 billion in 2010 in favor of China) and restrictions imposed on the Indian companies in the Chinese market. This issue was raised during President Patil's visit to Beijing in 2010 and subsequently during several high-level meetings. A forward momentum in this regard by China could assuage Indian feelings and bring further mutually beneficial economic ties.

Second, as the first strategic economic dialogue had envisioned discussing macro-economic issues, there is a need to look at possibilities of collaboration in offshore joint manufacturing and Research and Development areas. As the Indian government's recent national manufacturing sector policy had indicated, India plans to expand the manufacturing sector role from 16 to nearly 30% of the GDP. At the same time, Premier Wen Jiabao has suggested recently that the growth rates of China would be repositioned up to about 7%, in addition to restructuring the Chinese domestic consumption share. Both of these provide opportunities to both countries to expand cooperation.

Third, to overcome the global financial crisis in 1997 and 2008, China had invested heavily in the infrastructure projects across the country, specifically in the western areas recently. Thus it gained enough experience in the last three decades of reform and opening up in this sphere. At the same time, India has also announced the policy of attracting investments in the infrastructure projects to the tune of USD1 trillion. Both then have an opportunity to cooperate in this sphere extensively.

Fourth, maritime areas are becoming major areas of attention for both rising China and India, given their dependence on the export and import of goods and services. China has become the net importer of oil and now trades roughly 60% of its GDP through maritime routes. In 2010, it imported 200 million tons of oil, mainly through the Indian Ocean Region. India, likewise, is expanding its maritime role with trade and investments. Thus, while both China and India have been concerned about maritime security, very few initiatives were made to cooperate in the maritime domain, except in search-and-rescue and counter-piracy operations.

Finally, as India and China are the most populous countries in the world, there are enormous opportunities in learning from each other in sustainable development experience as well as mitigating poverty levels, overcoming water scarcity, and providing inexpensive housing. Ingenious and cost-effective ways could be explored for the betterment of the majority of Indians and Chinese by sharing and working together in several sectors. Ideas abound among Indians and Chinese. The task is putting them into practice.

10

Chapter

Emerging Markets in the Dawn: China and India to Play Important Roles in Driving the Demand for Solar Power

Sun Wei

Origins of the Sino-India Relationship

China has had diplomatic ties with India for more than 2,000 years. Buddhism and the Silk Road served as the cultural and geographic bridges between the two ancient, neighboring civilizations. The introduction of Indian Buddhism to China spurred the development of Sino-India relations. Chinese Buddhism originated from ancient India and was brought to central China across west Asia, and this led to the spread of Mahayana Buddhism to the Korean Peninsula and Japan. Under the influence of China, the creed of Mahayana Buddhism was introduced to the Korean Peninsula, Japan, and Vietnam. This movement also influenced Tibetan Buddhism.

Development of the Global Photovoltaic Market

So far, the economic take-off of both China and India and their increasingly frequent economic communications have led to the rising demand for energy supply. As such, the two countries, in addition to their efforts in developing traditional energy, have been more aware of the significance in developing other renewable energy sources, such as solar energy, after taking into account the imperative of global environmental protection. The chart below compares the estimated global demand for photovoltaic power generation in February 2011 and September 2011 (see Fig. 10.1). According to analysts, the demand for installation capacity of photovoltaic power generation looks promising as the demand for installation increased from 18.6 GW in the beginning of 2011 to 20.6 GW in August 2011, and the demand for installed capacity of photovoltaic power generation in 2012 is expected to reach 23.3 GW as a result of the continuous reduction in installation costs.

Photon, an influential photovoltaic magazine, also made the following analysis of the estimated installed capacity of the top 10 photovoltaic markets in 2011 and 2012 (see Fig. 10.2). European countries will still represent a dominant share of 50%, but other markets such as the U.S., China, Japan, and India will gradually take the important positions in the photovoltaic industry in the future.

Fig. 10.1 The estimated global demand for photovoltaic power generation in February, September of 2011 and 2012 (Unit:GW)

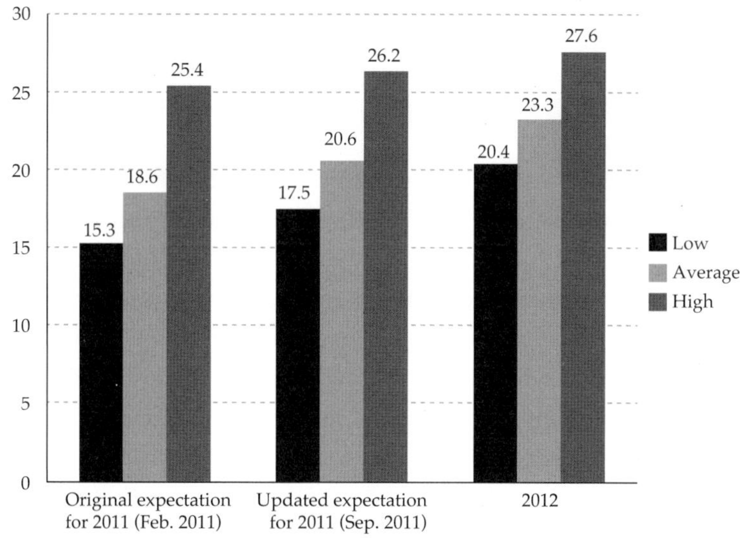

Source: Photon.

Fig. 10.2 The estimated installed capacity of the top 10 photovoltaic markets in 2011 and 2012 (Unit:MV)

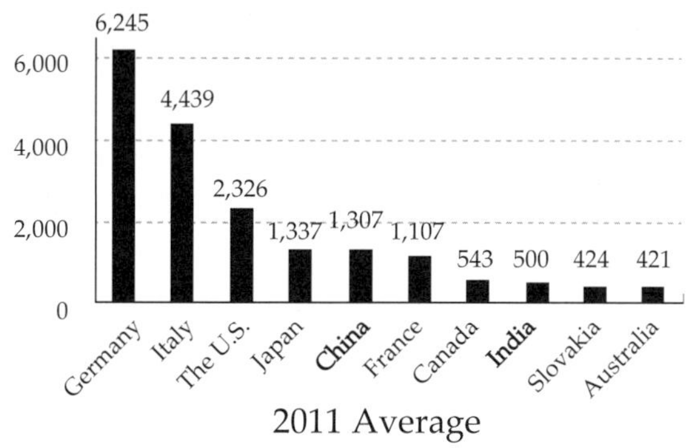

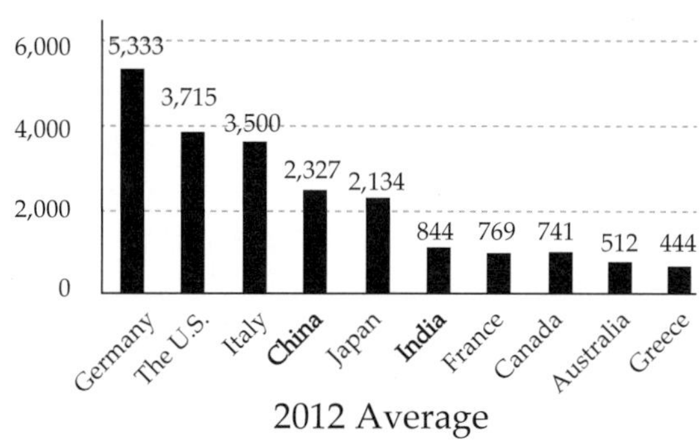

Favorable Policies on the Photovoltaic Industry from the Chinese and Indian Governments

Policies from the Chinese government

In 2011, the "Notice of Solar Feed-in-Tariff Policy from National Development and Reform Commission" issued by China's National Development and Reform Commission (NDRC) set the nationally united benchmark on-grid tariff for solar photovoltaic power generation. For the solar photovoltaic power generation projects that obtained construction approval before July 1, 2011, projected to complete construction and commence operation no later than December 31, 2011 but the tariff of which is yet to be approved by NDRC, an on-grid tariff of RMB1.15 per kWh (tax inclusive) will be adopted upon approval. For the solar photovoltaic power generation projects that obtained approval on and after July 1, 2011, and projects that obtained approval before July 1, 2011 but which are still under construction by December 31, 2011, an on-grid tariff of RMB1.15 per kWh, will still be adopted in Tibet, and RMB1 per kWh in other provinces (regions and cities), respectively. For solar photovoltaic power generation projects that won the bidding of concession rights, the on-grid tariff is subject to the bidding price, which shall not be higher than the benchmark tariff of solar photovoltaic power generation.

As a matter of fact, the new policy introduced in the "Notice of Solar Feed-in-Tariff Policy from National Development and Reform Commission" is more favorable than the prevailing one, as it marked the first benchmark photovoltaic tariff to be promulgated nationwide, which is subsidized by electricity end-users and subject to adjustments in line with changes in the cost of photovoltaic power generation and other factors. What's more, it is more targeted than the previous one in terms of both geographic coverage and subsidizing methods, which is basically in the same mode as Germany. It is a milestone heralding the large-scale expansion of China's photovoltaic market. In addition, thanks to the abundant solar energy resources in northwest China — the annual sunlight duration is more than 2,500 hours — Tibet, Inner Mongolia, and some other regions, such as Shandong and Jiangsu, under additional subsidy support are likely to have access to the market in a short time. Besides, the photovoltaic market in the next two years will not be affected by the subsidy capability. Taking Qinghai Province as an example, the benchmark tariff ranging from RMB1 to RMB1.15 per kWh and sulfur-free benchmark tariff of approximately RMB0.35 per kWh imply a subsidy of approximately RMB0.80 per kWh. At present, the national power consumption amounts to approximately 4,000 billion kWh and the additional subsidy for renewable energy is RMB0.004 per kWh. Accordingly, the annual renewable energy subsidy aggregates to RMB16 billion, half of which, i.e., RMB8 billion, will be adequate enough to support the photovoltaic power plants and provide subsidy for photovoltaic energy generation of 10 billion kWh. The current subsidy capability may support 5 GW installed capacity of photovoltaic power generation on the basis of 2,000 effect sunlight hours per year. Furthermore, considering the descending curve of photovoltaic power generation, it is anticipated that the rapid rise of the domestic market will not be affected by the subsidy capability in the next two years.

Policies from the Indian government

For the efficient use of solar energy, the Indian government carried out the Solar India policy, pursuant to which, the Indian government expects to ramp up its photovoltaic installed capacity to 20 GW by 2020, and 30 GW, or 10%–12% of the total annual power generation capacity, by 2030; and anticipates achieving grid parity for photovoltaic power generation by 2020, coal-based thermal power by 2030 as well as photovoltaic installed capacity of 4–5 GW by 2017.

At the end of August 2011, the Ministry of New and Renewable Energy of India published new rules concerning photovoltaic power generation under Jawaharlal Nehru National Solar Mission. In particular, the second stage of the first phase includes the 350 MW photovoltaic projects, representing an increase over the 150 MW for the first stage (2010–2011). In addition, the installed capacity of each project will rise from 5 MW to 20 MW. The permitted contracted capacity will increase from 5 MW to 50 MW, hence attracting major construction companies and power plants to take part in the project construction. Batteries and modules for crystalline silicon photovoltaic projects, excluding silicon wafers, are to be provided by Indian manufacturers as required. However, thin film equipment and products are exempt from such requirements. Project developers may complete relevant financing arrangements within seven months, one month extended from the original arrangement.

Background in Respect of Energy Demand in China and India

To accommodate future economic development, both China and India are desperate for an abundant energy supply. Given the exponential economic growth, China and India have become the two largest energy consumers across the globe. According to "BP Statistics Review," China and India have consumed 20.3% and 4.4% of the primary energies of the whole world in 2010, ranking the first and fourth, respectively. As China and India consumed mainly fossil fuels, their carbon emission during the same period accounted for 25.1% and 5.1% of the total global emission, respectively, while China has a higher utilization rate of hydro-power and other renewable energies, as compared to India. Since both China and India aspired to climate change and environment protection, these two countries have great potential to utilize renewable energies.

Composition of Primary Energies in China and India

Fig. 10.3 Composition of primary energies in China and India in 2010

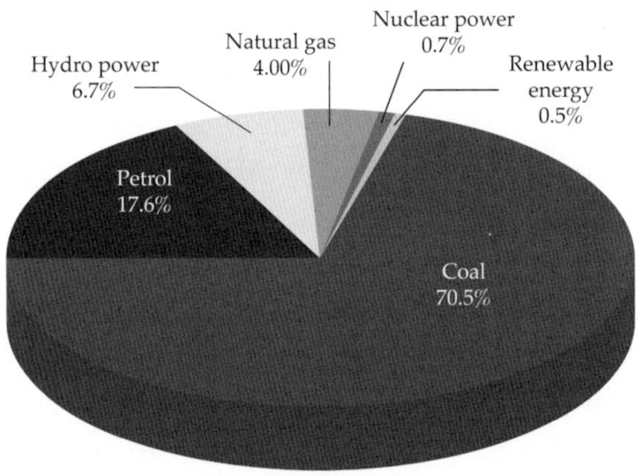

China: Composition of primary energies (2010)

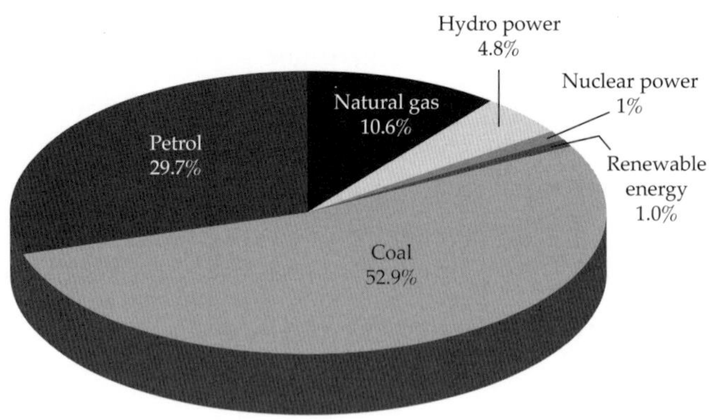

India: Composition of primary energies (2010)

Sources: CEIC data, and China Electricity Council.

In 2010, energy supply in China and India chiefly relied on conventional energies, with coal power and petrol representing 85% and 83% of their energy supplies, respectively, whereas renewable energies only accounted for 1% or below. Therefore, the potential for expansion of renewable energy utilization is huge.

China aims to have 15 % of its total energy supply from non-fossil fuel sources by 2020. China Electricity Council (CEC) estimated that the production capacity of wind energy, nuclear energy, and solar energy will increase from 44 GW in 2010 to 290 GW in 2020 (see Fig 10.4). Electricity demand mainly comes from: Industrial (75%); Residential (12%), Commercial (11%), and Agricultural (2%). The on-going development of industry and commerce makes the demand for energy ever-increasing.

Fig. 10.4 Composition of primary energies in China (Unit:GW)

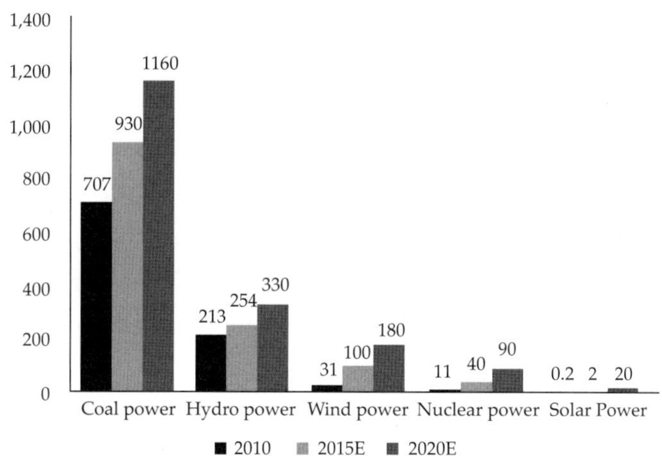

Sources: CEIC data, and China Electricity Council.

India aims to have 15 % of the total energy supply generated from renewable energies by 2020, whilst at the same time India has to step up its coal power production capacity in order to materialize its GDP growth of 7–8% per annum. As the power operations are still loss-making enterprises, a leap in production capacity in the near term is barely possible. Electricity demand mainly comes from: Industrial (38%); Residential (24%), Agricultural (21%), Commercial (9%), and others (8%). By the same token, the on-going development of industry and commerce fuels the growing demand for energy.

Fig. 10.5 Composition of primary energies in India (Unit:GW)

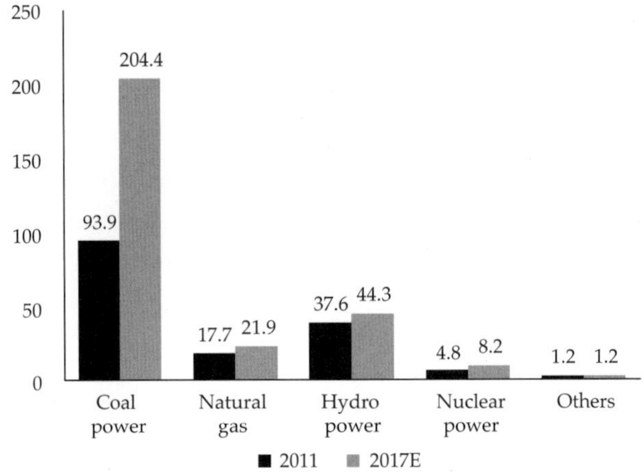

Sources: Central Electricity Authority (CEA), and Daiwa.

Distribution of Energy Demand and Supply

China was beset by an energy shortage from 2000 to 2004. It saw, however, an increase in power generation capacity from 2004–2010, thereby keeping electricity shortage in check for the past few years. Owing to China's fast implementation capability to expand power generation capacity, the expansion targets it set for 2007 were basically fulfilled (see Fig. 10.6).

The energy shortage in India became most severe in 2009, reaching 11%, which saw a fall back to 8.5% in 2011 (see Fig. 10.7). Power generation capacity grew in the past three years. Yet due to the operating losses incurred by the power companies during the same period, electricity demand was lowered accordingly. Since India provides an unattractive amount of capital to enhance electricity production capacity, at present it can only meet the capacity targets set five years ago, which was mainly attributable to the crippled operation of power enterprises and domestic shortage of coal supply.

Fig. 10.6 Distribution of energy demand and supply in China

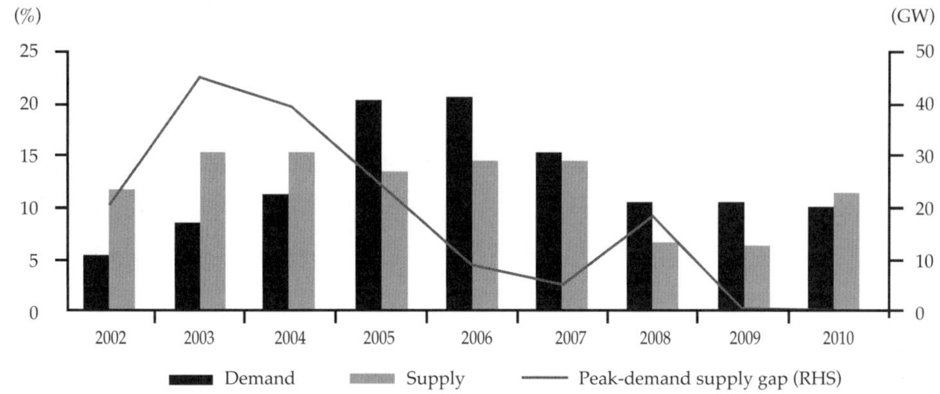

Source: CEIC.

Fig. 10.7 Distribution of energy demand and supply in India

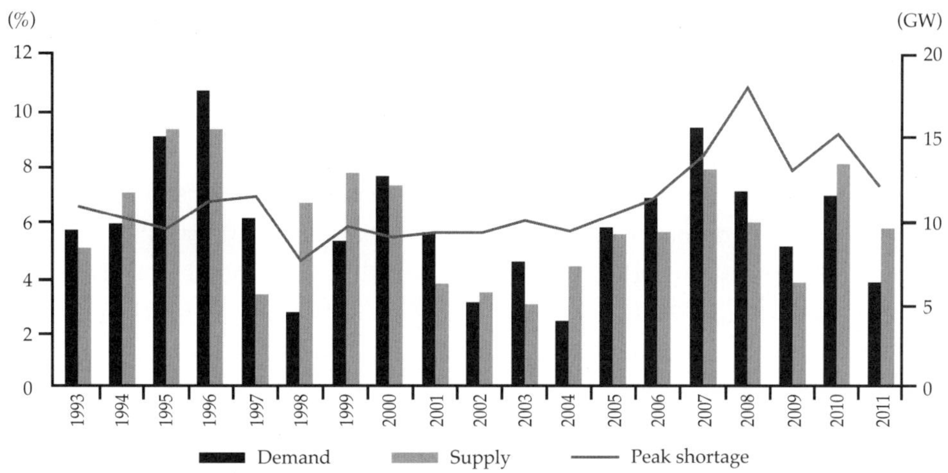

Source: CEA.

Encountering the challenges in expanding electricity production capacity in the future, China Electricity Council anticipates a shortfall of electricity in China up to 50 GW and 70 GW in 2012 and 2013, respectively, and wind power will still face the on-grid problem, with approximately 26.5% production capacity left unconnected to the power grid at the end of 2010. The situation, however, is likely to improve. According to a spokesman of State Grid, national power enterprises will invest RMB2,550 billion in power-grid construction under the "twelfth five-year plan," which is estimated to be completed in 2012–2013. Upon completion, an additional 60 GW of electricity can be transported each year, which serves to improve the shortage problem caused by the power grid bottleneck. Because of the high borrowing rate, power enterprises need to find alternatives to improve their profitability.

For India, power enterprises are still suffering losses. Central Electricity Regulatory Commission (CERC) estimated that power tariff might have to be increased by 5–40% to cover losses which will put the plan to purchase additional electricity on hold, and an intended decrease in electricity demand will be required to cut losses. Meanwhile, coal supply fails to satisfy ongoing demand and it is estimated that India will suffer a shortfall in coal supply up to 132 million tons by 2015.

Contributions Made by GCL-Poly to the Photovoltaic Industry

Introduction to solar business

GCL-Poly Energy Holdings Ltd. has engaged itself in the value chain of the solar business, such as polysilicon, ingots/rods, wafers, and solar farms. Regarding polysilicon, its production capacity for 2010 reached 21,000 metric tonnes and it ranked No. 1 nationwide and No. 3 worldwide. Its anticipated production capacity for 2011 is likely to hit 46,000 metric tonnes, which may secure it the first place globally. Its domestic and global market share for 2010 was 45% and 21%, respectively, and the production cost for polysilicon dropped to USD21.4/kg (as at the end of June 2011). In respect of ingots/rods and wafers, its production capacity for 2010 stood at 3.5 GW, rated No. 1 worldwide, and its anticipated production capacity for 2011 is 6.5 GW, which will further strengthen its leading position in the world. Its domestic and global market share for 2010 was 40% and 16%, respectively, while the processing cost for wafers declined to USD0.20/watt (as at the end of June 2011), with a slicing yield rate higher than 94%. In respect of solar farms, GCL-Poly owns a 20 MW operating solar farm in Xuzhou and the total installed capacity of its overseas solar farms reaches 10.8 MW.

Introduction to solar farm business

GCL Solar Energy is a solar power developer with extensive experience in engineering, procurement and construction (EPC), operation and maintenance (O&M), and upper-stream manufacturing. Located in China, GCL Solar Energy is dedicated to developing, constructing, and operating commercial and power-station solar power generation facilities in North America, Europe, and other emerging markets. It is most differentiated from its rivals in its ability to develop solar projects with very competitive prices, as supported by the joint development strategies formulated along with leading solar power enterprises in each area, the core design team based in China, lower-than-market purchase prices by leveraging its relationship with middle-stream manufacturers, and low-cost funding through its strong collaboration with Chinese and international banks. With its clear-cut investment screening criteria, GCL Solar Energy has realized an average rate of capital return of 15%. In 2010, it established a joint venture with Solar Reserve, a North American developer, to develop over-1 GW projects. In the same year, GCL Solar Energy and Wells Fargo jointly announced a special cooperation project under which Wells Fargo would provide funding of more than USD100 million to GCL's solar farm business in 2011. Having completed and commenced operation of its 20 MW solar farms in Xuzhou, China, GCL Solar Energy is currently setting its eyes on becoming one of the world's leading solar power developers.

Development vision and mission

By focusing on the challenges and pressure of customers' concerns and providing competitive wafers, GCL-Poly has continuously committed itself to maximizing the value for its customers and becoming one of the most respected leading new energy enterprises in the world. GCL-Poly will devote itself to providing high-quality energy and services to the public, improving the living environment of mankind, and bringing green energy to daily life.

Comprehensive strategic positioning

GCL-Poly's core business includes polysilicon, ingots/rods, and wafers. It is estimated that, by the end of 2011, polysilicon production capacity will reach 46,000 metric tons; wafer production capacity already hit 6.5 GW as at the end of July 2011. Under its "Co-location" strategy, GCL-Poly is building wafer plants around the bases of downstream cell customers to meet the demands of such customers. The distance of these wafer plants from downstream customers is all within 200 km by highway, which ensures efficient and convenient transportation, lower costs and lower products wear-and-tear during transportation. In respect of cells and modules, GCL-Poly chooses to forge a strategic alliance with its partners instead of making direct involvement. In respect of the end-user market, GCL-Poly assists its partners to promote the application of module products in system integration and solar farm construction business. At the end of 2009, GCL-Poly has completed the construction and commenced operation of its 20 MW solar farm in Xuzhou City, Jiangsu Province. In addition, GCL-Poly's on-grid power generation projects in the U.S. totaled around 11 MW, with pipeline projects of more than 1 GW in the U.S.

Social responsibilities

As an enterprise that has long been engaged in the development of renewable energy, GCL-Poly is well aware of its responsibilities to environmental protection and social contribution. We effectively recycle 100% of various by-products during polysilicon production, and ensure that our manufacturing facilities comply with national standards. All our cogeneration power plants are equipped with desulphurization facilities, which can significantly reduce the emission of sulfur dioxide. Meanwhile, we have actively served society by creating jobs, making charitable donations, and taking an active part in public welfare. We have extended our sincerity, love, and care to rehabilitation centers, orphanages, and schools in mountain areas in Mainland China via our annual "Sunshine Love and Care Action." We also donated photovoltaic power generation facilities to schools in Qinghai to provide a stable power supply to the students and good conditions for their study.

Last but not least, it is our hope to build a better living environment for the people of China and India, where the sky is bluer, the water is purer, and living is nicer. Thank you!

11

Chapter

The Energy–Poverty–Climate Nexus: A Tale of Two Countries

Sudhakara Reddy

Abstract

Close to two-thirds of the world's poorest people live in developing countries. Eradication of poverty depends on the increased access to goods and services. However, alleviating poverty is hindered by two interlinked phenomena: Lack of access to modern energy services and worsening environmental shocks due to climate change. In this context, the present study develops a framework for energy and climate security considering India and China as case studies. First, it analyses the state of energy deprivation in India and China and then presents the climate dilemma concerning the developing countries. It provides a framework to help policy-makers and business enterprises to identify options that are region-specific while cost-effective. A structured "public-private partnership" business model is conceived for various supply-side technologies — biogas, solar, and decentralized electricity — to facilitate their large-scale dissemination. It analyses actor linkages and their impact on energy and climate policies.

Introduction

Current energy systems are inadequate to meet the needs of the world's poor and are jeopardizing the achievement of the Millennium Development Goals. Worldwide, approximately 3 billion people rely on traditional biomass fuels for cooking and heating and about 1.5 billion have no access to electricity. Up to a billion more have access only to unreliable electricity networks (United Nations Development Programme [UNDP] 2010). The energy-deprived poor suffer the economic consequences of insufficient power for productive income-generating activities and for other basic services such as education. They also face problems because of inefficient combustion of solid fuels in inadequately ventilated buildings. There is also a nexus between energy use and climate change since CO_2 emissions, originating from energy use, result in climate change. The key link between poor people and the environment is the extreme dependence of the poor on low-quality fuels which degrade the environment. The more depleted the resource base is (e.g., little rain, polluted water, few trees, and soil erosion), the more meager the livelihoods of the poor become.

India and China, the rising economic powers, are classic examples of this nexus between energy, poverty, and climate change. They have to seek a balance between economic development and environmental protection. To achieve high growth as well as to bridge the prevailing energy access gap, the annual demand for energy, in particular for petroleum products, will significantly rise with time. In the near future, securing access to an adequate supply of safe, reliable, and affordable energy resources is going to be the most important policy consideration for India and China. However, the issue of energy access is not just limited to supply and demand. For sustainability of such an energy supply, the issues of climate change need to be taken into consideration. According to United Nations Framework Convention on Climate Change (UNFCCC) (2007), developing countries face climate risks in terms of the shortage of food and water and the negative impacts on health and life; but their economies have fewer resources — socially, technologically, and financially — to adapt to such risks. Hence, there is a need to look for alternative energy sources and mechanisms without compromising on the quantity of energy used.

The general perception is that meeting the challenges of access to modern energy services, reducing poverty, and tackling climate change need different policy prescriptions. However, they are part of the wider sustainable development agenda which requires social equity, both amongst communities and across nations. Thus, in seeking sustainable solutions to the challenges of climate change, an approach which embraces social justice is essential. Despite this, concern has been expressed that carbon reduction and poverty alleviation are often treated separately in practice, with the former concerned with the impact of energy policy on future generations and the latter more focused on the needs of the present population. Also, planners and policymakers face a dual challenge since energy plays a significant role in development and at the same time contributes to climate change. This has led to calls for a more integrated approach which would allow both environmental and social goals to be met.

In this backdrop, the present paper examines the nexus among energy, poverty, and climate change. It analyses the developing country's perspective of climate concerns. Taking India and China as case studies, the paper has done a comparative analysis of the energy situation. Focusing on the household sector, the paper looks at the social, economic, and technical factors that determine fuel choice and the impacts on livelihoods, the economy, the environment, and the health of the people. The study provides examples from the Indian perspective to show that modern energy services can be provided in a cost-effective manner, offering the potential to address aspects of poverty while also transitioning away from fossil fuel dependence. It suggests specific policies to target rural households and the urban poor. The energy efficient low-carbon energy systems have the potential to produce greater human development, employment potential, and carbon mitigation returns. The findings will constitute a guideline on how to formulate energy and environmental policies for the successful implementation of these programs in a way that is sustainable, enhancing economic performance practices to achieve the broad goal of reducing poverty and achieving energy and climate security.

Energy Poverty Nexus in Developing Countries

The energy–poverty nexus is one of the least discussed aspects of our current energy challenge. Among the world's population, nearly 1.5 billion people do not have access to electricity; 404 million in India alone. Three billion people, almost half of the world's population, rely on bio-fuels such as wood, dung, and agricultural waste for cooking and heating purposes (UNDP 2010). From an economic perspective, lack of access to modern energy services is a serious hindrance to households and countries trapped in poverty. Low per capita energy users tend to have low life expectancies, a high infant mortality rate, and a low literacy rate. Energy services are essential to both social and economic development and much wider and greater access to modern energy services is critical to achieve all of the Millennium Development Goals and thereby sustainable human development.

It is not surprising to see a strong relationship between per capita energy use and social indicators. Using 1997 data from 60 countries, Pasternak (2000) analyzed the relationship between electricity consumption and the Human Development Index (HDI). According to the study, to achieve an HDI value of 0.9 or greater, a threshold of per capita electricity consumption of 4,000 kWh per annum is required. Of the 60 countries, nearly half had 1,000 kWh consumption whose HDI values are less than 0.6. It is not just a matter of "quantity" of energy but the "quality" aspect is also an important factor that contributes to human development. The poor not only use small amounts of energy, they also tend to rely on lower quality bio-fuels (fuel wood, dung, and agricultural waste). The low efficiency of utilization of these fuels limits the amount of service that can be obtained (Najam and Cleveland 2003).

Household energy poverty is very different from national energy poverty as the latter focuses on self-sufficiency and trade, whereas for the former, disparity and the pattern of usage are important. At the micro level, energy poverty affects the efficiency of household activities and lessens the productive working hours. At the macro level, lack of energy affects a country's ability to engage in manufacturing and services to support critical agricultural activities. Poor nations and poor households are in an energy-poverty trap as they cannot afford to have modern energy carriers nor can they come out of the poverty trap in the present state of energy starvation. Energy poverty in developing countries needs to be tackled both at the household and national levels. Against this background, strategies to mitigate climate change should not limit the ability of developing countries to meet their basic energy needs for development and they should support access to cleaner energy services

Fig. 11.1 Relationship between energy use and HDI

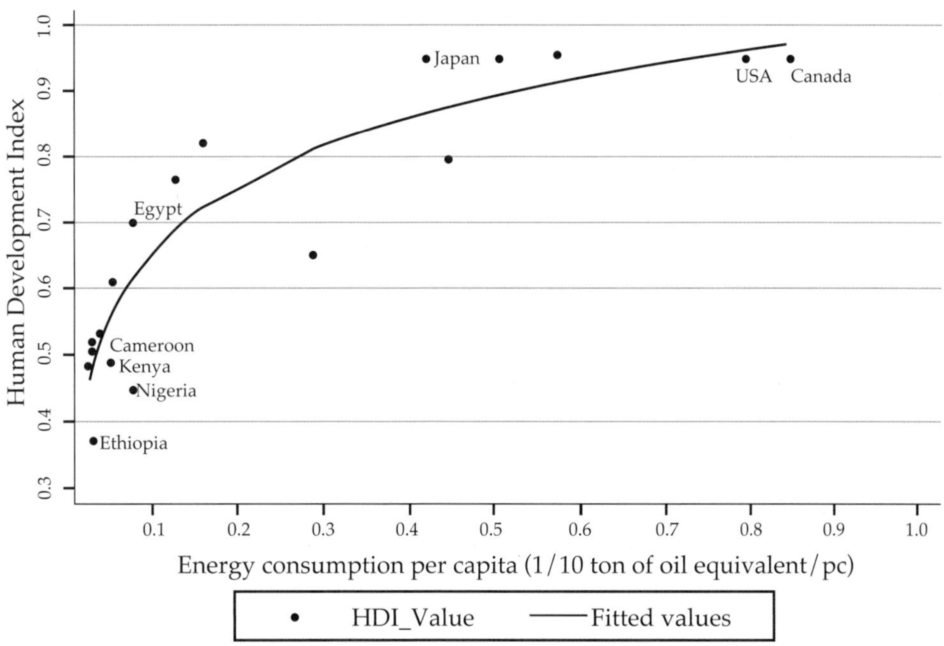

Source: Reddy (2002).

The Climate Scenario

There is a great climate divide in the world. This divide coincides with the economic divide of the world, i.e., the division between the developing and developed economies. The developing countries constitute 80% of the world's population, but they have contributed only 20% of the cumulative emissions since

1751 (Global Carbon Projects 2008). Being a relatively new entrant in the sphere of industrialization and urbanization, the developing countries are pumping pollutants into the atmosphere only for the last couple of decades, whereas the developed Western world has done this for centuries. Even today, the per capita CO_2 emission of developing countries like China, Brazil, and India is lower than the world average (Reddy and Assenza 2009). When compared to developed countries, the per capita CO_2 emission of developing countries is around one-fourth.

It is worth mentioning here that the philosophy of "pay-and-pollute," which emanated from the concept of a fixed emission quota for countries, is inherently debatable. This is because in developed economies excess energy is used for luxurious needs, whereas in developing countries there is a shortage of energy to address basic needs. So, acknowledging the fact that energy resources are limited, a stricter constraint on developed economies is the need of the hour. However, in recent years the developing countries are increasing their emission levels, while the developed countries are growing slowly. Even with a temperature rise of 1–2.5°C, the International Panel on Climate Change (IPCC) predicts serious effects including reduced crop yields in tropical areas leading to an increased risk of hunger, the spread of climate-sensitive diseases such as malaria, water stress, and the increased risk of floods (UNFCCC 2007).

India and China: Classic Cases

Energy utilization patterns

India and China are classic examples of developing countries which suffer from energy deprivation and climate vulnerability. Both countries depend on dirty fuels like coal and bio-fuels (see Table 11.1). The data shows that the share of bio-fuels is declining steadily with development — from 48.8% in 1980 to 32.1% in 2005 in India, and from 33.5% to 12.5% during the same period (Shonali P. and Leiwen J. 2008). The period of rapid reduction could be observed through 25 years, the period of industrialization when coal substituted traditional biomass fuels and became the most important fuel for power generation. The share of coal increased rapidly since 1980 and reached nearly 60% of total primary energy in 2005 in China and 39% in India. The rapid increase of oil consumption during the same period can be observed from Table 11.1.

Table 11.1 Primary energy use in India and China (MTOE)

Energy source	China				India			
	1980	Share (%)	2005	Share (%)	1980	Share(%)	2005	Share (%)
Coal	242	48.4	1000	59.80	77	32.6	207	38.6
Oil	60.5	12.1	350	18.20	31	13.3	114	21.2
Gas	10	2	100	4.30	2	0.9	27	5.1
Electricity	20	4	80	5.20	10	4.4	16	3
Bio-fuels	167.5	33.5	220	12.50	115	48.8	172	32.1
Total	500	100	1750	100	236	100	537	100

In the case of household consumption, although the share of bio-fuels in the energy system declined, the absolute quantity of biomass consumed in India continued to be high (69% in 2005). On the other hand, in China, both the share and absolute quantity of bio-fuels have decreased steadily as the process of industrialization caused a switching away from low-quality wood. In the case of modern energy carriers like gas and electricity, their share overtook bio-fuel share in China while the low income of Indian households did not allow any significant growth. The use of different sources is reflective of the non-uniform availability of resources and uneven access to infrastructure to avail the same. Even if the required energy carrier is available and accessible, households do not use them as they simply cannot afford it. Households are forced to use traditional forms of energy, i.e. bio-fuels as higher-quality energy carriers are unavailable or inaccessible or are unaffordable (see Table 11.2).

Table 11.2 Household energy use in India and China

Energy source	China				India			
	1980	Share (%)	2005	Share (%)	1980	Share (%)	2005	Share (%)
Bio-fuels	152	73.1	174	47.6	113	90.1	145	69
Coal	43	20.5	45	12.4	4	3.5	2	1.1
Kerosene	6	2.7	12	3.2	6	4.6	16	7.7
Gas	5	2.3	45	12.2	1	1.1	25	12
Electricity	3	1.4	90	24.6	1	0.7	28	13.2
Total	208	100	366	100	125	100	216.3	100

Energy accessibility indicators

Households use energy for many purposes. Their consumption and the types of energy sources depend on a variety of factors. These include the availability of energy sources and disposable income. However, they also include many factors that can be understood only by analyzing the real needs and behavior of energy consumers. A household's total energy consumption and mix of energy sources is the result of its attempt to meet its various energy needs. In rural areas, bio-fuels (fuel wood, charcoal/coal, dung, etc.) are the major sources for cooking while in urban areas LPG, along with kerosene, is the dominant fuel. In many households, the same energy carrier is used for both cooking and water heating. Similarly, multiple carriers are used for a particular end-use. Thus, a large number of households simultaneously use a variety of cooking fuels spanning both middle and lower levels of income. As shown in Table 11.3, accessibility plays a significant role in the use of a particular energy carrier. Carriers like LPG and electricity are accessible mostly in urban areas and hence their share is high both in India and China. As for lighting, approximately 412 million people in India live without access to electricity and 668 million depend on traditional biomass fuels for cooking. These numbers make up about a quarter of the people in energy poverty worldwide; 1.5 billion people in developing countries have no access to electricity and 3 billion people rely on solid fuels for cooking (UNDP 2009). As far as the urban–rural divide is concerned, 80% in India and 54% in China do not use clean cooking fuel. In India, 45% of rural households and 7.7% urban households do not have access to electricity (NSSO 2007).

Table 11.3 Energy accessibility indicators for cooking and lighting

Energy source	Cooking				Lighting			
	China		India		China		India	
	Rural	Urban	Rural	Urban	Rural	Urban	Rural	Urban
Bio-fuels	54.0	10.2	79.3	23.4				
Coal	20.3	12.9	1.8	1.4				
Kerosene	3.9	2.0	2.3	10.2	3.9	3.7	54.9	92.3
Gas	19.0	58.9	12.6	57.1				
Electricity	6.8	16.0	2.0	7.9	96.1	96.3	45.1	7.7
Total (million households)	232	127.0	145	63	232	127	145	63

Energy affordability indicators

Table 11.4 shows the data on households using various energy carriers for cooking in different income categories from India and China. There is a strong positive relationship between income and household demand for commercial fuels. High-income households have greater choice in selecting an energy carrier and many opt for cleaner, comfortable, and more efficient modern energy carriers such as electricity or liquefied petroleum gas (LPG). LPG is safe, reliable, portable, and flexible. Electricity suits a variety of end-uses such as air-conditioning, refrigeration, radio, TV, and other electronic appliances. Thus, electricity and LPG demand tends to increase with income, reflecting an increasing desire for comfort and discretionary energy consumption.

Table 11.4 Energy affordability indicators

	Energy source	Income groups		
		Low	Middle	High
China	Solids	79.8	52.6	27.5
	Liquids	1.1	1.8	0.7
	Gas	16.9	41.7	65.0
	Electricity	2.2	3.9	6.8
Total households (million)		180	144	36
India	Solids	81.0	61.7	31.1
	Liquids	7.8	5.0	4.9
	Gas	9.1	30.3	60.8
	Electricity	2.1	3.0	3.2
Total households (million)		108	68	30

Energy–Poverty–Climate Nexus

The traditional form of energy, bio-fuels, which dominates the energy spectrum, is different from its counterparts such as kerosene, LPG, or electricity in one respect. Unlike others, the preparation (collection, transportation, cutting, etc.) of bio-fuel is done by the households themselves. Women, being the primary cooks in the households, by default have the responsibility for fuel collection, preparation as a cooking-related activity, and the fetching of water. Labor households, who are the poorest among the lot, spend the maximum time in collection (10–20% of time). These responsibilities often constrain their capacity to undertake other employment activities.

The use of traditional biomass fuels has other impacts. Due to inefficient use, these fuels, when burnt, give off significant quantities of smoke and particulates which have an adverse effect on the health of women and female children. The indoor air pollution acts as a slow poison in the kitchen and affects the health of women. According to an Indira Gandhi Institute of Development Research (IGIDR) study (Laxmi, et al. 2003), the health impacts of the use of bio-fuels are quite high for adult women. The losses incurred because of cooking fuels, including work days spent expenditure on illness and lost working days due to illness are INR 29 billion per year in the rural areas of Rajasthan. Smith (2000) has shown that high risks such as respiratory infections (ARI), chronic obstructive pulmonary disease (COPD), lung cancer, and also tuberculosis (TB), asthma, and blindness are prevalent in India on account of indoor air pollution. Conservative estimates indicate that some 400,000 to 550,000 premature deaths can be attributed annually to the use of biomass fuels in these population groups. Using a disability-adjusted lost life-year approach, the total is 4–6% of the Indian national burden of disease, placing indoor air pollution as a major risk factor in the country. As per the World Health Organization (WHO), indoor air pollution, which is referred to as the "killer in the kitchen," is responsible for 1.6 million deaths per year, i.e., one life is lost every 20 seconds (UNDP 2007).

In addressing energy poverty, it is crucial to understand the gender dimension. The UNDP (2001) reports reveal that when women are overburdened, they are more likely to keep their daughters at home and away from school to assist with household activities, including fuel and water collection, thereby limiting opportunities for girls to move forward through education, thus increasing the likelihood of their families remaining in poverty. Education and literacy levels are positively correlated with a decrease in fertility rates. Women, with more education, tend to have fewer children, and to be better able to care for them.

A significant portion of the rural population relies on employment in either the informal or the manufacturing sectors which are energy intensive and require electricity for their sustenance. The lack of a continuous power supply leads to an increase in production costs and subsequently to a shutting down of operations. These outcomes have a negative impact on the overall performance of the economy which in turn reduces the employment potential. The availability of electricity services allows the use of machines for the tasks which were previously performed by hand or animal power, even more efficiently. Electric lighting allows individuals to extend the length of time spent on production and hence on income-producing activities. It also allows children time to read or do homework.

At the other side of the spectrum, conventional fuels like coal have a significant impact on the environment. India and China rely heavily on unclean coal particularly in the power sector[1] because of its relatively stable price and large availability.[2] They also depend heavily on imported oil. Moreover, since renewable sources are largely untapped, it has a very low (1%) share of zero-carbon fuels. Additionally, in India, biomass consumption, which satisfies 72% of the domestic energy and 90% of all rural energy needs, contributes to climate change through black carbon emissions. India's contribution to climate impact is going to be significant. According to International Energy Agency's (IEA) statistics and base line scenario (IEA 2007), China and India together account for nearly 20% of world energy consumption in 2005. Between 2005 and 2030, China and India will account for 45% of the increase in world consumption of primary energy. China will quadruple its oil imports while those of India will triple. World CO_2 emissions could rise by 57%, resulting in an increase of 6°C in average temperature. China and India could account for 60% of this increase in emissions. Furthermore, China's emissions will exceed those of the U.S. in 2008, while India will become the world's third largest emitter in 2015. In 2005, China's per capita emissions were 3.9 tons, compared to India's 1.4 tons. Thus, India and China are typical cases of developing countries whose developmental goals need to be integrated with energy-climate security.

Table 11.5 Environmental scenario in China and India (2005)

Country	CO_2 emissions			GDP (PPP)/ cap (USD)	HH without electricity (million)
	Per capita (tons)	Accumulated emissions (1984–2004) as a % of total emissions	Per capita accumulated (tons)		
China	3.8	8.1	68.9	6757	8.5
India	1.2	2.3	23.3	3452	412
Developing countries	2.4	24.9	53.9	5282	1569
Developed countries	13.3	75.1	843	33,082	

Sources: 1. UNDP, *Human Development Report 2007*, Tables 1, 22 and 24;
2. World Resources Institute, Climate Analysis Information Tool (CAIT).

Energy Access: A Business Approach

Access to modern energy services is a crucial precondition for development and the elimination of poverty.[3] These services are the last link in the "energy chain." This concept emphasizes end-use service and the satisfaction of human needs, rather than the energy supply source. Energy is the lifeblood of the modern economy and development has been historically linked to the widespread use of modern energy services. It is not possible to reduce poverty without a significant increase in the use of modern energy services that provide higher quality energy services. The linkage extends also to the capacity to adapt to climate change, since those countries and regions with lower poverty, greater levels of human development, and greater energy access will have more options and greater adaptive capacity.

People without access to modern energy services live mainly in the most remote and sparsely populated regions with limited access to roads, markets, and other services. In these areas renewable energy technologies, such as small hydro, wind energy, and PV, are the most technically viable and, in many cases, the most cost-effective options. Access to electrical power improves living standards in rural communities. For cooking and heating, biogas leads to improved social conditions (Table 11.6). However, provision of these services must be on a sustainable basis, economically, socially, and environmentally, if it is to ultimately improve living standards and lift people out of poverty.

Table 11.6 Technology options for universalization

Electricity source	Quality of power	Capital cost	Running cost	Technology reach	Impacts
Through Grid	High	High	Low	High cost to reach sparse rural areas	Environmentally not sound
Diesel	High	Medium	High	Supply of diesel is uncertain	Causes atmospheric pollution; Noise
Micro hydel	High	Medium	Low	Good option; Long life time	Spending on water availability; Issue of displacement of people
Solar	Low	High	Low	Provides power to lights and TV	Pollution-free

(Cont'd)

Electricity source	Quality of power	Capital cost	Running cost	Technology reach	Impacts
Wind	Low	Medium	Low	Both large- and small-scale; Can compete with traditional power generation	Pollution-free; Depends on wind availability
Biomass	Low	Medium	Low	Small scale generation	Environmental impact

Small amounts of energy can make a huge difference to the lives of poor people. The cost of providing energy depends on many factors such as where people live and the type of energy provided. We estimate that the average cost for a low-wattage electrical connection suitable for a poor family would be in the region of USD10. This cost will be much less for switching to alternative fuels and low-pollution cooking methods. With an average family size of five people we can assume that approximately 100 million homes will need new electrical connections to satisfy the needs of the 0.5 billion who do not have electricity. The total cost of these electrical connections (including meters and street lighting) will be USD12 billion. Spread over 10 years, this would cost just USD1.2 billion a year. This is significantly higher than the estimated annual subsidy of USD2.5 billion on fossil fuels and nuclear power in India (Reddy, et al. 2010).

It must be stressed that these are upfront costs. Running costs will be minimal if using renewable sources such as sun, wind, and water. These costs need to be spread over the lifespan of the energy installation, and financial support, such as "smarter" subsidies and soft loans, need to allow this. Cost will come down due to economies of scale as more systems are installed. How much funds would be required from international aid, government grants, private investment, local community, and individuals would depend upon the model of finance chosen. To reach them will require sustained subsidies and support.

Improving energy access will have positive impacts on households. This will result in a significant reduction in the time for collection of firewood as well as for cooking. Time savings can result in increased agricultural productivity and thereby contribute to a more secure food supply and income generation. According to a study, in Malawi's Mulanje District 34.3 % of the beneficiaries are spending their additional time on farming activities, and 8.4% on small-scale businesses. It was also observed that, depending on fuel resources, savings in fuel consumption also reduce households' financial outlays. Households with modern energy carriers spend less on fuel than those without. Numbers vary from EUR4 per month in Uganda to EUR6 per week in Peru, depending on living standards and the proportion of people who buy their firewood (instead of collecting it for themselves). This indicates that most of this money is then used for household items or food. This indicates that, at the household level, the main contribution of energy access is to improve living standards, and decrease poverty in economic terms.

According to United Nations Environment Programme (2008), there is significant job creation potential in clean energies, with over 2 million jobs accounted for per year, and the potential for 20 million more jobs by 2030. The study indicates that an expansion of renewables and investments in energy efficiency could generate employment that is 20% higher than business as usual by 2050. Bioenergy is among the renewable energy sources that provides the highest job potential, largely in rural areas in the agricultural sector. If planned and implemented sustainably, modern energy services can be a cornerstone not only for the economy but also for the environment.

These experiences tell us that adopting business approaches and encouraging the entrepreneurs to provide rural energy services are essential to ensuring the sustainability of the systems in the long term. But any form of energy has always needed some form of government subsidy. In China, non-governmental organizations are playing a unique role in rural energy supply due to their flexibility, accessibility, and creativity. There are numerous examples of projects which are developing sustainable and business-oriented approaches to rural energy supply[4] (Greenpeace 2003).

Fig. 11.2 shows the China model to finance energy services in rural areas. Apart from the government controlling the financial model, market elements are included in the policy options. In 2001, the Chinese government launched a village power program to install 700 village power systems with central and local government financial inputs. In this model, the government is the financial agency and the installation company and the local service company play a crucial role for supplying energy service in the rural areas. However, the sustainability of this model depends very much on continuing government support (Anon 2010).

Fig. 11.2 Government-led model: China's financial flow

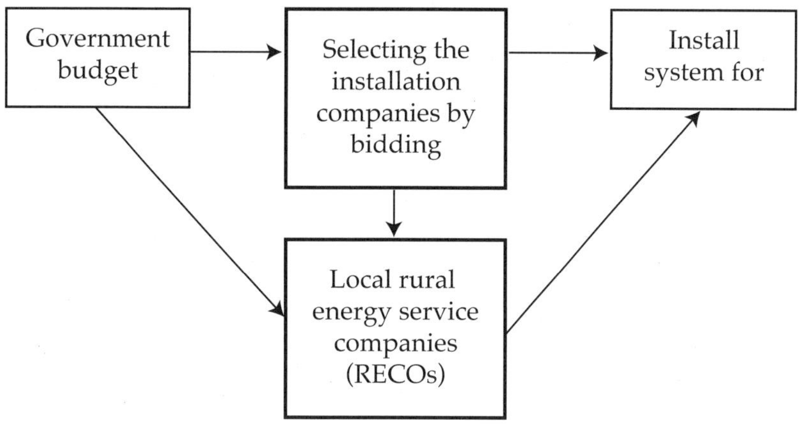

The most important determinant of the response to climate change, from the perspective of developing countries, is the substitution of traditional fuels with modern carriers. If supported by the government, these technologies could spread rapidly and usher in energy leapfrog. This can be the most cost effective way to deliver opportunities for income generation and poverty reduction. As consumers wield their financial power, so will investors, with growing attention paid to business approaches for climate change.

Lessons Learned and the Way Forward

The energy–poverty–climate nexus is one of the most important social issues of our time that has been neglected for too long and the time has arrived to bring half of the world's population out of energy poverty. Innovative policies and financial mechanisms are needed to bring modern energy services to people who live away from the grid.

Increasing energy access, alleviating rural poverty, and mitigating climate change, can all be complementary, their overlap defining an energy–poverty–climate nexus. The problem is that practice has not matched the rhetoric. Both India and China are considering these issues as separate ones and so too the policies and mechanisms. These programs are marketed as tools to address either poverty or climate change. It so happens that each one automatically benefits the other's agenda. Through the provision of modern energy services, there are financial benefits and we save energy supplies, reduce our carbon footprint, and boost local business. Hence, there is an urgent need to link poverty and climate change which should be made more explicit and policy-makers working in both arenas need to fuse their work and targets much more. Given the cross-sectoral nature of the problem, what is needed is the adoption of a strategic and coherent approach to this task linking different sectors and scales. Policy-makers should identify the strategies that can be used to provide environmentally sustainable and socially just energy services to deprived populations. There are other stakeholders in these areas and each has a role to play in targeting the poor and improving guidance on the programs and the costs to achieve this.

To overcome the twin challenges facing developing countries like India and China (poverty and climate change) they should make a transition from traditional energy sources to modern, renewable, and diversified ones. They should also design mechanisms for meeting the increasing energy demand resulting from increasing industrialization and growing populations. It is equally important to remove all institutional and financial barriers that hinder the development of renewable energies and energy efficiency, while at the same time addressing the future adaptation strategies and the path to low-carbon development. To achieve this, India and China should follow the principle of common but differentiated accountability recommended by IPCC. The poor can access modern energy services that would allow them to achieve their development priorities and at the same time adapt to present and future climate changes.

Notes

1. Coal is considered relatively unclean compared to other fossil fuels. In 2005, among fossil fuels, coal accounted for less than 57% of energy needs, but its CO_2 share was more than 67% (IEA 2007).
2. Coal-based thermal power forms 70% of India's power generation.
3. Modern energy services are the desired and useful processes / services that result from the use of modern energy, such as gas or electricity to produce heat for cooking; power for transportation, water pumping, grinding, etc.
4. The WWF initiated a program of small credit loans for rural households to promote small-scale biogas systems in rural areas of Hubei Province. The W. Jones Foundation and the Shell Foundation have supported a small-scale biogas program in the remote areas of Yunnan province, and the Greenstar Solar Community Centre has initiated a joint venture entity with villagers in Tibet to deliver solar powered handicrafts for sale internationally, to ensure the economic viability of the solar power systems.

References

Anon. 2010. *Increasing Access to Energy Services in Rural Areas*. http://africa-toolkit.reeep.org/modules/Module10.pdf.

Global Carbon Project. 2008. *Carbon Budget and Trends 2007*. http://www.globalcarbonproject.org.

International Energy Agency. 2007. *World Energy Outlook*. Paris, France: OECD / International Energy Agency.

Laxmi, V., Parikh J., Karmakar S., and Dabrase, P. 2003. "Household Energy, Women's Hardship and Health Impacts in Rural Rajasthan, India: Need for Sustainable Energy Solutions." *Energy for Sustainable Development* 7(1):50–68.

Najam, A., and Cleveland, C. J. 2003. "Energy and Sustainable Development at Global Environmental Summit: An Evolving Agenda." *Environment, Development and Sustainability* 5(1–2):117–138.

National Sample Survey Organization (NSSO). 2007. *Energy Used by Indian Households 2004 / 2005*. NSS 61st round. NSSO, Ministry of Statistics and Program Implementation, Government of India.

Reddy, A. K. N. 2002. "Energy Technologies and Policies for Rural Development." In Johansson, T.B., Reddy, B. S., and Assenza B. G., "Climate Change: A Developing Country Perspective," *Current Science* 97, no. 1 (2009):50–62.

Reddy B. S., Balachandra P., and Nathan H. S. K. 2009. "Universalization of Access to Modern Energy Services in Indian Households: Economic and Policy Analysis." *Energy Policy* 37(11):4645–4657.

Shonali P., and Leiwen J. 2008. "The Household Energy Transition in India and China." Interim Report, IIASA.

United Nations Framework Convention on Climate Change (UNFCCC). 2007. *Climate Change: Impacts, Vulnerabilities and Adaptation in Developing Countries*. Bonn, Germany: Climate Change Secretariat, UNFCCC.

United Nations Development Programme (UNDP). 2010. *Energy for a Sustainable Future: The Secretary-General's Advisory Group on Energy and Climate Change Summary Report and Recommendations*. United Nations Development Programme, New York.

12

Chapter

Engaging China: An Indian Perspective

Rup Narayan Das

Every time I visit Hong Kong, I am awestruck by its incredible spirit of resilience and dynamism, which to me is the hallmark of its spectacular growth and success. Look at the human ingenuity and spirit of entrepreneurship that has converted this tiny territory, once described as a "barren island," into one of the world's leading financial hubs and one of the most successful cosmopolitan cities in the world. Its resilience is not only limited and restricted to the domain of economy, but also to the political realm. How else can one describe the innovative "One Country, Two Systems" policy and its successful working for more than 15 years now? The Chinese mind is not only fertile in technological innovation, but also in political innovation. Mankind has fought wars on the basis of ideology. Although there is no comparison, we had in the past two Germanys, two Vietnams, and now two Koreas. The point that I am trying to make is that through the creative application of the human mind, one can solve the problems leftover by history. Hong Kong is a case in point.

Before I turn to the topic of my presentation, let me flag India's historical link with Hong Kong and the contributions of Hong Kong Indians in the early years of the founding of Hong Kong. I had written a paper on this aspect, which was published in *The Other Hong Kong Report* (1990), edited by Joseph Yushek Cheng and Richard Wong and published by the Chinese University of Hong Kong.[1] Since India was under British rule, India's link with Hong Kong can be traced back to as early as early as 1841 when the Union Jack was hoisted in Hong Kong. When the British established the administrative set-up in Hong Kong, they recruited Indians in both police and administration. The Hong Kong regiment also consisted of some Indians.

A nodding Indian connection can also be discerned to Hong Kong's oldest trading house, Jardine, Matheson, and Co. William Jardine was a surgeon in the East India Company and James Matheson was working in an accounting house. Together they founded the Jardine and Matheson Company. The names of two Indians are associated with the Star Ferry. While Ebrahim Noordin started the first cross border ferry between Hong Kong and Kowloon in 1842, Dorabji Naoroji started the Star Ferry in the mid-1880s.

Yet another rich Indian, Harmuji Mody, a stockbroker and opium merchant, donated HKD180,000 to help set up the University of Hong Kong. A road in Kowloon has been named after him and his portrait adorns the senate hall of Hong Kong.

In contemporary times, one man whose name automatically comes to mind, and who made a seminal contribution to Hong Kong as a patron of Hong Kong

Baptist University, is the formidable and renowned Hirleila family and patriarch Hari N. Harleila, the doyen of the Indian community often regarded as the "Sindhi Onassis."

Now let me very briefly throw light on Sino-Indian relations which are multilayered. There are many facets to this topic which in fact reinforce one another. The relationship has linkages of cultures and civilizations, political resonance, strategic and security dimensions, and robust economic content. This paper attempts to posit this complex and yet dynamic relationship in a new perspective. Every text has a context. In order to understand and appreciate the present state of the relationship between the two countries, it is essential that its moorings be put in the proper perspective. This paper argues why the Sino-Indian relationship is special and what is so unique about it, why this relationship has the potential to be sustained in the long run, and what could be done to make it more robust. At a time when China has risen in the world stage and everyone talks about engaging China or — borrowing the jargon from the management discipline — to "managing" China, India has had the unique experience of bonding with China. It was not out of any political expediency, but what can be called as the linkage of civilizations.

My earliest impression about China, like most India children, came from the textbook account of Fa Xian, a Buddhist scholar from western China, who traveled to India in 399. Fa Xian spent about a decade in India traveling widely and visiting major cities and Buddhist sites, collecting documents which he would later translate into Chinese. He wrote a highly illuminating account of India and Sri Lanka, *A Record of Buddhist Kingdoms*. Fa Xian's years in India, particularly near the ancient Pataliputra, were devoted to studying language and literature in addition to religious texts, and also the healthcare system in India. The erudite scholar returned to China by sea sailing from the Ganges, India's much revered river, via Sri Lanka and Java.[2]

Yet another passionate scholar who left an indelible imprint in the annals of the Sino-Indian relationship was the formidable Xuanzang, who traveled to India in the seventh century. Xuanzang, a connoisseur of Buddhist learning, collected a treasure trove of Sanskrit texts and, like Fa Xian, translated them into Chinese. He traveled throughout the country for 16 years and studied medicine, philosophy, logic, mathematics, grammar, and astronomy in addition to Buddhism at the famous seat of learning, Nalanda. The erudite scholar also met the Buddhist emperor of India, Harsha Bardhan, and had a conversation with him on Sino-Indian relations. Xuanzang's visit has been well remembered for many centuries, both in India and China. In China there were a great many legends about Xuanzang, which became quite popular by the 10th century and were frequently performed as plays later on. The best known and most popular of these semi-fictional accounts is a sixteenth-century allegorical novel, *Xi You Ji* (*The Journey to the West*).[3]

As is well known, there was a regular stream of Buddhist missionaries from India to China, beginning in AD 65 with Kashyapa Matanga, who was followed by such scholars as Kumarajiva, Dharma Kashama, and Paramartha.

Nalanda has thus become the icon of this great heritage and civilizational bonding. To commemorate and celebrate, and to carry forward this legacy, a sprawling world class university, with the moral and material support of the governments of India, China, and Singapore is being built at the historic site under the mentorship of no less a person than Nobel laureate Amartya Sen. It is gratifying that China has welcomed India's efforts to revive the Nalanda University and has committed to contribute USD1 million for the Nalanda University. Thus the claims of historical linkages are not rhetoric or pious platitudes, but are backed up with political intent. It is unfortunate, however, that "the ancient path," to quote Nobel Laureate Rabindranath Tagore, "be obliterated by the inertia of forgetful centuries."

It may be recalled that at a time when both India and China were passing through a churning process of history, there was a connection between the two countries. In the historic 1911 Revolution, the nationalist Kuomintang (KMT) under the leadership of Dr. Sun Yat-sen came to power and ended feudalism and imperialism in China. In India, the situation was not very different. It was a coincidence that the year republicanism came into being in China, India's capital was transferred from Calcutta to Delhi to signal the consolidation of colonialism and, correspondingly, the clamor for freedom grew louder in the country. There was a new awakening in both India and China. The idea of nationalism, freedom, and liberty had stirred the hearts and minds of the people of the two countries separately and independently. The two countries were passing through a cataclysm. In China, an old and archaic order gave way to republicanism, and in India resurgent nationalism was brewing in the length and breadth of the country. It is not widely known that the yearning for freedom in India had its echo in China.

Sun Yat-sen, one of the guiding spirits of the 1911 revolution, helped Indian nationalist leaders like M.N. Roy, Rash Behari Bose, and Lala Lajpat Rai to establish contacts in Japan, where he had considerable goodwill and influence, to mobilize support against British Colonial rule in the subcontinent. The credit for being the first Chinese leader to call for a China-India partnership against imperialism, however, goes to another leader of the 1911 revolution, Zhang Taiyan. Writing in 1906, Zhang argued that "Unless China and India embrace each other and support each other, Asia will not become secure." He further wrote "When they become independent, China and India must form a holy alliance."[4]

The great Indian revolutionary M.N. Roy of COMINTERN INTERNATIONAL (C.I.) fame, who later propounded his theory of "Radical Humanism" in the revolutionary struggle of China, also played a very crucial role in the revolutionary struggle of the Chinese people during the second "united front" struggle of the Communist movement in China. In his book on the revolution and counter-revolution in China, Roy wrote:

> The meeting of the Executive Committee of the Communist International in November 1926 adopted a new thesis on the Chinese question, the central point of which was that the Chinese Revolution must from that be developed as an agrarian revolution The leadership of the Chinese Communist Party, as well as the representatives of the CI in China, were of a different view. They still maintained that the nationalist bourgeoisie should be helped to lead the revolution and class struggle should not be accentuated for the sake of national unity. I was alone to advocate a different point of view that the China Revolution had reached a critical moment in which it must strike out a new course and a fetish should not be made of the alliance with the Kuomintang. The Executive of the C.I. adopted my point of view, which was opposed in the beginning by Stalin himself. But Stalin was brought around to my view and the Thesis adopted by the C.I was drafted by me. Immediately afterwards, I left for China as the head of a new delegation of the C.I.[5]

Whatever the fact, Roy was sent to China towards the end of 1926 as the Special Representative of the C.I. to oversee the implementation of the new theses.[6]

The civilization linkage and cultural linkage between the two nations and their people have been carried forward in modern times. An eloquent statement of India's support and solidarity for China was evident even prior to India's independence. The first joint action plan against imperialism was by India and China, when their representatives signed and made a joint-declaration at the International Congress against Imperialism, and for national independence, held in Brussels in February 1927. Jawaharlal Nehru, who became independent India's first Prime Minister, represented the Indian National Congress at the Brussels National Congress.

Besides Buddhism, which is a perennial source of bonding between India and China, two towering figures have epitomized and carried forward India-China friendship and amity to greater heights. One is Dr. Dwarknath Kotnis, the legendary doctor who served in China during a very critical juncture of its national life in the late 1930s and died there leaving behind an indelible imprint. Nobel Laureate Rabindranath Tagore, whose 150th birthday was celebrated in 2011 by both China and India, was yet another iconic figure who continues to nourish and nurture the relationship between the two countries and their people. Tagore is rated by a leading Chinese daily *People's Daily* as one of the 50 important personalities who have influenced modern Chinese thinking.

The award of Nobel Prize in literature to Rabindranath Tagore in 1913 found resonance in China as well. As soon as Tagore was catapulted to international fame immediately after winning the Nobel Prize, he received accolades and recognition in China as well.

The most enduring contribution of Tagore for Sino-Indian friendship was the establishment of Cheena Bhavan in 1937 at Shantiniketan in West Bengal. The aims and objectives of the Cheena Bhavan were to promote cultural exchanges between India and China; to conduct research studies in Indian and Chinese learning; to join and unite the people's of India and China; to jointly promote universal peace and harmony of humanity; and to help in building up the "great unity" of the world. Mahatma Gandhi, revered as the "Father of the Nation" in India, whom Tagore had invited to inaugurate the Cheena Bhavan, could not come for the occasion as he was stuck up elsewhere on the very day. In his message, he hoped that "May the China Hall be a symbol of living contact between China and India."[7]

Prime Minister Jawaharlal Nehru, who also could not turn up for the occasion as he was ill, deputized his daughter, Ms. Indira Gandhi. In his message Nehru said, "China and India, sister nations from the dawn of history, with their long tradition of culture and peaceful development of ideas, have to play a leading part in this world drama, in which they themselves are so deeply involved." In his inaugural address, Tagore said, "The most memorable fact of human history is that of a path opening, not for the clearing of a passage for machines or machine guns, but for helping the realization by races of their affinity of minds, their mutual obligation of a common humanity. Such a rare event did happen and the path was built between our people and the Chinese in an age when physical obstruction needed a heroic personality to overcome it and the mental barrier a moral power of uncommon magnitude. The two leading races of that age met, not as rivals on the battlefield each claiming the right to be the sole tyrant on earth, but as noble friends, glorying in their exchange of gifts. Subsequently, relationships relapsed into isolation, covering up the path with the accumulated dust of indifference. Today, our old friends have beckoned to us again, generously helping us to retrace that ancient path obliterated by the inertia of forgetful centuries and we rejoice."[8]

The legendary doctor Dwarkanath Kotnis was yet another iconic figure who continues to be the harbinger of Sino-Indian amity and friendship. It may be recalled that Jawaharlal Nehru, who weaved the foreign policy of India, even prior to independence, was pained when the war broke out between China and Japan in 1938. He raised his voice for the Chinese people and aroused mass support for them. In this context, Marshal Zhu De, the Commander of the Eight Route Army, wrote a letter to Nehru expressing gratitude for the moral support of the Indian people, and appealed for the medical supplies, surgical instruments, and training for doctors and nurses. Zhu De's appeal stirred Nehru to give a call for China Solidarity Day throughout India on January 9, 1938. He also took the initiative to send a medical team with necessary supplies and instruments to China as a token of the Indian peoples' sympathy and solidarity with the Chinese people in their struggle against colonialism and imperialism. The medical team, selected by a committee headed by Dr. Jivraj Mehta, was led by Dr. M. Atal and had in it Dr. M.R. Cholkar, Dr. Bijay Kumar Basu, Dr. Deben Mukherjee, and the young doctor Dwarkanath Kotnis.

When the People's Republic of China was formally proclaimed on October 1, 1949, India was the second non-Communist country to accord recognition to it. The birth of Communist China found its echo and resonance in the Provisional Parliament of India. Though the two countries followed different political paths — India, a democratic path and China, a Communist path — the birth of Communist China was welcomed by the members of the Provisional Parliament. President Rajendra Prasad in his Address to the House on January 31, 1951 referred to the Government of India's recognition of the People's Republic of China and hoped for an early exchange of diplomatic representation. Pointing out that India and China had friendly relations in the past for more than 2,000 years, he expressed his optimism that those friendly contacts would be carried forward in the interest of preserving peace in Asia and the world.

Initiating a debate on external affairs on March 17, 1950, Nehru asserted that "it was not a question of approving or disapproving; it was a question of recognizing a major event in history and appreciating it and dealing with it." Articulating the policy of Independent India in the broadened Asian Context, he said, "It affects us, because we are in Asia. It affects us because we are in a strategic part of Asia, set in the center of the Indian Ocean with intimate connections with western Asia, with southeast Asia, and with far eastern Asia. We could not ignore it, even if we would, and we do not want to ignore it."

It was just coincidence that when India recognized the birth of the People's Republic of China around the same time, a crisis loomed large in the Korean Peninsula. A Special Session of Parliament was convened in July 1950 to discuss the Korean crisis. Later, when participating in a debate and referring to the problem relating to the admission of the Peoples' Republic of China to the United Nations, Nehru maintained that after having recognized the new regime, it would have been seen as exceedingly unreasonable not to accept the logical consequences thereof. He said, "It is not for us to criticize what they do internally in their country, as it is not for them to criticize internal happenings in our country." What a nuanced approach! He bequeathed that which is being followed even today with renewed freshness. The debate that followed witnessed a near unanimity of views with regard to China's admission to the United Nations.

In fact, India was the one of the first Asian countries to sponsor a resolution for the admission of China into the United Nations, and when a resolution was moved by the Soviet Union in the Security Council to unseat the Kuomintang representative in favor of the People's Republic of China, India extended its full support. The Government's advocacy of China's admission into the United Nations was generally supported by all political parties.

However, the issue of China's bid to become a member of the United Nations got entangled with the unfolding Korean crisis in 1950 as the war broke out in June 1950 in Korea. India voted for the United Nations (UN) resolution condemning North Korea's aggression on South Korea and calling for withdrawal of the Korean forces to the 38th parallel, and also supported UN intervention to restore peace and security in the region. India was of the opinion that no settlement of the East Asia imbroglio would be durable and permanent without China's concurrence. Speaking in Parliament on August 3, 1950 Nehru categorically expressed the view that China's entry into the United Nations might well have prevented the Korean crisis, and also made it clear that while India had accepted the UN resolutions, it completely disassociated itself from any American action with regard to Formosa (Taiwan).

While India hailed the birth of the People's Republic of China as a major event in world history, tension started surfacing between the two countries with regard to development in Tibet. It was against this backdrop that the Chinese Premier Zhou Enlai visited India in 1954 at the invitation of the Government of India. The high point of the visit was the ratification of the Sino-Indian Agreement on Trade and Intercourse between Tibet and India which was signed earlier in April the same year. Under this agreement, India gave up all the extraterritorial rights enjoyed in Tibet by the British Government of India and recognized that Tibet was a region of China. The Agreement, which was to be in force for eight years, specified trade agencies, markets, and pilgrim routes and laid down regulations for trade and intercourse across the common border.

Moreover, in the preamble of the Agreement, the two countries affirmed that they would abide by the Five Principles of (i) Mutual respect for each other's territorial integrity and sovereignty, (ii) Mutual non-aggression, (iii) Mutual non-interference in each other's internal affairs, (iv) Equality and mutual benefit, and (v) Peaceful coexistence.

Chinese Premier Zhou Enlai was given a warm reception in New Delhi. In a joint statement issued at the conclusion of their talks, the two Prime Ministers re-affirmed the Five Principles and declared, "These principles are to be applied not only between various countries but also in international relations generally."

The war of 1962 marred the relationship between the two countries and left behind a scar that still haunts. The two countries restored diplomatic relations in 1976 when India appointed K. R. Narayanan, who later became the President of India, as India's Ambassador in 1976 and ever since then there has been no looking back. The relationship between the two countries is growing from strength to strength and there is broad political consensus in the political spectrum about India's engagement with China. While the Congress Party under the leadership of Mrs. Indira Gandhi restored the diplomatic relationship between the two countries, the Foreign Minister of the erstwhile Janata Government, Atal Behari Vajpayee, who later rose to become Prime Minister of the country, visited China in 1979 to signal the continuity of the country's foreign policy towards China. When the Congress Party returned to power, Prime Minister Rajiv Gandhi took the bold initiative to visit China in 1988 and signed a slew of agreements taking the relationship between the two countries to a greater height. The most significant of the agreements signed during Prime Minister Rajiv Gandhi's visit to China was the one on the establishment of the Joint Working Group (JWG) on border dispute between the two countries.

When the National Democratic Alliance (NDA), which included the BJP, came to power, Prime Minister Atal Behari Vajpayee not only continued the policy of the previous government but also gave further impetus to it when he visited China in 2003. Political consensus among political parties in India is of crucial importance in India's dealings with China, particularly in the context of the unsettled border issue with China. It is no wonder that China itself is also courting leaders from India cutting across political lines. In the recent past, a number of leaders from political parties have visited China and have had discussions which have a bearing on the bilateral relationship between the two countries. They include the President of Bharatiya Janata Party (BJP), the single largest opposition Party, Mr. Nitin Gadkari, the Chief Minister of Bihar and leader of Samata Party, Mr. Nitish Kumar, former Chief Minister of Karnataka, and the BJP leader Mr. S. Yedurappa, and the Communist Party of Marxist (CPM) leader Mr. Sitaram Yechuri. Recently, the Chief Minister of Gujarat and very towering leader of the BJP, Mr. Narendra Modi, visited China and held talks with the Chinese leaders.

The sideline meetings on the margins of multilateral meetings like the UN General Assembly, the Asia-Europe Meeting, the Association of Southeast Asian Nations (ASEAN), the BRIC (Brazil, Russia, India and China), and the G-20, etc., have also provided over the years excellent opportunities for Prime Minister Dr. Manmohan Singh and Chinese President Hu Jintao or Premier Wen Jiabao to interact and share each other's views having a bearing on the bilateral relations. These meetings have assumed added significance in the context that we are yet to have an institutional mechanism of summit-level meetings. Prime Minister Dr. Manmohan Singh and the two top Chinese leaders so far have met 12 times, which includes the visits of each to the other's capital city. Thus, there is perfect chemistry and a comfort level between the two. When there is a connection between the two heads of the government, it produces magic. In the era of the media blitz, the photo opportunities provided by such sideline meetings, when the media expects some deliverable result, have magical effects. Just to give some illustrations, when Prime Minister Dr. Manmohan Singh met President Hu Jintao on his way back from Japan on the sidelines of the Asia-Europe Meeting in Beijing in October 2008, the sideline meeting took place against the backdrop of the Nuclear Supplies Group (NSG) meeting in Vienna concerning India's nuclear issue, which had cast a shadow on Sino-Indian relations. Beijing assuaged India's feelings when President Hu Jintao instead of Prime Minister Wen Jiabao met Prime Minister Dr. Manmohan Singh on the sidelines of the meeting. The meeting thus removed the strains of the Vienna hangover.

Yet another such fruitful sideline meeting between Prime Minister Dr. Manmohan Singh and Hu Jintao was on the occasion of the BRIC and Shanghai Cooperation Organization (SCO) summit meeting in Yekaterinburg in Russia in June 2009, where it was declared to set up a hotline connection between the two to have faster coordination and consultation. It was reported recently in the media that the hotline would be set up soon. Prime Minister Dr. Manmohan Singh the same year met his Chinese counterpart Premier Wen Jiabao in October in Hua Hin, Thailand on the margins of the East Asia/ASEAN Summit. The Minister for External Affairs S.M. Krishna met the Chinese Foreign Minister Mr.Yang Jiechi at Phuket, Thailand in July 2009 on the margins of the East Asia Summit Ministerial Meeting, and thereafter in Bangalore in October on the sidelines of the Russia-India-China (RIC) trilateral meeting. During these meetings, there was a fruitful exchange of views and the leaders agreed to continue and strengthen efforts to build mutual political trust and understanding in the spirit of the Strategic and Cooperative Partnership between the two countries. Prime Minister Dr. Manmohan Singh and his Chinese counterpart Wen Jiabao again met on the sidelines of the ASEAN/East Asia meeting in Hanoi in October last year against the backdrop of the controversy relating to the "stapled visa" issue. The bonhomie that the two leaders exuded on the sideline meeting allayed the nagging concerns and anxiety when Wen declared that he would be visiting India in December to discuss all issues including the difficult ones.

The last such sideline meeting between Prime Minister Dr. Manmohan Singh and Chinese President Hu Jintao was at Sanya in China in April 2011 on the occasion of the BRICS meeting, where the two leaders discussed various issues including the bilateral ones. The most significant outcome of the meeting was the decision regarding the resumption of defense exchanges between the two countries, which was suspended in the wake of the controversy regarding the "stapled visa" issue. The two leaders also reiterated their idea of the setting up of a border mechanism to address incidence of alleged border intrusions in the context of the undefined and undemarcated line of actual control (LAC).

Having listed all of these is not to say that everything is alright in the bilateral relationship between the two countries. There is a persistent security dilemma, an unsettled border dispute giving rise to occasional hiccups, and the galloping trade imbalance, to name a few irritants in the bilateral relations between the two countries. But given the level of political understanding between the two countries, the chemistry between Prime Minister Dr. Manmohan Singh and the Chinese leaders, and the groundswell of goodwill between the two countries, these issues are not insurmountable. What is required is the spirit and vigour of the "Asian Renaissance" and the Asian identity. In this endeavour, the think-tanks, the scholarly community, media, and the civil society have a collective responsibility.

Notes

1. Richard Wong and Joseph Cheng, eds., "A nationality issue: Ethnic Indians in Hong Kong," *The Other Hong Kong Report* (Hong Kong: The Chinese University of Hong Kong, 2006).
2. Amartya Sen, *The Argumentative India Writing on Indian Culture, History and Identity* (New Delhi: Penguin Books, 2005), 161–190.
3. Ibid.
4. C. Raja Mohan, "India and 1911," *Indian Express,* http://www.indianexpress.com/news/india-and-1911/858585/.
5. V. B. Karnik, *M.N. Roy: Political Biography* (Bombay: Nav Jagriti Samaj, 1978), 255–256.
6. Ibid.
7. Dwijendra Nandi, *Sino-Indian Border Dispute: A New Realization* (Calcutta: Book Mark, 1988), 29–36.
8. Ibid.

13 Chapter

The China-India "Energy Bottleneck" Breakthrough Strategy and Mutual Cooperation

Yu Jianhua

In the contemporary world, China and India are all in the process of increasing their comprehensive national strength under the background of reform and opening up. As the two most populous developing countries, China and India are also facing the problems of energy demand inflation, the oil-gas shortage, and the conflict of energy growth and environmental protection. In order to solve the problem of energy security, the two countries based on their own national conditions, strives to better exploit the energy resources while advocate energy saving, and pay attention to environmental protection and sustainable energy development strategy at home; actively carry out energy cooperation and energy diplomacy abroad to make oil-gas resources pluralistic while easing the "Energy Bottleneck" in the process of peaceful development. And then, this helps the two countries' healthy and peaceful development and begins the growth of a prosperous strategic partnership.

China's Energy Situation and Developing Strategy

Essential feature of energy resources

As the largest developing country, China is one of the largest energy reserve countries and also one of the largest energy producers and consumers.

China's gross energy reserves are considerable. According to relevant statistics, China's gross reserves of proven conventional energy (such as raw coal, crude oil, natural gas, hydraulic power, and so on) are more than 845 billion tons of standard coal, of which gross reserves of remaining recoverable energy (economically feasible) are 159 billion tons of standard coal, accounting for approximately 2.6% and 11.5% of the world's total, respectively.[1] Gross reserves of hydraulic power and coal rank first in the world. China's hydraulic power theoretically amounts to 6.19 trillion KWH generated yearly, of which 1.76 trillion KWH generated yearly is economically feasible, accounting for 12% of the world's hydraulic power and ranking first worldwide.[2] Coal plays a dominant role in China's fossil energy resources. Gross reserves of remaining coal are 114.5 billion tons, which rank third next to the U.S. and Russia in the world.[3] Gross reserves of remaining oil and natural gas are 2.788 billion tons and 3.03 trillion cubic meters all ranking the 13th in the world.[4] In addition, China's resources of nuclear fuel resources, biomass energy, solar energy, wind energy, water-electric energy, and geothermal energy are rich.

Table 13.1 Reserves constituent of conventional energy in China

	Raw coal	Crude oil	Natural gas	Hydraulic power
Gross reserves constituent of proven energy	85.1%	2.7%	0.3%	11.9%
Gross reserves constituent of remaining recoverable energy	51.4%	2.9%	1.1%	44.6%

Source: Lin Boqiang, *Report on China's Energy Development 2008* (Beijing: China Financial and Economic Publishing House, 2008): 262.

Table 13.2 Reserves of conventional energy in China

Energy / Project	Gross reserves of energy (100 million tons of standard coal)	Raw coal (100 million tons)	Crude oil (100 million tons)	Natural gas (100 million cubic meters)	Hydraulic power (100 million KWH)
Gross reserves	40,466.4	50,592.2	1,000.0	381,400.0	59,221.8
World reserves	1,048,809.7	1,195,748.4	51,172.8	79,330,827.1	413,095.0
China's share (%)	3.9	4.2	2.0	0.5	14.3
Gross reserves of proven energy (Technically feasible)	8,231.0	10,077.0	160.0	20,606.0	19,233.0
World reserves	329,697.5	352,749.6	25,674.6	26,630,075.2	117,549.0
China's share (%)	2.5	2.9	0.6	0.1	16.4
Rate of proven resources	20.3	19.9	16.0	5.4	—
Service life of resources	766.8	1,007.7	98.2	74.3	—
Annual output in 2000	10.9	10.0	1.6	277.0	2,224.0
Gross reserves of remaining recoverable energy (economically feasible)	1,391.9	1,145.0	32.7	13,668.9	12,600.0
World reserves	—	9,842.1	1,402.8	1,493,811.0	73,053.0
China's share (%)	10.1	11.6	2.3	0.9	17.2
Service life of resources	129.7	114.5	20.1	49.3	—

Notes: Rate of proven resources is defined as gross reserves divided by gross reserves of proven energy. Service life of resources is defined as annual output in 2000 divided by gross reserves of remaining recoverable energy.

Source: The energy strategy research team, Chinese Academy of Sciences, *Strategic Research Reports on China's Sustainable Energy Development* (Beijing: Science Press, 2006): 19.

However, per capita resources quantity is to be cut far lower than the average level in the world because of more than 1.3 billion people. The per capita quantities of raw coal, oil, natural gas, and water account for 79%, 6.1%, 6.5%, and 25% of the world total, respectively.[5]

Regional distribution of China's energy resources is obviously unbalanced. Four-fifths of the mineral resources are distributed in the north. 60% of raw coal is distributed in northern China. Oil is mainly distributed in the northeast and northwest. Natural gas and about 70% of water-electric energy is concentrated in the southwest. East China, central China, and southern China with densely populated areas only have 5% of the whole energy resources.

The resources feature of being rich in raw coal, poor in oil, and weak in gas make China a coal-based energy production and consumption structure. Since the end of the 1980s, China has been the world's largest raw coal producer. With the successful development of Daqing Oilfield, the growth rate of oil production was up to 230% from 1964 to 1979 and the volume of the net export of oil reached a peak in 1985 (35.4 million tons). Natural gas development accelerated apparently in the 1980s with an average annual growth rate of 3% from 1982 to 1995. The Qinshan Nuclear Power Plant in Zhejiang Province designed and manufactured by China and the Guangdong Daya Bay Nuclear Power Station (GNPS) with a nuclear reactor of France were put into commercial operation one after another in 1994. At the same time, new electricity generation technology like wind, solar, tide, and geothermic resources were developed. At present, China has formed a grand energy production system mainly based on coal and other complementary energy, ranking second only to America. China's raw coal output ranks first in the world. Generated energy, oil output, and natural gas output rank second, fifth, and seventh, respectively, worldwide. In the meantime, China's whole energy consumption ranks first in the world, and the total primary energy consumption was 2.43 billion tons of standard oil in 2010.

Gradually prominent energy bottleneck

China's comprehensive national strength has been greatly enhanced thanks to its 30 years of reform and opening up. Total economic output in 2010 was up to USD5.88 trillion, accounting for 9.3% of the world output, which was more than 16 times that in 1978 where it was only 1.8%.[6] China's great achievements of energy play a foundational support role in the speedy development of the national economy. China's energy consumption was at an average annual growth rate of 5.6% supporting an average annual national economy growth rate of 9.8% in 1980–2006.[7] But China's energy development has faced more and more difficulties in meeting the demands of the speedy growth of the national economy and the quick improvement of national life since the new century. Energy constraints become a big "bottleneck" factor of carrying out Scientific Development Concept and building a well-off society in an all-around way.

First, supply-demand contradiction is more and more serious. For many years, the growth speed of China's energy production has failed to cope with the growth speed of its energy demand. The annual average growth rate of GDP was, respectively, 9.36% and 11% during 1979–2003 and 2004–2007. But energy production was 3.82% and 9.53% while energy consumption was at 4.4% and 11% in the meantime. The annual average growth rate of GDP and the growth rate of energy consumption was, respectively, 11.9% and 7.8% in 2007, but the energy production was only 6.5%. The total volume of energy production has been less than energy consumption since 1992. The balanced differences between energy production and energy consumption were a positive value (52.19 million tons of standard coal) in 1990, but it became a negative value in 2001 (–140.14 million tons of standard coal). And it was –301.38 million tons of standard coal, twice that in 2001. The year-on-year growth of energy consumption was up to 16.1% and 10.6%, respectively, in 2004 and 2005, while the annual rate was 9.6%, 7.8%, 4%, 6.3%, and 5.9%, respectively, during the Eleventh Five-Year Plan.[8] Although growth speed is slowing, the absolute total number of energy consumption is increasing. Not only is the supply-demand contradiction more and more serious, but also a series of challenges, such as the serious shortage in power supply, are caused by the development of extension mode. The power supply of 20–30 million KW was short in covering 21 provinces and cities in the peak time in 2004.[9] Although national power supply-demand is integrally balanced, a short time of poor power supply or limitation in some seasons, periods, and local areas also forms a severe impact on some enterprises and urban inhabitants' life.

Second, oil demand inflation and substantially increased import dependence. China's oil supply gap has been expanding fast for more than 10 years because the growth speed of its oil consumption is far faster than its oil production. According to Chinese customs' statistics, China has been a country of net importer of oil since 1993 and 9.88 million tons of oil (the number of petroleum is larger than crude oil) were imported. Trade value of petroleum and crude oil was negative in 1996 with the country fully becoming a net importer of oil (net import volume of oil was 13.95 million tons).[10] In 2010, the annual net volume of oil was as high as 253.67 million tons, annual growth was 16.2%, and net volume of crude oil was as high as 236.27 million tons, with annual growth of 19%.[11] In 2010, the dependence degree of petroleum and crude oil was 59% and 54%, respectively. Professor Zhang Kang predicts that by 2020, China's gap between oil supply and demand would reach 400 million tons while the dependence degree of imported petroleum would be up to 70%.[12] Additionally, according to the forecast of the International Energy Agency, by 2030, China's import volume of oil would be up to 10 million barrels per day (500 million tons) and the dependence degree of oil would be as high as 74%.[13] Under the situation of high oil prices, trade balance is influenced by a sharp increase of oil imports, which has an adverse effect on China's long-term economic development, employment, and consumption.

Again, the contradiction of energy structure emerges. There are not only contradictions of gross balance but also hysteretic energy structure in China's energy supply and consumption. Because China's economic growth mode is influenced by energy, there is a tendency which has existed for a long time that stresses "thinking highly of quantity and capability" while "ignoring the optimization of quality structure" in China's energy industry development. Although the proportion of coal was below 80% after the 1970s, about 70% around the turn of the century in energy production structure after many years' hard work, it was over 75% in the last 5 years because of high oil prices and, accordingly, the proportion of coal was about 70%. In China's energy consumption structure, the proportion of coal is too high, but the proportion of high efficient energy like oil, natural gas, nuclear power, and water-electricity is low compared with other major big countries of energy consumers, or the world's average level. However, the development of new energy is just beginning, but it is still not good enough. The poor situations of energy structure bring the problems of environmental pollution, low energy efficiency, and poor economic benefits described in the following passages.

In addition, the contradictions between energy development and environmental protection are acute. The proportion of green energy and renewable energy of the conventional energy are low and coal plays an overwhelmingly dominant role. Most of the coal consumption, especially the raw coal burning with low efficiency directly causes atmospheric pollution of the areas around the city. The coverage of acid rain, sulfur dioxide, and smoke is enlarged yearly and the degree of pollution rises up. According to the relevant materials, 80% of the coal in China is directly combusted, producing 90% of SO_2, 67% of NO_x, and 70% of CO_2. There are situations of atmosphere-water-soil interaction pollution in the Yangtze River and the Pearl River Delta areas, which make up a growing threat to the ecological system, food security, and human health. With the signing of the *United Nations Framework Convention on Climate Change* in 1992, which went into effect in 1994, the global climate control movement shifted into high gear to form a growing challenge for the growth limit of China's greenhouse gas emission.

Finally, the utilization efficiency of energy is low. Long-term extensive production results in low utilization efficiency of every part from production to use, which makes waste a serious problem. In China, there is a large proportion of energy-intensive enterprises, few large-scale enterprises, and fewer high-tech enterprises. So, there is a huge gap between China and many other countries in the world in terms of energy consumption per unit product and energy efficiency of equipment. During the Tenth Five-Year Plan, China's average annual energy consumption elasticity coefficient was 1.04, twice as much as before. It is estimated that if the average annual energy consumption elasticity coefficient is 1.0 over the next 15 years, the whole country will consume 5 billion tons of standard coal. And China's resources cannot afford this. It is estimated that China's level in the number of GDP coming from unit energy consumption is about 1/5–1/16 of the developed country's average level.

Energy is the foundation and motivation of China's economy and social development. China currently is in the stage of industrialization. So, the degree of dependence on energy for China's social economic development is far larger than the developed countries. Mitigation of the energy "bottleneck" has a direct bearing on social economic development, people's quality of life, climate change, and even national security.

Sustainable development strategy of domestic energy

The Chinese government came to realize that it must take energy as the strategic focus of economic development on which it would provide stable, economical, sanitary, reliable, and secure energy to entirely build a moderately prosperous society and support the sustainable development of China's economy and society with the sustainable development and efficient utilization of the energy. On June 30, 2004, Premier Wen Jiabao chaired the Standing Meeting of the State Council, deliberating and approving in principle *The Medium- and Long-Term Development Plan for Energy (2004–2020)*. The plan indicated that to solve China's energy problem, the country must implement the correct guidelines which apply to national conditions, respect the laws of nature and the economy, learn from world experiences, and set the country on the course of energy development with Chinese characteristics. On March 16, 2006, the Fourth Session of The

Tenth National People's Congress approved *The 11th Five Year Plan of National Economic and Social Development*. Based on the general requirement to build a moderately prosperous society, during the period of the 11th Five-Year Plan, the GDP per capita would double that of 2000, the utilization ratio of energy would obviously increase, the energy consumption of unit GDP would reduce by 20%, and the gross of main pollutant discharge would reduce by 10%.[14] So far, the Chinese government has confirmed medium and long-term strategies for energy development with the guidance of Scientific Outlook on Development, fostered new industrialization with Chinese characteristics, and implemented a sustainable energy development strategy, which is "energy conservation, multiple-structure, environmentally friendly, and developing internally and externally." The strategy was implemented as follows.

First, China's goals should follow the following path. To put energy conservation as a priority, the country needs to carry out a comprehensive and strict energy conservation system and measures to obviously improve the efficiency of energy utilization. To firmly carry out development and energy conservation simultaneously as basic state policy, energy conversation is to be made a priority. To encourage the development and application of new energy-saving technology and reduce consumption, the equipment and products of high energy and high consumption need to be eliminated; To formulate and implement the *Medium- and Long-Term Energy Conservation Plan*, China should define the standard, target, and policy measures of energy conservation in each industry. China should develop a recycling economy and accelerate the integrated and recycling utilization of resources through methods including resources exploitation, consumption, and utilization of waste and social consumption. To foster a culture of energy conservation, China should form a healthy, civilized, and economical consumption model. To publicize the meaning of energy conservation, popularize the knowledge of energy conservation, enhance the sense of urgency and the awareness of conservation, and make great efforts to establish a long-term mechanism of energy conservation in the whole society. With the readjustment of economic structure, and through technical progress and strengthening management, the performance of energy conservation and improving efficiency was obvious. Based on the fixed price in 2005, the energy consumption of GDP at RMB10,000 was reduced from 3.39 tons of standard coal in 1980 to 1.21 tons in 2006. The annual energy savings rate was 3.9% and the overall efficiency of energy processing, converting, storage, and transportation, and terminal utilization was 33%, 8% higher than that of 1980.[15] In order to relieve the conflict of national energy resources and the development of economy and society, we must at first focus on our own country and stick to the leadership of the government. The market and enterprises are the keys to improving the efficiency of utilizing energy resources and fully propel and build an energy-saving society.

Second, to greatly adjust and optimize energy structure, China should stick to the strategy of focusing on coal, electronic power, and oil and gas and new energy development in an all-around way. The resource structure determines that coal will be China's main basic source of energy for a long time. China is now enhancing the exploitation of coal resources, accelerating the construction of large-sized coal bases, increasing coal technical transformation, strengthening the security management of coal production, and improving the capability of coal transportation. In terms of electric power construction, the major task is to build important projects of the power supply and power grid, and to carry forward the independent research and development of key electric power equipment. Meanwhile, another goal is to enhance the exploration and development of oil and gas, while promoting the technical progress of the oil and gas petrochemical industry. China has greatly improved its energy structure by taking diversity as the principle to actively search for alternative energy and increase the proportion of hydroelectric power, nuclear power, and gas power. As clean excellent energy, natural gas is vigorously promoted to utilize efficiency. The utilization of nuclear energy is from "moderately developed" to "actively developed." The potential of using renewable energy sources is huge, such as small hydroelectric power, wind energy, solar energy, and biomass energy, etc. The exploration and utilization play important roles in increasing energy supply, improving energy structure, and promoting environmental protection which is also a strategic choice of solving the conflict of energy demand and supply and realizing sustainable development. In 2009, the proportion of renewable energy sources consumption in the total energy consumed was 9.9% which was 3% five years ago.[16] Therefore, it has a chance to realize the target that the proportion of renewable energy sources should be 10% of the total energy consumed in 2010 and 15% in 2020 according to the goals proposed by the government in the *Medium- and Long-Term Development Plan for Renewable Energy Sources*.

Third, to make a rational layout for the energy sources development, give consideration to the coordinated development of the eastern and mid-western regions, and comprehensively consider the reasonable allocation of energy production, transportation, and consumption. In terms of economic policy, capital investment, and industrial development, the government enhanced support to the development of the mid-western region and stressed that it should fully emphasize resource superiority, develop characteristic industry, and enhance self-development capabilities. Xinjiang has become a key region to explore and develop national oil and gas resources and in recent years it has made great progress. The output of crude oil in Xinjiang increased from 15.677 million tons in 1998 to 27.215 million tons in 2008, an annual growth rate of 5.7%. At the same time, the gas production in Xinjiang increased from 2.548 billion cubic meters to 23.614 billion cubic meters, an annual growth rate of 22.4%. Besides, the government also paid great attention to the coordination of the transportation of electric power, oil, and gas which organized and combined supply and demand. Over the years, the construction of the comprehensive energy transportation system had made great progress. Special railways that transported coal from the western area to the eastern areas and ports were established to form a pipe network that transported oil from the north to the south. And the west-east natural gas transmission project was established to realize the transmission of the electricity from the western to the eastern region and the interconnection of the regional power system. As an important part of China's natural gas development strategy, the momentum project of west development from the west toward the east natural gas transmission was fermented in 1998. The decision was made in 2000 and the construction was started in 2002. On December 30, 2004, the first-line natural gas transmission project from the west of Lunnan, Xinjiang to the east of Baihe Town in Shanghai realized the whole line commercial operation. Taking the gas field in Tarim, Xinjiang as the main gas source, the Yangtze River Delta in the mideast as the targeted consumer market, main pipelines, important branch lines, and gas storage as the main concerns, users along the line were connected and the natural gas air supply system traversing the west and the east of China was formed. On that basis, the second-line project was started in 2008 from the west of Khorgos which connected the natural gas pipelines of Central Asia and China to the south of Guangzhou and the east of Shanghai. By way of 14 provinces and cities, including Xinjiang, the main line was 4,895 km and the whole main line was completed on June 30, 2011.[17] The natural gas in Central Asian countries, such as Turkmenistan and Kazakhstan, etc., was imported as source gas, and the gas in China as standby and complemented source gas. The natural gas produced from Xinjiang and imported from Central Asia was transmitted to central and western regions along the line, the Yangtze River Delta and Pearl River Delta, etc., to meet the energy demand in the Pearl River Delta and the Yangtze River Delta.

This is significant in changing China's energy structure, guaranteeing the supply of natural gas, protecting China's energy safety, promoting energy conservation, and reducing emissions, optimizing energy consumption structure and boosting the cooperation and mutual benefit of international energy. It is very conducive to meet the growing demand of natural gas and environmental protection in the east. Besides, the construction of oil-gas pipelines on land was smooth, connecting the northwest of China and Central Asia, the northeast of China and Russia, and also connecting the southwest of China and Myanmar.

Fourth, China must greatly rely on scientific-technical progress and innovation and explore the path of new industrialization. Utilizing the concept that science and technology are the primary productive forces, the government is gradually increasing capital investment, actively developing and promoting advanced applicable technology related to energy conservation, substitution, cyclic utilization, and pollution management. The government gradually established a technological innovation system focusing on enterprises, market, and connections to production, study, and research. Here are the five aspects. To vigorously promote the technology of energy conservation: Overcome key technology of energy conservation in high consumption areas; improve the utilization ratio of primary energy and terminal energy; implement technical policy and the outline of energy conservation technology; lead to the investment in the application of energy conservation technology. Second, to boost the innovation of key technology: Encourage and develop clean coal technology and poly-generation technology based on coal gasification; give priority to develop the technology of large-scale utilizing renewable energy. Third, to enhance the standard of equipment manufacturing: Rely on national energy major projects to improve the technological progress in the equipment manufacturing industry; encourage the development of comprehensive mining equipment, large-scale coal chemical industry kit, large efficiency power generation equipment, high-tension power transmission and transformation equipment, oil-gas exploration and drilling, especially large offshore oil engineering equipment. Fourth, to enhance the study on cutting-edge technology: Lead the energy industry and energy technology to realize great-leap-forward development; focus on fossil energy, biomass energy, hydrogen production with renewable energy, the technology of hydrogen storage with efficiency and transmission and distribution; and accelerate the development of gas-cooled faster reactor and its core technology; actively study the technology of magnetic confinement fusion and natural gas hydrate. Fifth, to develop the study on basic science: Stress the basic theory of efficient and clean utilization and transformation of fossil energy, the basic principle of high performance of heat into power and high efficient energy conservation and storage, basic technology of scale utilization of renewable energy, basic theory of scale utilization of nuclear energy and hydrogen energy, etc.

In the last 30 years, China's industries of energy, science, and technology have made great progress. Technologies such as exploration for fossil fuel sources and the development of oil and gas, and increasing recovery ratio in oilfields took the lead in the world. The degree of mechanization of key coal mining was obviously improved. The design of hydroelectric station, the engineering technology and equipment manufacturing are advanced in the world. Nuclear power has the capability of autonomously designing million-kilowatt pressurized water reactor and engineering construction. The research and development of high temperature gas cooled reactors and fast breeder reactors have made a significant breakthrough. The pollution regulation of flue gas desulfurization and the technology of developing and utilizing renewable energy improved rapidly. International Thermonuclear Experimental Reactor (ITER, also named as the project of "Artificial Sun") was launched successfully. In November 2006, the European Union, India, Korea, Russia, the U.S. and China signed *The Agreement on the Establishment of the ITER International Fusion Energy Organization for the Joint Implementation of the ITER Project*. In January 2010, China signed the agreement on implementation of international thermonuclear experimental reactor.[18] The ITER at present is one of the largest international scientific research projects in the world. Its goal is to establish a thermonuclear experimental reactor to verify the scientific and technical feasibility of the peaceful utilization of thermonuclear energy.

Fifth, to integrate energy development with environmental protection. In order to feasibly solve the problems that affect the development of economy and society, especially jeopardize people's health, to build ecological civilization, reduce pollutant emission, and protect the environment has become China's basic state policy. The government proposed that during the period of the 11th Five-Year Plan, the environmental deterioration should be under control and the quantum of main pollutant emission reduced by 10%. The control of greenhouse gas emissions should obtain the effective goal. The 11th Five-Year Plan stressed taking precautionary measures, treating comprehensively, reinforcing to prevent and control pollution, and protecting the ecology at the source, and firmly changing the situation that first caused pollution. While entirely promoting energy conservation, China mainly prevents and deals with the prominent problems of environmental pollution in four aspects as follows. The first is to entirely control the emission of greenhouse gas. The second is to actively prevent ecological damage and environmental pollution. The third is to actively control the pollution of vehicle emissions. The fourth is to strictly control energy projects and environmental management.

What we stress is that as a responsible developing country, China is highly aware of the severe problem of global climate change. In combination with fighting climate change, implementing sustainable strategy, and accelerating to establish a resource-saving, environmentally-friendly, and innovation-oriented country, China set up a cooperating agency to deal with national climate change and formulated *China's Climate Change Program*, drawing up specific objectives, basic principles, key areas, and policies. In September 2009, President Hu Jintao addressed the United Nations Climate Change Conference and proposed the methods to fight climate change with international cooperation while also announcing on behalf of the Chinese government a series of significant moves to fight climate change that in 2020 the carbon dioxide emission of unit GDP would be reduced from that of 2005, and the proportion of non-fossil fuel in primary energy consumption would be 15%.[19] On November 25, 2009, the State Council decided that by 2020 the carbon dioxide emission of unit GDP, as an obligatory target incorporated into the medium-long planning of the national economy and social development, should be reduced by 40%–45% than that of 2005. This was the first time a clear and quantitative goal for greenhouse gas emission was put forward. On December 18, 2009, Premier Wen Jiabao addressed the Copenhagen Climate Change Summit *Build Consensus and Strengthen Cooperation to Advance the Historical Process of Combating Climate Change*, and announced that China would not attach any conditions to reduce greenhouse gas emissions and he fully committed the country to achieving and even exceeding the target.

Sixth, to deepen the reform of the energy system. In order to enhance the process of energy marketization, complete the energy macro-control system, and ameliorate the environment of energy development, China has to gradually carry forward and deepen the reform of the energy system, and the main aspects are described as follows. The first is to propel the legal energy system building, issue *Law of the People's Republic of China on Energy Conservation* and *Renewable Energy Law of the People's Republic of China,* formulate *Energy Law* and *Circular Economy Law*, revise *Mineral Resources Law*, *Law of the People's Republic of China on the Coal Industry* and *Electricity Law,* and actively deliberate the legislation in the fields of energy, including petroleum and gas, crude oil market, and atomic energy. The second is to improve the reform of energy commercialization, entirely complete the coal market system, build a power market with separation of government functions from enterprise management, encourage fair competition, open to the outside in a well-organized way, accelerate the structural reform of petroleum and gas circulation and boost the healthy development of the energy market, and in this order. The third was to improve the reform of the price system. In the situation that properly dealt with the relationships among different interest groups and fully considers the tolerance capability of all quarters of the society, to actively and steadily promote the reform of energy price, the pricing mechanism will be gradually formed which can reflect the degree of energy scarcity, supply and demand in the market, and the environmental cost. The fourth was to complete the national energy management system and decision-making system, enhance coordination of each side, intensify the overall plan and macro-control of national energy development, put forth effort to change functions, rationalize relationships, optimize structure, improve the performance, and form a management system which is properly centralized. The division of work is reasonable, decision-making is scientific, execution is smooth, and the supervision is forceful. In January 2010, the National Energy Commission was established and its main responsibilities are: Be responsible for deliberating and drawing up national energy development strategy; deliberating on major issues on energy security and energy development; planning and coordinating major issues on national energy exploration and international energy cooperation.

Seventh, to accelerate the construction of strategic oil reserves. In recent years, China has built a reasonable strategic oil reserve system in stages and relevant work including strategic site selection and formulation of the related system has been rapidly started. From March 2004, the four strategic oil reserve sites decided in the first stage — Zhenhai in Ningbo, Zhejiang, Daishan in Zhoushan, Huangdao in Qingdao, Shandong and Dalian New Port in Liao Ning — have come into operation. By the end of 2008, the four bases in the first stage had been established and put into operation. The gross oil reserve in the first stage was 16.4 million cubic meters, or about 14 million tons of crude oil. Meanwhile, based on the *Medium- and Long-Term Plan of National Oil Reserves* which had been approved, the infrastructure construction of strategic oil reserves in the second and third stage will be finished before 2020, which will be equivalent to the total scale of net import volume of oil within 100 days. Besides crude oil, the construction of petroleum products and natural gas reserves are carried forward. To match it, the national oil management system was also under construction.

In December 2007, China's Oil Reserve Center was established and *The Plan for Oil Reserves* was drafted to promote the systematization legislation and standardization of the oil reserve which was turned into the safeguard of energy resources needed by national economic development.

"Going Out" strategy and international energy cooperation

It is obvious that to fundamentally solve the issue of China's energy, we must take a "Scientific Outlook on Development," rely on scientific advancement, and stick to the guideline that "energy conservation is the priority, the structure is varied, and the environment is friendly," as well as persist in new industrialization and energy sustainable development. Meanwhile, in consideration of abundant international energy resources, huge development potential, good resource condition, and the lower cost of development, China has taken an active part in the rational development and utilization system of energy worldwide, vigorously promoting a mutually beneficial and win-win international energy cooperation strategy while being based on the domestic energy exploration, development, and construction.

China's international energy cooperation went through three phases since its reform and opening up. The first phase was from 1978 to 1992 which was the fermenting and exploratory stage of international energy cooperation. The target was to develop and utilize China's native place resources, open up to the Western developed countries, and introduce foreign capital, equipment, technology, and services in the field of energy resources. From 1993 to 2005, it was the phase to steadily boost the "Going Out" strategy in China's international energy cooperation. Along with the change of national and international situations, the foreign cooperation of China's energy gradually went towards exploring the overseas energy market and implementing the "Going Out" international operation. In March 1993, China National Petroleum Corporation (CNPC) won the bidding in the project of 6/7 region in TALALA oilfield in Peru, where the Chinese oil industry started to move into the international market. After that, CNPC went to Venezuela, Sudan, Kazakhstan, Iraq, etc. Its overseas oil shares increased from 520,000 tons in 1997 to 10.18 million tons in 2002.

During that period, Sinopec and China National Offshore Oil Corporation (CNOOC) successfully "went out" to the Middle East and Southeast Asia, achieving performances in the investment and operation of international oil and gas. Not only did the scale, reserves, and output of the investment projects of national overseas oil increase substantially, but the multinational operation of overseas energy formed a unified industrial chain, especially because CNPC had established a complete oil industrial chain in the Sudan, including oil and gas production — pipeline operation — oil refining and end-product sales. Meanwhile, the international investment projects of national oil and gas enterprises drove the flourishing development of overseas oil engineering, technological service, and supplies export. The enterprises are booming in the international operation. In this phase, China's oil enterprises not only successfully implemented the "Going Out" strategy to lay a solid foundation for the development of national energy overseas operations, but China gradually carried forward the international energy dialogue and multicultural communication. China has taken an active part in the interchange activities and mechanism of international energy cooperation. In October 1996, China and the International Energy Agency signed the *Policy Memorandum of Understanding on Cooperation in the Field of Energy*, and agreed to improve the cooperation in terms of energy conservation, efficiency, energy development and utilization, peripheral investment and trade of the energy industry, supply guarantee of energy, and environmental protection, etc.[20] In January 2005, China took part in the Ministerial Roundtable Meeting of Asian Oil Economic Cooperation in New Delhi; in December 2005, China and OPEC announced to establish the "Dialogue Mechanism on Energy."

It was the third phase of boosting China's international energy cooperation strategy since 2006. The failure of CNOOC's acquisition of Unocal Corporation in 2005 made us rethink profoundly about how to further promote the "Going Out" strategy and we became clearer about the profound changes in the international energy situation. In July 2006, the Group of Eight and the leaders from developing countries held the dialogue meeting in St. Petersburg. Chairman Hu Jintao put forward that China should set up and implement a safety outlook of new energy that involved mutually beneficial cooperation, diverse development, and collaborative protection in order to guarantee the security of global energy. The security of Chinese and global energy is inseparable, and China will strengthen the coordination with the energy policy of each country. In order to guarantee the safety of global energy, the new energy security outlook of mutually beneficial cooperation, diverse development and collaborative protection should be set up and implemented. The first goal is to strengthen the mutual cooperation of developing and utilizing energy sources. The second is to shape the research and development system of advanced energy technology. The third is to maintain the good political environment for the security and stability of the energy. The security outlook of new energy complies with the trend of economic globalization. It exceeds the traditional zero-sum thinking and combines the mutually beneficial cooperation among countries, the establishment of research and development system of advanced energy technology, and the harmonious international political environment which creates energy safety. And it indicates a correct direction to realize global energy safety and finally solve the energy issues. The explicit announcement of a new energy security outlook provides a significant theoretical guide towards China's comprehensive and multicultural international energy cooperation.

In this phase, with strong policy direction and support of the central government, Chinese energy resource enterprises increased the force to go abroad, and actively, comprehensively, and widely participated in the global energy cooperation. And relevant authorities also provided active cooperation and coordination. The Ministry of Foreign Affairs also emphasized that one of its key points in the diplomatic work was "to promote diplomatic relations of energy and help energy enterprises expand [the] international market."[21] Since launching the "Going Out" policy in 1993, China's international energy cooperation strategy gradually developed and became mature in the changeable world. During the period of the 11th Five-Year Plan, the Chinese oil enterprises developed over 130 international oil and gas cooperation projects in more than 40 countries and regions, including exploration and development of oil and gas, construction of pipelines, refining, and technical service contracts. Five large international oil and gas cooperation zones have been basically built up in Africa, Central Asia-Russia, South America, the Middle East, and the Asia-Pacific region. By the end of 2008, Chinese enterprises had accumulatively acquired over 1.2 billion tons of residual recoverable old reserves and over 220 billion cubic meters of residual recoverable reserves of natural gas abroad. In 2008, the equity output of overseas crude oil of Chinese enterprises was 45 million tons and the equity natural gas was 6 billion cubic meters.[22] In 2008, the overseas equivalent equity output of oil and gas overseas was for the first time to surmount 70 million tons and the amount of the merge deal was nearly USD30 billion.[23] Today, the business scope of China's international oil and gas cooperation covered a complete oil and gas industrial chain, including exploration and development, oil refining, and chemical industry, pipeline transportation, sales and trade, and engineering and technical service.

Table 13.3 Regional coverage of China's petroleum enterprises' overseas oil and gas business

Region	CNPC	Sinopec	CNOOC	Sinochem	Total
Africa	29	12	5	2	48
Middle East	6	2	4	2	14
South America	13	9	0	1	23
Central Asia	16	8	0	0	24
South Asia	7	1	13	2	23
North America	1	1	1	0	3
Total	72	33	23	7	135

Sources: 1. Consultancy center of CNPC, *The Strategic Studies on National Oil-Gas Exploration in the Major Fluctuation of Oil Price* (Study Report, 2008).
2. Mu Xianzhong, *The Development Studies on the Globalization of China's Oil and Gas Industry* (Beijing: Economy and Management Publishing House, 2010): 164.

It is worth mentioning that currently China's international energy cooperation strategy is demonstrating some outstanding features. The first is the diversification of collaborating objects of international energy. The cooperation between China and foreign countries is not limited to the energy producing countries, such as the Middle East, Central Asia, and Latin America, and China has closely cooperated with developed and developing energy-consuming countries. The second is the diversification of cooperative models of international energy, that is, to take part in the cooperation of international energy resources at multiple levels. China's cooperation of international energy and resources has broken through the singular situation that bought oil and gas in the international market, but widely participated in each phase, including exploration, production, processing, distribution, and consumption of energy resources. After the international financial crisis, China signed loan cooperation agreements with the oil- and gas-producing countries successively, including Kazakhstan, Russia, Brazil, etc., initiating a new win-win model for mutual benefit. And then, the channel and path of international cooperation increasingly becomes long-term and mechanized. In recent years, a large part of overseas cooperation projects launched by China's energy enterprises have been long-term strategic cooperation ones. The energy cooperation between China and some other countries or regional cooperative organizations has been gradually mechanized and normalized. The last step is to reach cooperation principles and value orientations of equality and mutual benefit. The cooperation of China's energy enterprises towards outside is different from the Western oil oligarch's predatory mining towards host countries of resources. It pays high attention to the benefit of two parties involved and seeks for the confluence of the profit, sticks to mutual benefit and development, and enhances communication, collaboration, understanding and trust with host countries of resources and other cooperative partners, in the meantime pursuing profits, striving to show humanistic concern and social aid, and setting up a good international image to create a beneficial atmosphere for its international operation.[24]

Nowadays, the Chinese government has paid great attention to highlighting the strategic position of the work of energy. On June 27, 2005, General Secretary Hu Jintao stressed to the 23rd collective study of the Political Bureau of the Central Committee of the Communist Party of China that the issue of energy resources was a major strategic one concerning the overall situation of China's economic and social development. Accomplishing the work of energy and taking the work of conservation as priorities should become the basic train of thought to solve the issue of China's energy resources. In January 2010, the National Energy Commission was established and Premier Wen Jiabao was appointed to be its chief. It plays a more effective role in the strategic policy of directing the coordinated growth among national energy, economy, society, and the environment. The formulation and implementation of the policies in the field of energy has become a more powerful and effective system basis that is obviously conducive to relieving the current bottleneck of energy and enhancing the strategic management ability of energy sources in China.

China shall continue to persist in its basic national principles, strengthen the exploration of national energy, encourage the development of new energy and renewable energy, optimize the energy structure and establish resource-conserving society. At the same time, it shall actively launch international cooperation in the field of energy resources, and fully utilize international and national markets and resources to provide reliable energy resources for realizing the ambitious goal of building a well-off society in all all-around way and the long-term development of China. Naturally, the "Going Out" strategy of China's overseas energy cooperation in the past decade has achieved progress along with numerous hardships and setbacks. Although the cooperation of international energy development is challenged by competition, even conflicts, the world needs cooperation due to competition while economic globalization is rapidly developing. Either China's "Going Out" strategy or its "Oil Diplomacy," which attracts the world's attention, will stick to the policy of equality, cooperation, and mutual benefit, respect the interest of each country in the cooperation, and enlarge the profit confluence in order to strive to realize the target of mutual development and common prosperity.

China's Peaceful Development (White Paper), published by the Chinese government in June 2011, emphasized that China would focus on breaking through the bottleneck of developing resources and the environment, setting the development concept of green and low carbon dioxide with the key point of energy conservation and emission reduction, accelerate the energy-conserving and environment-friendly mode of production and consumption; promote the development of a circular economy, improve environmental quality, construct a secure, stable, economical, clean and modern energy industrial system, upgrade the guarantee of energy, facilitate the harmonious development between human beings and nature, realize the coordination between economic development, human beings, resources and the environment, and continue to explore a new industrial path with Chinese characteristics featuring high technology, high economic profit, low energy consumption, and less environmental pollution, and the superiority of human resources will be given full play. It is obvious that the comprehensively coordinated and sustainable development of the Chinese economy will provide a wide space for the world's economic development.

Status Quo and Development Strategy of India's Energy

Rising major energy consumer

India is another rising major power in the East. Since it launched the reform and adjustment in the 1990s, India's economy has developed dramatically. Its GNP increased to 9.8% in the fiscal year 2006–2007 from 0.8% in 1991–1992 and its yields increased to USD1.101 trillion in the fiscal year 2007–2008 from USD278.5 billion in 1991–1992.[25] Since 2008, although the increase of its economy has slowed down due to the impact by the global financial crisis, India's GNP increased rate still reached 8.6% in the fiscal year 2010–2011. India also mentioned that it should be the third largest economy in the world. However, along with the rapid development of the economy, its demand for energy increased strongly; India is turning into an increasingly important consumer in the world energy market. In 2001, India was the sixth largest consumer of energy in the world. But from 2002 onwards, it surpassed Germany and Japan, and became the fourth largest one after China, the U.S., and Russia according to the latest *BP Statistical Review of World Energy 2011*. Its total consumption of energy in 2010 accounted for 4.4% of the world's, rising 9.2% from 2009, and 77.2% from 2000.[26]

India's energy consumption structure fully presents the characteristics of developing countries. In its primary energy consumption in 2009, coal took up 52%, petroleum 32%, natural gas 10%, nuclear energy 1%, and hydroelectric power 5%. India's increase rate of energy consumption was 4 times that of the world on average. Along with the rapid development of its economy, population, and per capita energy consumption, India's total energy demand will continue to speed up and its demand for energy sources of all kinds will increase significantly. According to the forecast of the International Energy Agency, during 2000–2030, India's annual demand of primary energy would increase by 3.1% on average, and the ultimate demand for petroleum, natural gas, and electric power would rise sharply.[27] During 2002–2030, India's annual supply of primary energy will increase by 2.3% on average, which is much lower than its annual average increase of 3.6% during 1971–2002.[28] After 2010, thanks to its economic development and slowing increase of population, India's increase rate of energy demand is expected to drop. But the absolute increase capacity is still a challenge. At present, biomass and waste take up the majority of primary energy sources in India but are being replaced by coal and petroleum. During 2002–2030, India's ultimate aggregate consumption of energy will rise by 2.1% annually. The proportions of biomass and waste would drop to 36% by 2030 from 54% in 2002. By 2030, the civil purpose would take up 48% of the ultimate aggregate consumption of energy. After giving up traditional biomass energy, local residents would turn to using liquefied natural gas, kerosene, natural gas, and electric power. By 2030, the civilian consumption of petroleum would double, and that of natural gas quadruple. Its population-reaching electricity would rise up to 68% by 2030 from 44% in 2002, and the coal used for generating electric power would take up nearly 3/4 of the total. The industrial percentage of aggregate energy consumption of India's ultimate total would rise up to approximately 32% by 2030 from 27% in 2002. As the leading fuel of industry, petroleum would take up 43% of industrial aggregate energy consumption by 2030 when the sum of natural gas and electric power would take up 27%, and the proportion of coal and renewable energy sources drop dramatically.

In terms of resources, India boasts abundant reserves of coal with a huge mine ranging from the east of Maharashtra State, Central State, and Bihar State to West Bengal State. In 2010, its national demonstrated reserves of coal reached 60.6 billion tons, accounting for 7% of the total in the world and ranking the world's fifth largest coal resources after those in the U.S., Russia, China, and Australia thanks to China's reserves/production (R/P) ratio of 106 years. Before 1973, petroleum had been the main energy of India. After the first global oil crisis in 1973, India had to use coal as the alternative to petroleum and became the third largest coal producer in the world after the U.S. and China. In recent years, it has lagged behind Australia and been the fourth largest. Thanks to its abundant domestic reserves, the Indian industrial system basically relied on coal that will be the major energy source for a longer term. But the quality of coals in India is low with high ash, low sulfur content, and low calorific value. What's more noticeable, in recent years, is that there has been a big gap between production and supply of coal in India. In 2010, the coal yield of India was 216 million tons of oil, equivalent to an annual increase of 2.5%. However, in the same year, the coal consumption was 278 million tons of oil, equivalent to an annual increase of 10.8%.[29] India has a huge potential of water resources, which is 150,000 MW. But at present it has developed only 17%. Its hydroelectric outputs are unstable because of emigration, environmental protection, and monsoons. Thorium reserves in India top the world due to its demonstrated reserves accounting for 1/3 of the world's supply and this is the nuclear fuel for the atomic industry. But its domestic uranium deposits are insufficient.

Security of energy supply and environment

As a traditional agricultural country, non-commercial energy sources with biomass as the majority in rural areas and small towns weigh significantly in India's public energy consumption. Coal is the main type of its commercial energy. But since the 1980s, the demand of petroleum has increased rapidly in India and so has the natural gas consumption, which unveils India's serious shortage of oil and gas resources. So far, the energy issue has become the current and future bottleneck for the economic development in India.

The petroleum yield was only 0.45 million tons when India was independent. In 1974, the large oil field near Bombay on the west coast and that of the KG oilfield on the east coast were discovered in succession, which made India's petroleum reserve and production increase dramatically. In particular, the Bombay High oil field once supplied nearly 70% of petroleum outputs of the country. However, since the 1990s, the yield of Bombay High oilfield had dropped. The outlook for the exploration of petroleum and natural gas in India is not optimistic while the reserve has decreased remarkably and the outputs have not increased. But the domestic consumption of energy increases rapidly and the gap between supply and demand is gradually growing. During 1990–2003, the Indian primary energy consumption increased by 4.6% annually on average (the world annual average increase rate was 1.4%), and at the same time the Indian petroleum consumption increased to 113 million tons from 57.9 million tons. In 2010, it rose to 156 million tons and its domestic yield was 38.9 million tons, while the degree of its dependence on external petroleum was 75%. In the same year, the remaining demonstrated reserve of petroleum in India was 1.2 billion tons, only accounting for 0.7% of the world's, which would be completely exploited within 30 years at the rate of current production.[30] Now, India has become the fourth largest country of petroleum consumption and import worldwide.

Two main reasons contribute to the sharp increase of petroleum consumption in India. On one hand, since 1991, India has launched the overall economic reform especially for establishing the market-oriented fiscal and economic structure, its economy has increased rapidly. Over the past year, the annual increase rate of economy has maintained more than 6%, while that of oil consumption was 6–7%, surpassing the 2% of the global level on average. On the other hand, as the population grew, there was an increased demand for cars and this increased oil consumption. From 1991 to 2001, the increase rate of the Indian population was up to 21.34%.[31] About 70% of the increase of demand for petroleum resulted from the transportation sector, i.e. passenger and commercial vehicles including farming tractors that were the main reason for consuming newly increased petroleum. According to the objective of the Indian government, its GDP per capita would reach the level of a moderately developed country by 2020, which would lead to an abrupt increase of energy consumption, in particular, the consumption of oil and natural gas by 2020. It is estimated that in the next 20 years, in India's primary energy demand, oil and natural gas will still take up 40%-45%. By 2020, India's domestic demand of oil and natural gas would reach to 195 to 245 million tons and 64.7 to 70.8 billion cubic meters, respectively.[32] According to the forecast of International Energy Agency (IEA), against the background of speeding up the growth of the population and economy, India would import more petroleum and natural gas and its dependence on imported oil would rise to 94% by 2030 from 65% in 2000 and 76% in 2003 because of its limited domestic resources and outputs of domestic oil and natural gas. India's self-sufficiency rate of natural gas would drop to 60% by 2030 from 84% in 2004.

In 2003, India imported oil and gas at the cost of USD17.685 billion, accounting for 1/3 of its total import value.[33] The fact that India's petroleum depends on imports heavily has challenged its tight foreign exchange, which even caused several economic crises. Because the petroleum is priced basically by the government in India, each price rise of international petroleum might mean a potential crisis to it. The lack of energy is a key constraint on India's economic development. In 2003, the shortage of power supply in India reached 40,000 MW while the shortage rate at a normal time was 7.5%, and at peak time 12.1%.

On the other hand, India also faces the increasing challenge on environmental protection. The dramatic increase of energy consumption in India has accelerated the pollution in air and water, the overexploitation of forestry and the increasing emission of CO_2. The air pollution in urban areas largely results from fossil fuels like petroleum. At present, in the majority of Indian cities, the density of carbon dioxide and inhalable particulate matters (PM) has already surpassed the international criteria mainly thanks to the rapid increase of fuels for transportation and the charcoal used in power generation and industry. The massive consumption of petroleum, charcoal, and coal has turned India into the fifth largest source of carbon dioxide emission in the world. New Delhi, Bombay, and Kolkata have been the most polluted cities in the world. The famous ancient Taj Mahal is losing its charming color of white. The polluted environment has badly damaged the forestry and the field fertility in India, which hinders the sustainable development of its agriculture. India needs to lower the ratio of charcoal and coal in its energy composition so as to focus its economic structure on those industries of low energy consumption.

Therefore, India's energy security is mainly challenged in terms of supply and environment.

Energy development strategy for opening sources and saving costs

Along with the rapid development of the national economy, the Indian government has paid important attention to the security of energy since the 1990s. Under the principle of safety, high efficiency, environmentalism, and equality, it has fostered the reform and adjustment in the energy sector and the like, worked out, and implemented a complete strategy of energy development with the characteristics of opening sources and saving costs.

First of all, fostering the development of domestic oil and natural gas industry with the significant support of investments and policies. In the *India Vision 2025 of Petroleum and Natural Gas*, it is indicated that the guideline for the long-term development of its domestic petroleum and natural gas industry is to increase the investment on the yields of domestic petroleum and natural gas and overseas equity oil for realizing the general self-sufficiency rate of energy and securing national energy, to improve the global competitiveness of its petroleum and natural gas industry relying on technical progress, to complete the market economy and foster orderly competition, to improve the product standard, to enhance the environmental protection, and to improve living quality. The Indian government declared that during the period of its 10th Five-Year Plan (2002–2007), it would invest INR1.7 trillion to help domestic enterprises to purchase the most advanced equipment and technology of exploration and exploitation as well as encourage them to be listed public as joint ventures to be merged with energy multinationals or lead to the establishment of strategic partnerships with them.

Second, emphasizing the domestic exploration and exploitation to improve the self supply of petroleum and natural gas. The Indian government has encouraged the overall exploration in its territorial lands and seas with the latest technology. The undergoing 10th Five-Year Plan puts forward a more concrete objective for extensively exploring those new lands and seas including deep waters where there are no fields of oil and natural gas in addition to intensive exploration in the existing production areas such as Bombay High, improving the recovery efficiency by 3–4% in large oilfields as well as undertaking lab research and small field experimentation to improve the successful exploration and recovery. In order to compensate the state-owned enterprises' shortage of funds and technology in terms of exploration and development, the Indian government launched the New Exploration Licensing Policy (NELP) in 1997 to encourage private and foreign investors to explore and develop its petroleum and natural gas, which revised it in 1999 to be a standardized contract of exploring and producing oil and gas in line with international financial and contractual criteria for the purpose of offering more competitive favors to investors. So far, the NELP has attracted USD4.3 billion in private and foreign investments to develop 70 fields of oil and gas.

Third, establishing strategic petroleum reserves and strengthening oil refineries. The Indian government has started to explore and implement the strategic reserve mechanisms of crude oil and petroleum products. It has planned to build up three petroleum reserve tanks in Mangrol Port in the west, the Port of Visakhapatnam in the east, and Rajkot. At the same time, it has improved the domestic refinery level via delivering favored policies and impetus to investors. India's self-sufficiency rate of petrochemical goods has reached over 90%.

Fourth, adjusting energy structure and developing environmentally-friendly energy. Realizing that natural gas is more friendly-environmentally and more stably-supplied than petroleum, the Indian government has carried out the measures of replacing oil with gas, focused on the exploration and development of gas fields, paved natural gas pipelines across the country, and implemented associated research and development (R&D) for the aim that its gas consumption will have taken up 20% of the total national energy consumption by 2025. India has established the Ministry of Non-conventional Energy Sources (MNES) to promote the programs for developing solar and biomass energy sources across the country. Its application technology of renewable energy is world class, its utilization of wind power ranks the fourth in the world, and it is the third largest producer of solar-thermal and photovoltaic batteries worldwide.

Fifth, actively developing nuclear energy and speeding up the R&D of alternative energy. In order to fulfill the various supplies of energy, India has made the development of nuclear power an important part of its energy strategy. By 2004, 14 nuclear power plants had been built with installed nuclear power capacity of 2,200 MW and another 8 plants were being built in India. It also plans to build another 20 ones in 2020 to achieve its objective of installed nuclear power capacity of 20,000 MW. India's design and application technology of nuclear power, as well as recycling technology of nuclear fuels, have reached world class levels. Simultaneously, India is actively developing coal-bed methane (CBM), ethanol-blended gasoline, and gas hydrate.

Finally, increasing effect and enhancing energy conservation and environmental protection. The Indian government has started production, transportation, and consumption to foster energy conservation, increase benefits, and protect the environment. It has introduced tremendous donations and loans as well as technical assistance projects delivered by international organizations and developed countries to aid the research and development of new technology, techniques, and equipment for energy conservation, whose outputs are transferred to the enterprises for commercialization in turn. Moreover, the government has promulgated related laws to define the principle that those who lead to pollution should be responsible for it. The Indian government has also established a number of regulations for controlling fume emissions. In 2003, Euro-III standard was launched in India.

Positive energized diplomacy and international energy cooperation

India is another example of a developing country which lacks oil and gas resources. Having 16% of the world's population, the demonstrated reserve of oil and gas in India is no more than 0.6% of that of the earth; over 70% of its energy market relies on imports. Along with its speeding up consumption of energy, its dependence on external energy is worse and worse. According to the forecast of its authorities, by 2030, 90% of India's oil and gas will be supplied by foreign countries. What's more, India suffers a terrible challenge due to its serious shortage of power supply and other energy sources. The two priorities for India's national security are border safety and the long-term stable supply of oil and gas to secure the safe and sound social and economic development. Therefore, India had to promulgate a new plan of comprehensive energy policy in September 2005. The most remarkable feature of the plan is the prioritization of energy safety as India's most important external strategy via emphasizing the overall construction of an energized diplomacy strategy to secure the country's energy supply for achieving three objectives. First, India shall expand petroleum supply area and new import channels to ensure the long-term stability of the energy supply at home and abroad. Second, India shall gradually establish an extensive energy network in South Asia to ensure the mutual delivery of power supply, oil and natural gas among South Asian countries. Finally, it shall encourage the Indian petroleum companies to purchase more stakes of foreign oilfields to safely obtain long-term overseas energy supply at reasonable and stable prices rather than being affected by the price fluctuations of the international oil futures market.

Compared to other energy consumers in Asia, India's energy security greatly benefits from its special geography so that it can foster its security strategies of energy and national defense synchronously. Therefore, energy security is an important and practical part of its overall national strategy. India's existing strategy of external energy security can be summarized as one line and three regions, namely the international energy shipping route of the Persian Gulf, the Indian Ocean, and the Persian Gulf-the Indian Ocean-the Strait of Malacca as well as the three directions of north, west, and east to India. At present, India's energy strategy develops in the T shape, namely, obtaining the license of developing oilfields in Russia, building up a safe energy channel west to Iran and to the east, taking over the majority of export of natural gas in Myanmar. In addition, India also extends its influence to Africa and Latin America to form its global energized diplomacy,[34] which is shown as follows.

1. Constructing supply network of petroleum and natural gas via pipelines in the neighborhood to ensure the stability of energy supply

In order to transport the available oil and gas back to India from its neighboring regions, India has planned to build up three oil and gas pipelines.

It will pave the TPI (Turkmenistan, Afghanistan, Pakistan, and India) pipeline to the north, the IPI (Iran, Pakistan, and India) pipeline to the west, and the MBI (Myanmar, Bangladesh, and India) to the east. India has talked with Turkmenistan and Afghanistan about the need to extend the natural gas project of Turkmenistan, Afghanistan, and Pakistan (TAP) to the border between India and Pakistan after being accepted as an observer to the TAP project. In January 2005, the IPI project was officially launched. Its pipelines run 2,775km with a total investment of USD4.16 billion. India has reached a primary agreement with Myanmar and Bangladesh to launch the MBI project. In February 2005, the energy ministers of India, Myanmar, and Bangladesh reached a common understanding in Rangoon to transport the natural gas of Myanmar to Kolkata in the east of India via Bangladesh. The pipeline runs 290 km and is estimated to cost USD1 billion. Upon its completion, Myanmar is able to supply 60 billion cubic meters of natural gas to India annually. In addition to the three natural gas pipelines mentioned above, India is concerned with various strategic channels of transporting petroleum out of the Caspian Sea, for example, active participation in the Egyptian oil pipeline project connecting the Mediterranean Sea and the Red Sea, the "Blue Stream" pipeline project that covers the Caspian Sea, the Black Sea, and Kazakhstan, the project to deliver crude oil from the Caspian Sea to the Persian Gulf via Iran, etc.

2. Promoting regional cooperation and establishing energy center in south Asia

In order to carry out its new strategy of overseas energy, India positively adjusts and improves its relations with its small neighboring countries and attaches importance to the regional cooperation in South Asia. First, in order to ensure the early operation of the three pipelines, India promises it will offer road tolls of USD100 million to Bangladesh annually, and compromises on the distribution of the Ganges water to win Bengal support for the MBI project. Second, in line with the strong complementary feature of energy sources in South Asian countries, India proposes to set up an energy coordination agency in this region, and build up the South Asian energy network based on three pipelines for the purpose of realizing the complementary and cooperative development of the countries in this region. India seeks the cooperative development of the Bay of Bengal with Bangladesh, which boasts abundant natural gas. Apart from the demonstrated net reserves of 15 trillion cubic feet, the undiscovered reserves of 32.1 trillion cubic feet are estimated according to the United State Geological Survey (USGS). India also plans to import power supply from Nepal and Bhutan.

In 2002, India Petroleum Corporation invested USD100 million to enter the oil market of Sri Lanka. In 2003, India exported petroleum products of 480,000 tons valued at USD130 million to Sri Lanka. In 2004, India supplied Sri Lanka 1.5 million tons of petroleum products to meet the requirement of building 100 gasoline stations there. India has been licensed to hire the oil tank in Trincomalee for 35 years, which has an oil reserve capacity of 1 million tons.[35] All the activities mentioned above not only sped up the economic cooperation in South Asia, but also consolidated India's leadership in that region to a certain extent.

3. Actively attending the development of overseas resources of petroleum and natural gas with a focus on the Mideast and Russia

Because 60% of its imported oil and gas is produced in the Mideast, India broke the U.S. and other Western countries' sanctions imposed on Iran and developed a close relationship with the country. India has agreed to jointly develop the oilfield in South Pars with Iran.[36] In January 2005, India and Iran reached an agreement of natural gas trade that lasts 25 years valued at USD40 billion based on which India would import 5 million tons of liquefied natural gas from Iran, and help Iran to develop two oilfields and one natural gas field. Moreover, India Oil and Natural Gas Corporation (ONGC) holds 20% of the stake of Iran's biggest marine oilfield in Yadavaran.[37] India and Saudi Arabia have founded a number of joint ventures of petroleum, and it imports 24 million tons of crude oil from Saudi Arabia every year. In January 2006, India and Saudi Arabia signed the *Delhi Declaration* aimed at enhancing the mutual energy cooperation. The Indian enterprises would invest the chemical fertilizer industry in Saudi Arabia, and Saudi Arabia, in turn, will invest the petroleum refinery and oil product sales as well as the construction of oil tanks in India. In April 1993, India and Oman signed the agreement to jointly pave a submarine gas pipeline of 900 miles long to import natural gas from Oman. Besides, India Petroleum Corporation takes over 20% of the stake of an oil and gas area in Oman where it operates jointly with Total-Fina-Elf Corporation.

At the same time, India attaches high importance to expanding its cooperation with Russia on energy strategy based on its traditional ally relationship with Russia. The two countries have maintained a good relationship since the period of the Cold War. India longs for Russian petroleum resources and advanced development technology. Russia focuses more on consolidating their partnership of strategic cooperation, so the energy cooperation naturally turns to be the new highlight of their relationship. The Indian Minster of Petroleum once mentioned to the public that over the past five decades Russia has guaranteed India's territory complete access and India expects that Russia will continue to secure its energy sources in the future 50 years. During Vladimir Putin's visit to India in December 2004, both countries signed an energy cooperation agreement that India would invest USD3 billion in two Russian oilfields, and at the same time Russia would provide India with technical support for its building the IPI project. In February 2005, the Indian minister of petroleum paid a visit to Russia when the India Natural Gas Corporation signed up a memorandum with the Russian Gazprom (Natural Gas Industry Ltd., Co.) for jointly developing in the sector of exploitation and refinery of oil and gas, and reached an overall agreement for Phase III of the natural gas project in Sakhalin and the like. As an important step of deepening the "energy strategy partnership" between India and Russia, India Petroleum and Natural Gas reached a memorandum with the Russian Gazprom (Natural Gas Industry Ltd., Co.) in the end of 2009 for the strategic joint development among India, Russia, and the third country in the sector of exploitation and refinery of oil and gas. In recent years, India has frequently appointed senior officials to visit the Central Asian countries, added diplomatic agencies and military bases there, and put forward the proposal of hosting the "Central Asian Meeting of Energy Producers."[38] Through the means of fostering economy with politics, India has reached a series of energy cooperation agreements with Central Asian countries including the stake purchase of exploiting four oilfields in Kazakhstan, the import of natural gas from Turkmenistan, etc.

In addition to setting up the energy transport network centered in India, it has also reinforced cooperation with those countries in Southeast Asia and Latin America, which have no direct geopolitical relations with it, in energy exploration, exploitation, refinery, and stake purchase as well as expanding the stable supply and reserve of energy, in particular petroleum and natural gas. India has also cooperated with developed countries in the fields of energy conservation technology and renewable energy. For example, it has cooperated with the U.S. for developing nuclear energy.[39] In July 2005, India and the U.S. reached the *Civilian Nuclear Cooperation Agreement*, which was officially signed in March 2006.

4. Exploring and fostering the Asian dialogue mechanism of energy

Aiming at the negative competitions among the Asian countries when they purchased petroleum in the Mideast and the so-called "petroleum premium for Asian countries,"[40] India initiated that the production and consumption countries of petroleum and natural gas should establish a regional market to secure the stable supply and reasonable pricing system. In January 2005, India held the first Asian ministerial roundtable of Petroleum Economic Cooperation in New Delhi where the participants from China, Japan, Korea, Kuwait, Saudi Arabia, Iran, Qatar, the United Arab Emirates (UAE), and other major petroleum production and consumption countries as well as the representatives from the International Energy Agency, the Organization of Petroleum Exporting Countries (OPEC), and the International Energy Forum convened for discussing the establishment of a dialogue mechanism, promoting cooperation in the energy sector, jointly developing the market and establishing strategic reserves among Asian countries.[41] At the conference, India and other energy consumption countries such as China, Japan, and Korea reached the important agreement to cope with the premium in Asia and the petroleum safety together. In January 2009, India hosted the Asian ministerial meeting of petroleum consuming and supplying countries again, probing and attempting the design of establishing the community of the Asian petroleum consumption countries.

In short, India's external energy strategy features three points, i.e. a variety of sources, a focus on pipelines, and a diplomacy-led approach. In an overall manner, it is actively striving to obtain overseas resources of petroleum and natural gas and undertaking energized diplomacy and international cooperation of energy.

Sino-Indian Energy Cooperation

At the same time, it is an important part of the Indian external energy strategy to carry out energy cooperation with its eastern neighbor, China. As a matter of fact, the two countries have supported each other in actively exploring and fostering the dialogue mechanism of international energy. In 2005, China took an active part in the first Asian Ministerial Roundtable for Petroleum Economic Cooperation held in New Delhi, India as well as the 2009 Asian Ministerial Meeting for petroleum consuming and Supplying countries. Also, India has actively joined the mechanism of the Energy Ministers' Meeting initiated by China, which was attended by China, India, Japan, the Republic of Korea, and the United States. China and India have worked together to explore effective international and multi-lateral cooperation for the purpose of avoiding the premium of petroleum in Asia, carrying out overseas cooperation, and developing alternative energies. What's more, in the past decade, the petroleum enterprises from China and India have actively boosted the overall development of overseas petroleum and natural gas. Their representatives can be seen at the same time in a number of negotiations of regional oilfield projects. Their common demand of energy leads to different cooperation of their petroleum enterprises in overseas projects.

Their cooperation in the Sudan project is regarded as a model. The Indian ONGC and China's CNPC jointly developed the oilfield in Malut, Sudan, which helped to reduce the cost, improve the benefit, and exchange technology. While the Chinese company was constructing its oil refinery in Khartoum, its Indian counterpart there built a pipeline for transporting oil product to the port. In Iran, the Indian ONGP and the Chinese Sinopec Group jointly exploited the oil field in Yadavaran where Sinopec holds 50% of its equity, ONGP 20%, and Iran the remaining 30%. In Russia, the petroleum companies from the two countries undertook cooperation with the Russian national oil company Rosneft in the petroleum and natural gas sector, respectively. In Kazakhstan, the Indian ONGP also expressed positive intent to join the foundation of the Sino-Kazakhstan petroleum pipeline.

In February 2005, the Indian GAIL and the Chinese CHINAGAS reached an agreement. The former would invest USD243 million to buy 9% of the stake of the latter, which was the first successful cooperation between the two countries in downstream energy activities. In August 2005, a senior delegation headed by Ahmed, who was responsible for the international cooperation at India's Ministry of Petroleum and Natural Gas, paid a visit to China to discuss the opportunity of mutual cooperation on the basis of securing their own energy, especially the joint purchase for overseas energy properties including petroleum and natural gas as well as jointly coping with the challenge of lacking energy. On December 20 of the same year, at the cost of USD573 million, China and India succeeded in jointly purchasing Petro-Canada's oil and gas properties in Syria, which is also a successful record[42] of the joint-venture founded by CNPC and India ONGC. In August 2006, China Petroleum Chemical Corporation (CPCC) and the overseas subsidiary of India ONGC succeeded in jointly bidding for purchasing 50% of the stake of Omimex de Colombia, each holding 25% of its stake. Under such encouragement, other Indian energy enterprises are keen to reach agreements with their Chinese counterparts to jointly purchase more oil properties from the third country.

In January 2006, when Mani Shankar Aiyar, minister of Indian Petroleum and Natural Gas headed a delegation to visit China, both sides signed the *Memorandum of Strengthening Cooperation of Petroleum and Natural Gas*, in which the two countries decided to reinforce their mutual energy cooperation, stabilize the pricing system of the Asian energy market involving crude oil development and refining, develop ethanol-blended gasoline, improve energy efficiency, establish a working group of energy cooperation for holding meetings at least once a year, and reach the common understanding of avoiding conflicts on bidding for the same international projects for the purpose of promoting the two countries to take an important further step in their energy cooperation. Aiyar mentioned that India could learn a lot from China in the field of developing energy sources, and China could also be inspired from India's experience in turn.[43] In 2006, during Chinese President Hu Jintao's visit to India, the two countries published the *Joint Declaration* as follows:

> Both sides agree to fully implement the provisions of the *Memorandum on the Cooperation in the Field of Oil and Natural Gas* signed in January 2006 and encourage the collaboration between their enterprises, including through joint exploration and development of hydrocarbon resources in third countries.
>
> Considering that for both India and China, expansion of the civilian nuclear energy programme is an essential and important component of their national energy plans to ensure energy security, the two sides agree to promote cooperation in the field of nuclear energy, consistent with their respective international commitments.
>
> Energy security constitutes a vital and strategic issue for oil producing and consuming countries alike. It is consistent with the common interest of the two sides to establish an international energy order, which is fair, equitable, secure and stable, and to the benefit of the entire international community. Both sides shall also make joint efforts, bilaterally as well as multilaterally, to diversify the global energy mix, and increase the share in it of renewable energy sources. Global energy systems should take into account and meet the energy needs of both countries, as a part and parcel of a stable, predictable, secure, and clean energy future.[44]

Naturally, facing their common challenge of lacking oil and gas, the mutual competition is inevitable. But for the two countries, the most advantageous option for them should be to establish a long-term partnership that benefits both of them so as to lower their cost of investment on overseas oil and gas projects and expand their chances of success by following the orderly competitions of the market instead of destructive ones that would harm both. Moreover, besides the cooperative bidding for overseas resources of oil and gas, their cooperation in energy can also expand to extensive sectors such as hydraulic power generation, nuclear utilization, development of new energy sources, and renewable energy as well as energy conservation and emission reduction. Besides bilateral cooperation, as the two major Asian energy consumers and importers, China and India can also reinforce their mutual coordination through available multilateral cooperation mechanisms such as the Asian Energy Ministerial Roundtable, the Energy Ministerial Meeting of China, India, Japan, Korea, and the U.S., the trilateral cooperation of China, Russia, and India, the BRICS (Brazil, Russia, India and China) cooperation mechanism, the Shanghai Cooperation Organization (SCO), and the East Asia Summit (EAS). Or, we can probe the establishment of multilateral energy cooperation mechanism by which China and India can play an active role in initiating the "Asian Energy Cooperation Organization" similar to the International Energy Agency. In addition, as for deepening energy cooperation between the two countries, the establishment of the joint coordination mechanism of regional strategic reserves for petroleum is the tendency for them to improve the utilization of energy, spread technology of energy conservation, develop new energy sources, and carry out mutual communication and collaboration. We are confident that the further cooperation in the energy sector between the two largest developing countries worldwide—China and India, the better the contribution to securing energy sources for the two countries, Asia, and even the whole world.

Notes

1. Lin Boqiang 林伯強, ed., *Report on China's Energy Development for 2008* 中國能源發展報告 2008 (Beijing: China Financial and Economic Publishing House, 2008), 262.
2. 國務院新聞辦, *China's Energy Situation and Policies (White Paper)* 《中國的能源狀況與政策》（白皮書）, Beijing, Dec. 26, 2007.
3. *BP Statistical Review of World Energy*, Jun. 2011, p.3.

   Most of the energy statistics data if not labeled specially in the paper came from this source. According to the statistical practices of energy, the data which refers to China is only from the Mainland China minus Hong Kong, Macau, and Taiwan.
4. *Oil & Gas Journal* (Dec. 20, 2010; Mar. 7, 2011).
5. Jiang Zemin 江澤民, "Thoughts on China's energy" 對中國能源問題的思考, *Journal of Shanghai Jiaotong University* 上海交通大學學報 3 (2008).
6. China's State Council Information Office 國務院新聞辦, *China's Peaceful Development (White Paper)* 《中國的和平發展》（白皮書）, Beijing, Sep. 6, 2011.
7. Refer to China's State Council Information Office, *China's Energy Situation and Policies (White Paper)*, 2007.
8. He Jun 賀軍, and ZhouWei 周偉, Saving costs is more urgent than opening sources "節流" 比 "開源" 更緊迫, *Social Sciences Weekly* 社會科學報 (Aug. 25, 2011).
9. Wang Qianhai 王前海, "Saving: Urgent call of resources, environment and development" 節約：資源、環境與發展的沉重呼喚, *China Information News* 中國資訊報, Aug. 11, 2005.
10. Ni Jianmin 倪健民, ed., *National Security Report* 國家能源安全報告 (Beijing: People's Publishing House, 2005), 58.
11. Tian Chunrong 田春榮, "Analysis of China's oil import and export in 2007" 2009 年中國石油進出口狀況分析, *International Petroleum Economics Monthly* 3 (2010).
12. Zhang Kang 張抗, *Geopolitics of Oil and Gas of the World and China* 中國和世界地緣油氣 (Beijing: Geological Press, 2009), 87.
13. International Energy Agency 國際能源署, *World Energy Outlook 2004* 世界能源展望 2004 (Beijing: China Petrochemical Press, 2006), 156.
14. "The 11th five-year plan of national economic and social development" 國民經濟和社會發展第十一個五年規劃綱要, *People's Daily* 人民日報, Mar. 17, 2006.
15. Refer to China's State Council Information Office, *China's Energy Situation and Policies (White Paper)*, 2007.
16. Tu Lufang 塗露芳, "Proportion of China's renewable energy consumption increased by 9.9%" 中國可再生能源消費比重升至 9.9%, *Beijing Daily* 北京日報, Jan. 21, 2010.
17. "Second-line of west toward east natural gas transmission is completed and natural gas in central Asia arrived in the pearl river delta" 西氣東輸二線幹線貫通，中亞天然氣運抵珠三角, *China News Service* 中新社, Guangzhou, Jun. 30, 2011.
18. "China signed the agreement on implementation of international thermonuclear experimental reactor" 我正式簽署國際熱核聚變實驗堆計畫聯合實施協定, *Xinhua News Agency* 新華社, Beijing, Jan. 27, 2010.
19. Hu Jintao 胡錦濤, "Join hands to address climate challenge" 攜手應對氣候變化挑戰, *Xinhua News Agency* 新 華 社 (Speech, United Nations Summit on Climate Change, New York, U.S., Sep. 22, 2009).
20. Wang Lianhe 王聯合, "China and the international energy agency: A standard study" 中國與國際能源機構：一項規範研究, *International Review* 國際觀察 4 (2009).

21. Xia Yishan 夏義善, and Fu Quanzhang 傅全章, eds., *Study on China's Development Strategy of International Energy Sources* 中國國際能源發展戰略研究 (Beijing: Word Affairs Press, 2009), 23.

22. Pan Jiping et al. 潘繼平 等, "Opportunity of China's overseas exploration and development of overseas oil and gas, challenges and measures" 中國境外油氣勘探開發的機遇、挑戰和對策, *International Petroleum Economics* 國際石油經濟, no.5 (2009).

23. Zhang Yichi 張一馳, "Study on the trend of industry to promote cooperative win-win" 研究行業大勢，促進合作共贏, *International Pertoleum Economics* 國際石油經濟, no.1–2 (2011).

24. Yu Jianhua et al. 余建華 等, *International Energy Politics and China's International Energy Cooperation* 國際能源政治與中國國際能源合作 (Changchun: Changchun Publishing House, 2011), Chapter 6.

25. Shen Kaiyan, et al. 沈開豔 等, *Indian Economic Reform and Development over 20 Years: Theory, Evidence and Comparison* 印度經濟改革發展二十年：理論、實證與比較 (Shanghai: Shanghai People's Publishing House, 2011), 140–141.

26. *BP Statistical Review of World Energy*, Jun. 2011, p.43.

27. International Energy Agency 國際能源署, *World Energy Outlook 2002* 世界能源展望 2002 (Beijing: China Petrochemical Press, 2004), 158.

28. International Energy Agency 國際能源署, *World Energy Outlook 2004* 世界能源展望 2004 (Beijing: China Petrochemical Press, 2006), 159.

29. *BP Statistical Review of World Energy*, Jun. 2011, p.30–33.

30. Zhang Kang 張抗, *Geopolitical Petroleum and Natural Gas in China and the World* 中國和世界地緣油氣 (Beijing: Geology Press, 2009), 342;

BP Statistical Review of World Energy, Jun. 2011, p. 6–8.

31. Sun Shihai 孫士海, and Ge Weijun 葛維鈞, *India* 印度 (Beijing: China Social Sciences Press, 2003), 26.

32. Xu Bo 徐博, and Shan Weiguo 單衛國, "India's Choice for Energy" 印度的能源選擇, *China Petroleum and Petrochemical Journal* 中國石油石化, no.11 (2003).

33. Chen Fengying 陳鳳英, and Zhao Hongtu 趙宏圖, eds., *Global Energy Structure* 全球能源大棋局 (Beijing: Shi Shi Publishing House, 2005), 255.

34. "Lessons learned from India's policies on energy" 印度能源政策對我國的啟示 (Dec. 25, 2007), http: / / www.in-en.com.

35. *The Economic Times*, May 28, 2003.

36. Pramit Mitra, "Indian diplomacy energized by search for oil," *Yale Global*, Mar. 14, 2005.

37. *China News Service* 中新網, Jan. 11, 2005, www.chinanews.com.

38. Subodh Atal, "The New Great Game" 新的中亞大角逐, *The National Interest (The U.S.)* 國家利益（美國）(Fall, 2005).

39. Zhao Gancheng 趙干城, *India: Status and Diplomacy as a Major Power* 印度：大國地位與大國外交, (Shanghai: Shanghai People's Publishing House, 2009), 200–212.

40. When selling crude oil, the Middle Eastern countries charge the Asian countries USD1 or 2 per barrel more than charge the American and European countries. Thus, the Asian countries have to pay extra USD10 billion annually.

41. Tan Dongyun 譚冬雲, and Zhang Kang 張抗, "Prospect of Sino-Indian Energy Cooperation" 中印能源合作前景, *International Petroleum Economics* 國際石油經濟, no.4 (2005).

42. *Reuters*, New Delhi, Dec. 20, 2005.

43. *Associated Press*, New Delhi, Jan. 10, 2006.

44. *Sino-India Joint Declaration* 中國和印度聯合宣言, website of the Ministry of Foreign Affairs of the PRC, Nov. 22, 2006, http: / / www.fmprc.gov.cn / chn / pds / gjhdq / gj / yz / 1206_42 / 1207 / t281112.htm.

14

Chapter

The Rise of China and India and the Future International Order[1]

Shang Huipeng

For a long time, the rise of China and India has drawn much of the world's attention.[2] However, due to the following simple but important facts, the significance of the simultaneous rise of the two nations in the future, whether to the world or to the two countries themselves, has not been recognized properly. The reasons for the needed recognition are as follows. First, the total population of the two nations is about 2.4 billion, which accounts for over 1/3 of that of the whole world. Second, the economies of both nations are growing at an annual rate of nearly 10%. Third, both of the countries are giant civilizations with long histories different from those of Western countries. Fourth, the two cultures are geographically adjacent and share a similar development path. Finally, the two civilizations have historically had a unique experience of peaceful interaction. Compared with the rise of either of the two countries, the rise of all the non-Western countries and regions together, or the rise of Japan and the "Four Asian Tigers," are not comparable. And, in this article, from a different perspective, three ideas will be elaborated on regarding the rise of China and India.

1. **Due to the influence of the concept of modernization, the world has not fully recognized the significance of the rise of China and India in regards to these two civilizations. The present development pattern of the two countries chasing the West is not sustainable, and the countries need to leap from thinking of "modernization" to consider the future from the perspective of a "new civilization."**

The total population of China and India is twice that of Europe and North America. This amazing number indicates numerous opportunities and markets for greedy investors. For example, if everyone there buys only one pocket of tissue or one bottle of shampoo, the market will be astronomical. But, we have to think about a question first: Is the present development pattern sustainable? The "modern" way of life which has its origin in the West and has been followed all around the world is established on the following two basic values; first, the happiness of people is established on the satisfaction of their constant desire for material goods; second, the reasoning of human beings is that they can limitlessly alter nature to create more material wealth. It must be noted, however, that such basic values are problematic. The affluence of the West has stimulated our various desires, but the desire of people to pursue enjoyment and comfortable life is endless. While we are celebrating our economic achievements, our mind and society are eroded unconsciously by the idea of "consumerism." Whether it is in China or India, some rich people began to live a life of luxury,[3] and the consumerism and hedonism found there have drawn more to follow. Many people are dreaming of leading a life like the rich Americans, i.e., living in a big house, having several cars, private yachts, and aircraft, using luxurious items and travelling around the world in Boeing airplanes. The dream is beautiful, but the problem is, can we achieve the same? The fact is, in his whole life, one ordinary American (with a life expectancy of 80 years) will consume 262.4 tons of oil and 1,000 trees. If the Chinese and the Indians want to reach the American standard of living, even without considering the factors of population growth (it is estimated that the population of India will exceed that of China in 2031), these figures would be astronomical if multiplied by 2.4 billion.

To give an example which may be indecent but common, in the past when the Chinese people and the Indians went to the toilet, they did not use toilet paper, for paper was expensive and rarely used in their daily life. Now, however, lifestyles have changed and tissues, toilet paper, napkins, and sanitary napkins are widely used in their daily lives. If the Indians and the Chinese reach the American standard of living, in terms of toilet paper alone, the amount of demand would be amazing. It has been estimated that if China and India catch up with the current American paper consumption, the total consumption will reach over 500 million tons, which is 3 or 4 times the world's current paper production (161 million tons). If the whole world reaches such a standard, there would never be enough paper even if we cut down all the trees. Another example, the annual food consumption per capita in the U.S. is about 1,046 kg, 6 times that of the Indians; the annual consumption of meat per capita in the U.S. is 124 kg, 30 times that of the Indians.[4] India has quite a lot of vegetarians (according to different sources, the proportion of the vegetarians in India varies from 30% to 60%, but on the most conservative estimate, the population of vegetarians in India is over 300 million), and the mainstream society in India does not eat meat. And in China, the annual meat consumption per capita was 4 kg 60 years ago, and as the lifestyles there have been westernized, this figure was 54.8 kg in 2008. Although this number is still less than half of the American per capita consumption, it has increased by 12.7 times compared with that of 60 years ago. At present, the world's population has reached 7 billion, and scientists estimate that if all the people are vegetarians, the 1.4 billion hectares of arable land on the Earth can support only 9 to 10 billion people. But there are quite a number of people who refuse to be vegetarians, and along with the "modernization" in the non-Western world, the consumption of meat is still on the rise. If this continues, the population which the Earth can support will be greatly decreased. Therefore, besides the health problems and mental problems caused by eating meat, just think of the issue from the perspective of protecting the environment alone when deciding whether to take a Western lifestyle or one like the Indians. Is not it a good question worthy of thorough consideration?

Mahatma Gandhi had once clearly recognized that if both China and India had lifestyles like those in the Western world, our Earth's resources would not be enough to support all the people. Continuing the present consumerist lifestyle, what comes would not be "the end of history,"[5] but the end of human civilization. The American way of life cannot be copied, for its current model of economic development is not sustainable, and its fossil fuel-based, car-centered, pursuit of comfort and convenience, and the disposable economic model of consumerism, do not apply to China and India. In the long run, the rising China and India should not follow the current model, the world should abandon this mode, and the affluent United States and Europe should take the lead. Recently, the "Occupy Wall Street" movement occurred across the U.S. with protests against the greed of Wall Street capitalists. The protesters accused the U.S. government of providing bailouts to a small number of financial institutions while leaving the majority of people in financial difficulties. In fact, greed is not only the sin of the Wall Street financiers, but the sin of the capitalist system which is spreading over the world. This system has stimulated the greedy nature in human beings to the maximum, and the Wall Street financial oligarchy is only pushed to the top of the waves by this system. The Americans should also criticize capitalism as a system and culture, and reflect on their own lifestyle of surviving on debt and on consumerism.[6]

In concern for the human race, we need to reflect on the entire human consumerism lifestyle, and to explore a solution from the traditions of China and India. In history, only the rise of Japan, a non-Western society, can be viewed as an example for the West, but its rise did not provide any noteworthy contribution to the integration of civilization. Japan achieved the modernization of society in a very short time, and became one of the Western countries. Seen from a linear and modern point of view, the rise of Japan is undoubtedly a success, an "excellent student"; from the perspective of civilization, however, it is a failure, for it completely took a Western road and wavered in its civilization identity, providing little practical experience for the integration of civilizations from the East and the West. And in this regard, it is a "poor student."

Unlike Japan, the profound cultural heritages of China and India can provide rich resources for the integration of civilizations to create a new civilization. The traditional heritage of these two civilizations has prevented the two civilizations from being modernized as quickly as Japan. But in terms of the integration of civilizations, it is not necessarily a bad thing, for it left enough time for the two countries to reflect on and to select and choose from their own experience and the modern civilization which originated in the West and which has now spread wildly over the whole world. The Western civilizations have contributed to the concept of freedom, independence, rights, equality, development, and progress, and these ideals, based on concern for the individual, have promoted personal development and brought well-being for humans. But problems such as consumerism, the plundering of the environment, the destruction of the family unit, poor interpersonal relationships, and mental loneliness have arisen. In contrast, the key concepts in Chinese civilization are filial piety, loyalty, favor, righteousness, respect, trust, and reward, among other ideas, with an emphasis on the harmony of interpersonal relationships. And the key words in Indian civilization are Brahma, Atman, Dharma, Maya, and Mokosa, among other terms, with an emphasis on the mental harmony of human beings. Neither of the two civilizations has focused on developing the individual, nor have they put any emphasis on how to satisfy the desire for materials, for both of them held that, compared with "the individual," the "mutuality" of people is more important; instead of meeting the desires for materials, Indian culture values more the harmony of interpersonal relationships and spiritual fulfillment. This cultural orientation has led to the weakness and poverty of the two civilizations in the modern world.

Having encountered the powerful Western civilization, the two ancient civilizations awoke and began to learn from the West, develop their economies, improve their material lives, and eliminate hunger and disease. We all hope to shake off poverty and lead a prosperous and decent modern life and our life does change in this way. This is not wrong in itself, for to make over 1/3 of the world's population get rid of poverty and live a decent life is a great contribution to the overall well-being of humankind. However, when China and India reach a certain level in the aspect of material development, their consideration should be beyond "modernization" but take a new look at the experience of the civilizations of China and India. The two civilizations have gained much experience in thriftiness and restriction, and placed emphasis on interpersonal harmony and mental harmony, but due to their degeneracy in modern times, all their experience has been ignored. The wise men of India (Buddha, Mahatma Gandhi, etc.) and China (Confucius, Lao Tzu, etc.) have a clear understanding of the serious consequences caused by human desires and the stimulation of those desires, and their warning is not out of date today. Today, the rise of China and India is never simply an economic rise, but a renaissance of the two ancient civilizations. These two civilizations in the world weigh far more than their GDP.

In this process, both China and India need to review the experiences of their own civilizations, and explore resources from which to find a way to make up for the defects of modern civilization established on over-consumption and over-production. These experiences can be integrated with the modern industrial civilization originating in the West to produce a new civilization which will restrain the human desires, pay more attention to interpersonal relationships, and lead to a more harmonious relationship between man and nature.[7] The rich cultural heritage of China and India is able to contribute to create this new civilization.[8] Of course, here I am just talking on the long-term results of the current mode of economic development, and I just want to mention that, if we go along the current mode of development, there will be serious consequences. In fact, the moderate economic development of China and India and the creation of a new civilization in the future should be aspects of a mutually reinforcing relationship. To eradicate hunger, poverty, malnutrition for China and India is very important, for, on one hand, if more than one-third of the world is in hunger and poverty, there would not be true well-being for mankind, and the rise of China and India could not take place. On the other hand, if we do not take the new civilization of sustainable economic development into consideration, the significance of the rise of China and India is out of the question.

2. **Influenced by geopolitics, the world does not have enough understanding of the significance of the rise of China and India for the future international order. There is a need to break free from the shackles of geopolitical thinking in order to think from a "geo-civilized" perspective about the rise of China and India and the future international order. The rise of China and India, while internalizing the existing international order, needs also to supplement the inadequacy of the existing international order to form a new international order which would parallel the current one.**

At present, most people view the impact of the rise of China and India on the international order from the geopolitical perspective. According to this thinking, all countries are in the fight for their own "living space," and the rise of new forces is bound to break the original balance of power and cause a redistribution of power, which will unavoidably be accompanied by conflict and finally be resolved through war and reach a new world order balance. Thus, conclusions would naturally be drawn that "the rise of China and India will challenge the existing international order," or that "the rise of China and India will challenge the U.S. position," and that "there will be a conflict of the dragon and elephant between China and India," and so on. With the two countries' increase of demand of resources, the public is asking a question, what is the impact of their rise on the world order? Can the two big countries get along?[9] If these two countries also think over the problem from the geopolitical point of view, chasing their own interests desperately to develop their own "hard power," there will not only be conflict between China and India and the existing international order, but also between the two countries themselves; according to the logic of the existing international relations, the final resolution to this problem is nothing but war. The changes of powerful forces of the world in modern times have all taken this road.

The geo-politics is actually the basis of international order. The existing international order was established after the signing of the Treaty of Westphalia in 1648. This order has contributed a lot for mankind in order to solve the relations between states. To be frank, the current international order itself is in question. First, the order places too much emphasis on national interests. The action organizations of each country are struggling to maximize their own interests. Second, this order emphasizes strength, "the law of the jungle" plays a significant role. The stronger has the right to say, and the weaker is bullied, and therefore the establishment of this order is filled with war, conquest, slavery, exploitation, and oppression. China and India, being poor and weak, have been ravaged in this order. After all, these features are based on the experience of Western individual social experience, and it is the externalization of the personal social relationships (originally, this order included only the Western countries; non-Western countries applied and joined this order later). Some of the current major international issues, such as the nuclear predicament, environmental destruction, terrorism, etc., are all rooted in the existing international order and international rules. The root of the difficulty to solve the nuclear weapons dilemma is that the rules of the game under the current international order is a rule for the stronger, i.e., the most powerful one is the boss, so it is unfair for those countries without nuclear weapons. If the countries who possess nuclear weapons do not abandon their nuclear weapons first, it can be expected that there will be more and more countries with nuclear weapons. Another example, to solve the pollution problems, unless the self-interested behavior of international actors is restrained, no optimistic prospect can be achieved. Notice that in human history, the two largest and most cruel wars occurred under the modern international order in which the emphasis was on benefits and power. Though a non-Western country, Japan has also taken such a road. When encountering the Western powers, modern Japan soon recognized that the modern international order is an order for the powerful, and they quickly internalized this order, and got rid of the colonial fate of Western powers, while they also embarked on a road of aggression and plundering colonies. The rise of Japan has already posed a challenge to the international order, but this challenge is just breaking the balance under the existing international order, but this rise occurred in the Western international order, and happened in the competition and the redistribution of rights among the great powers in the contemporary international order. It had crawled under the world power after its failure of waging the war. Japan does not have any doubt on the existing international order, nor did it participate in the formulation of international rules; it has been a passive recipient of international rules.

But the logic of the rise and fall of the big powers under the modern international order may not be applicable to the rise of China and India. China and India are state actors embedded in rich civilization systems, forming a world of their own. Neither of them is "a modern nation country" in the Western sense, and their behavior in the international arena cannot be completely interpreted from the perspective of the existing international order. Rather, it should be understood as a civilization body. Historically, for quite a long time, these two countries were in the unique center of the international sub-order which is implementing different principles of the modern international order. The East Asian order, centered on the ancient Chinese civilization, is characterized for its emphasis on the Chinese Confucian ideals of virtue and benevolence. And in certain periods in the history of the South Asian regions, there was also a South Asian order emphasizing the Hindu Grand Cult. The biggest difference between both the two orders and the orders of the Western world in history is that neither of them have had large-scale colonies as found in the Western order, and the maintenance of their order is not based on conquest with forces or slavery, but by their cultural attractions. The spread of China's Confucian culture, Buddhist culture of India, and Hindu culture in the surrounding areas was not through mandatory missionary work, but by peaceful means. In other words, these two civilizations' abilities to exert influence on the surrounding areas did not rely on hard power but soft power. In modern times, both of them have suffered from the historical experience of Western powers (colonial plunder), and thus it would not be possible for them to take the old road of external aggression and plunder, as was seen in the rise of the West. The rise of the two countries will not depend on the external conquest and plunder, but by their own peaceful development, and thus it would not be like the rise of Japan which caused violent conflict with the existing international order. To a certain extent, China and India have accepted the current international order and benefited from it, and therefore there is no need for them to challenge this order. For a long time in the future, China and India will focus more on the domestic affairs and economic development to ensure control of social unrest. It is no good for China and India to change the current U.S.-led international system, instead, to continue to follow the current global order will bring to them long-term interests. However, the unique experience of the civilizations of China and India makes it impossible to fully internalize the existing international order and become its passive recipients. In fact, neither China nor India has fully internalized the existing international order. Many of their beliefs and behaviors on the current international affairs are strikingly similar, and both maintain a certain distance from the existing international order originating in the West. The concepts, such as the "Five Principles" posed by China and India for jointly handling international affairs, the policy of nonalignment proposed and carried out for a long time by India's Nehru, Mahatma Gandhi's non-violent ideology, and China's non-hegemony idea in international affairs, and the present concept of the harmonious world, are all beyond the realm of geopolitical thinking. China and India should recognize the problems of the current international order and, while accepting the existing international order, retain their own unique experience and consider contributing to make amendments to the drawbacks of the existing international order.

Today, there are more and more calls on the ethical principles in the international order. China and India should inherit their tradition of emphasizing their own cultural attractions, and develop their "soft power." If we only focus on the development of hard power, just like the powerful countries in the world, it would not only fail to solve the problem, but also bring more trouble to the world. China's Lao Tzu once said: "I have three treasures which I hold firmly: The first is compassion, the second is thriftiness, the third is unimportance."[10] The principles embodied in the "three treasures" are completely different from the principles of the existing international order, and I think for China and India, this has great significance of reference for the two newly minted international actors. With the two countries being increasingly affluent and powerful, there may be conflicts with the existing international order; but because of its inherent civilized characteristics and a restrained model of development, their rise relies more on the successful resolution of internal issues rather than foreign war and plunder. This process is bound to be very slow and fraught with difficulties, but it is more peaceful and stable. In the future, the relationship between these two actors and the existing international order, may neither be a relationship between the challenge and the challenged, nor between the fully assimilated and the have yet to be assimilated. It is likely to bypass the existing international order, or to relatively weaken the current international order or reduce the "Western" rules component to form a new international order which parallels the existing international order. Some Western scholars have seen this and may worry that the future is "a world without the West."[11] In fact, this is unfounded. What is more likely is an international sub-order which is no longer Western-centered but parallel to the current international order.

3. **Because of the two reasons mentioned above, the two civilizations of China and India are still unclear of the importance of giving up geopolitical thinking and taking a new path of win-win cooperation.**

Under the current international order, the rise of one power is inevitably associated with external expansion, which will result in strained relations with other neighboring countries in the region. Take Japan as an example. Its emergence as a new power was accompanied with invasion and plunders and thus it was hated by other countries around it. Its process of rise is isolated and without cooperation. It is the price it paid for sticking to the geopolitical road under the current international order. China and India should learn from Japan's lesson. Instead of persisting in the geopolitical thinking mode, they have to ponder the significance of cooperating with neighboring countries by taking the viewpoint of geo-civilization.[12] China and India are two big civilizations as well as the core players in the framework of the one-Asia order. The rise of the two countries should never threaten the other countries of the region and they have to persist in the path of resolving problems in a peaceful way and seeking friendship wherever they turn. As big powers within the region, China and India cannot simply perform according to their own interests and depend on self strength when handling relationships with other countries, but need to provide certain "public benefits" to countries around them by behaving in a way taking into consideration their individual culture and the principle of humanity and decency. This is very important when it comes to establishing a stable regional order. The main features of the "geo-civilization" paradigm are: Far-sighted vision, tolerance, peace, being grateful instead of vengeful, equality and mutual benefit, harmonious co-existence, and awareness of the world's commonwealth.[13] Although these are somewhat idealistic, these concepts are actually already included in the experience of the civilizations of China and India and are carried out by the two countries in implementing foreign affairs in the region. Of course, I am not here advocating regaining the splendor of big powers in the golden old days. What I want to say is that China and India should take great care in dealing with the feelings of the comparatively smaller countries in the vicinity, keep a humble attitude, and avoid bullying by posing as big and powerful countries. In this sense, Lao Tzu made a good point about how we should treat smaller countries. He said: What makes a great state is its being (like) a low-lying, down-flowing (stream); it becomes the center to which tend all the small states under heaven. To use the Daoist idea of the female: The female always overcomes the male by her stillness. Stillness may be considered a sort of abasement. Thus it is that a great state, by condescending to small states, gains them for itself; and that small states, by abasing themselves to a great state, win it over to them. In the one case, the abasement leads to gaining adherents, in the other case to procuring favor. The great state only wishes to unite men together and nourish them; a small state only wishes to be received by, and to serve, the other. Each gets what it desires, but the great state must learn to abase itself.[14]

China and India should proceed from the perspective of geo-civilization and rethink about the meaning of bilateral cooperation. Specifically, the two nations should no longer threaten each other, nor attempt to conquer each other. They should walk out of the shadow of historical conflicts and take the road of cooperation and mutual benefit as soon as possible. In history, China and India were mainly living in peace and there were basically no wars between the two countries. A great number of Chinese intellectual scholars once went to India for study in spite of difficulties and there were Indian scholars coming to China. This kind of peaceful experience of mutual study is not only special in the history of civilization but precious. Armed conflict between China and India happened only after the arrival of modern times and there was only once, which might be the result of adopting the geopolitical thinking set. At present, China and India still have territorial problems to solve. Now the two countries harbor deep suspicions against each other and conflicts around boundary and trade issues arise constantly. However, fortunately, the decision-makers of the two countries all know well about the likely serious consequences brought by the opposition and conflict of China and India so they carefully avoid worsening the situation. Elites from intellectual and political circles in the two countries have reached understanding about the competition and cooperation coming along with "the double rises" of China and India. Indian scholar and former minister of commerce, Jairam Ramesh put forward a new concept of CHINDIA including the idea of China-India cooperation.[15] This concept was warmly welcomed by Chinese scholars. When the former Indian Prime Minister Vajpayee visited China, he stated in his speech made in Peking University that "It is unavoidable human nature that two adjacent and equal neighbors see each other as competitors. But we must clearly understand that healthy competition greatly differs from vicious competition...We should focus on the simple fact that there are no objective factors for our discord and the feelings of being threatened by each other are unreasonable. This simple but important principle should serve as the foundation of our future partnership." I wish the leaders of the two countries can keep this wise opinion in mind and practice it out. If the two world's biggest developing countries can collaborate with each other at the world's fastest speed, the "Asian Age" might arrive soon.

Notes

1. This paper is one part of the "Study on Spreading China's Soft Power to India," the sub-project of the programme of "Studies of Spreading China's Soft Power to Other Countries," which is the national-funded key program of social sciences in 2008. The project number is 08&ZD057.
2. The latest report by *The Age* in Australia on Oct. 12th said that Australian Prime Minister Julia Gillard is about to make a new pack of strategies in response to the upcoming "Asian Age" introduced by the rise of China and India and has appointed advisory group to assist with the writing of government's white paper named "Australia in the Age of Asia" (http://world.huanqiu.com/roll/2011-10/2080249.html).
3. According to KPMG, one of the four largest accounting firms in the world, China will surpass Japan as the first luxury consumer. For this, *China Week* published an article entitled "Luxury Fever: The Hidden Logic behind Crazy Consumption" in its 10th issue in 2011. Another report said that the richest man in India, Mukesh Ambani, has been constructing the most expensive private house in Bombay, which will cost nearly USD2 billion and measure 173 meters in height (http://finance.people.com.cn/GB/42877/14372430.html).
4. The original article is published on the website of *The Times of India*, see its Chinese version at http://www.xjjjb.com/html/news/2008/5/19922.html.
5. "The end of history" is a judgment about the world's development trend made by the Japanese-American scholar Francis Fukuyama after the Cold War. In his preface to the famous book *The End of History and the Last Man* (Chinese Version, China Social Sciences Press 2003), he described the development trend of the current world based on consumerism like this: "Science and technology make the unlimited accumulation of wealth possible, which in turn fulfill the ever-expanding desires of mankind. Such a process continues to assimilate the whole human society, regardless of their different origin and cultures. All the countries which have undergone modernization become similar in the end: they have all achieved the unity of the nation based on the basis of centralized power, they are all pursuing urbanization, and in term of economy, they have all replaced the traditional forms of organization of the tribes and families with efficient and functional social organizations, they all provide education for their citizens, and link up through the intermedia of the global market and spread the cosmopolitan consumer culture."
6. According to statistics, in 2004, Americans' after-tax income was approximately USD8.647 trillion, and USD8.532 trillion was spent that year. The money deposited in banks was very little, and the savings rate is only 1.3%, which means that when Americans earn USD100, they save only USD1.3 in the bank. And another thing is borrowing money from banks. Many Americans not only save no money, but often borrow money from the banks to buy big-ticket items, or go on vacations they cannot afford. According to the statistics of the U.S. Federal Reserve Board, by the end of June 2011, the total credit of U.S. consumers had been up to nearly USD2.15 trillion, which means an average debt of more than USD7,000 per person according to the country's population, which does not include the debt of more than USD5 trillion loans for buying houses (*Xinhua Net*, Nov.06, 2005, http://finance.sina.com.cn).
7. The new civilization mentioned here is similar to the concept of "ecological civilization" discussed by some Chinese scholars. See Huang Zhansen 黄栴森, "The philosophical foundation of ecological civilization" 生態文明建設的哲學基礎, *Xinhua Digest* 新華文摘, no. 10 (2012):38. Other articles include Pang Shiwei 龐世偉, "Revolution of consumption concepts and ecological civilization and the construction of contemporary ecological consumption view based on aesthetics" 消費觀變革與生態文明——兼論當代審美型生態消費觀的構建, http://khnews.zjol.com.cn/khnews/system/2011/05/14/013738105.shtml.
8. This idea of the author was expressed in other places too. See Shang Huipeng 尚會鵬, "Integration of civilizations and CHIDIA" 文明整合與CHIDIA, *Journal of Shenzhen University* 深圳大學學報, no. 2 (2007); also see Shang Huipeng 尚會鵬, *The Hindu Cultural Traditions: A Comparative Study with China* 印度文化傳統研究：比較文化的視野 (Beijing: Peking University Press, 2004), 304–331

9. Worries associated with the rise of China and India can be found in various reports and books. The latest article in this aspect is written by Gideon Rachman published in *Financial Times* in the U.K. The name of the article is "A Test of Will" in which the author talked about people's concerns regarding the rise of the two countries. See the Chinese version at http://www.ftchinese.com/story/001039944?page=1.

10. Lao Tze 老子, *The Tao Te Ching* 道德經, Chapter 67.

11. "A World without the West" 沒有西方的世界, *The National Interest* 國家利益 (Jul.–Aug 2007). See more at http://news.xinhuanet.com/world/2007-08/02/content_6463617.htm.

12. The author of this paper agrees with the famous Chinese Indian scholar Tan Zhong about applying the idea of "geo-civilization" to the study of international studies. Tan once said, "The Westerners are not neglecting the significance of 'civilization' but they are deliberately distorting it as Samuel Huntington did — he came up with the 'theory of the conflict between civilizations.' Meanwhile, the non-Western scholars of international studies (including those from China and India) do not emphasize 'civilization.' I think there is a strange division in the field of academic research in China. Scholars of Chinese ancient civilization seldom or never care about social science and social scientists, especially those studying international relations do not pay attention to the study of ancient civilization — they believe that Chinese tradition will imbue no inspiration or wisdom into their research. We should really break down these two camps and set the main tone with the concept of Oriental civilization, make the ideals of the two civilizations of China and India as the main line, and energetically promote the idea of 'geo-civilization' in the international studies and further push forward the relationship between China and India according to the 'geo-civilization' paradigm."

    See Tan Zhong 譚中, "Adopting 'Geo-civilization' Paradigm to Develop China-India Relations" 採用"地緣文明"範式促進中印關係發展, *South Asia Studies Quarterly* 南亞研究季刊, no. 2 (2008).

13. Ibid.

14. Lao Tze 老子, *The Tao Te Ching* 道德經, Chapter 61.

15. The famous Chinese Indian scholar Tang Zhong suggests to translate CHINDIA into "中印大同" in Chinese. He edited and published the book of *CHINDIA: Ideal and Reality* 中印大同：理想與實現 (Ningxia: Ningxia People's Publishing House, 2007), in which 28 scholars have made positive response to the concept.

15

Chapter

China's International Strategy and Its Relationship with India

Ting Wai

Introduction

China's economic rise has made it the focus of the world's attention, but it seems that China still does not have a complete "Grand Strategy" (i.e., international strategy) to respond to the constantly changing international situation and clear the doubts from the world. China is in a very complicated peripheral security environment with India occupying a pivotal position in South Asia. Ever since its independence, India has been committed to becoming a first-class power and the rapid development of the economy in recent years has filled New Deli with pride. As a democracy, India has maintained an increasingly close relationship with the United States in the past decade or so, and apart from its policy of "Befriending Distant States," it is also implementing the "Look East Policy" to make its way toward the West Pacific Ocean Region, cooperating with Japan, Vietnam, and East Asian countries in all aspects including national security, in an attempt to balance or even "contain" the development of China. This, on the one hand, relieves the pressure of India from the rising China, and on the other, paves the way for India to struggle to the leadership position in the Asia-Pacific region and rank among the great powers. What is India's position in China's "Grand Strategy" and how to identify the obstacles that exist in security and strategy in the current bilateral relations are the main subjects of this thesis.

China's International Strategy

In the past three decades since China started to open itself to the world, it has properly grasped opportunities to grow rapidly from a poor country lacking capital and technology to a power with high energy production capacity and rich capital. Although the booming economic relations with the foreign countries have boosted the shipping industry and thus facilitated exportation of manufactured goods and importation of raw materials and energy, it has also brought about challenges to the security and strategy of China's central government in Beijing. To guarantee safety of the waterway, the navy has to be enhanced, but to send troops to the waters of the Indian Ocean and the Bay of Bengal from the Arabian Sea and Malacca will inevitably arouse doubts from foreign countries, especially from India. Economic relations with foreign countries cause considerations of security and strategy, and then military enhancement arouses wariness of neighboring countries and great powers, thus putting China in a security dilemma. While China is rising, its first priority is to establish the Grand Strategy in terms of diplomacy and geopolitics.

The international strategy of China should address the following questions and considerations:

1. Does the policy of "hiding capacities and biding time," the core value of the "Grand Strategy," still work for this era?
2. China Image refers not only to the image of the nation (the government), but should also cover that of the Chinese enterprises (especially the large-scale enterprises) and the image of the Chinese people.
3. How to ensure the safety of properties and people in the foreign countries?
4. How to promote democratization of international relations and thus establish a democratic global order?
5. How to make a "responsible great power"?
6. Considerations of geopolitics and the various partnerships[1]

China-India Relations: Considerations of Geopolitics

At the end of the 20th century when China put forward "The Rise of the Great Powers," American scholars were keen to make historical comparisons. In the early 20th century, the greatest powers in the world were the U.S. and the UK, who were both playing leading roles in the international community as the so-called Status Quo Powers by the international political scholars; while two other burgeoning powers, Germany and Japan, were planning to expand their influence by constructing a powerful state machine to be dominant in the development of the world's situation and thus become the Revisionist Powers. The conflicts between the new emerging powers and the incumbent powers finally led to the outbreak of the two world wars, which irretrievably undermined the U.S. and the UK as first-class powers, but left Germany and Japan economically dead in 1945. In the 21st century, the Status Quo Power is undoubtedly the U.S. with China as the undoubted Revisionist Power. Although its economy is at a comparatively low ebb, the U.S. is still in a dominant position as the sole super power in the world. Will the new emerging China offer challenges to the supreme authority of the U.S., and will the two nations have conflicts?[2] This has been a hot topic among the Western scholars of international politics. What's interesting is that there is one thing in common between China and then Germany and Japan: not democracy but a powerful state machine.

Quite a few American and Indian scholars believe firmly that China is an expansive power and that it has caused the democratic countries in the Asia Pacific Ocean area to guard against it. These countries formed a coalition to counterbalance China, including America, Japan, Korea, Australia, India, and the small countries in Association of Southeast Asian Nations (ASEAN).[3]

Actually, India has also been rising since the 1990s, but why is not it regarded as a Revisionist Power by the Western scholars? Is it because India is not strong enough or there is no need to fear India as a democracy? While the mainstream view in the U.S. was that China posed a threat and was an important rival, they also firmly believed that India provided an opportunity for coalition. The two rising powers were treated in completely different ways: one was the rival that should be guarded against and the other was an ally that should be cultivated. Does that mean that there is something wrong with China in the positioning of the future international political order? We think that the low profile policy made by Deng Xiaoping after the Cold War should be emphasized, because China's soft power (culture, system, ideas, and values), is extremely weak though its hard power (the economic and military strengths) is increasing rapidly.[4] Apart from efforts in this, the Chinese people must be humble and cautious, guard against arrogance, and try to do their best in order to establish the lofty image of a great power.

On the one hand, it seems that China did not pay much attention to its neighbor India, in the process of its rise. Instead, it paid more attention to the other big powers, such as the U.S., Japan, Russia, and the European countries. On the contrary, India has long been covetously eyeing the development of China and remained on the alert for this assumed biggest threat. Other than the geopolitical benefits, as well as the long-term hostility and misunderstanding caused by the China-India border wars, this is partly due to the fact that India has long failed to realize its dream of becoming a great power ever since the Nehru era.[5] China attaches much importance to strengthening its alliance with the U.S., Japan, and the European countries in order to introduce their funds, technology, and talents to be used for its modernization, and Russia for its energy and weapons. Regarding international strategy, China is much more concerned that the Western countries will continue to rise but China has ignored India's role.

On the other hand, India has long regarded China as its strategic competitor. India cannot win in this one-to-one contest, so it is in a more inferior position when China is allied with Pakistan. In order to reverse this disadvantage, India developed a relationship with the Soviet Union and thus was stronger than China and Pakistan. In the 1970s, a thaw in China-U.S. relations appeared, and both countries were on good terms with Pakistan. Under this circumstance, India needed to rely on the Soviet Union more than ever to achieve a balance. After the dissolution of the Soviet Union, India claimed itself to be the biggest democracy in the world, and the U.S. was willing to improve its relationship with India to consolidate the democratic camp. India moved closer to the U.S. out of strategic consideration to achieve a position superior to China and Pakistan.

The *Agreement on Building Confidence Measures in the Military Field along the Line of Actual Control in the Border Areas* concluded by China and India, respectively, in 1993 and 1996 were intended to contribute to maintain the status quo and the stability of the boundary. However, given India's sensitive psychology, each policy taken by China seemed to be cautious. Even in the nuclear tests in 1998, when India's Defense Minister Abraham Fernandez was spearheading his attack on China and he said that Beijing was India's first enemy, China was still trying carefully to manage its relationship with this rising power.[6]

In the early 21th century, China and India no longer regard each other as threats or rivals. Instead, there was a substantial expansion of trade and economic relations between the two countries. In 2003, the two parties concluded *Principles on Sino-India Relations and Declaration of Comprehensive Cooperation*, according to which India recognized that Tibet is part of China and prohibited anti-China activities in India by the Tibetans. In April 2005, when Premier Wen Jiabao was paying a visit to India, the announcement was made to establish a strategic partnership for peace and prosperity and to establish a special representative's meeting mechanism. The two countries also concluded the *Memorandum of Understanding on Strengthening Exchanges and Cooperation in the Field of Defense*. In December 2005, the navies of the two countries conducted a joint search and rescue exercise in the Indian Ocean with the theme of "China-India Friendship 2005."

However, the year 2006 saw a sharp turn in the relationship of the two countries. Ambassador Sun Yuxi affirmed just before the visit by President Hu Jintao that South Tibet is part of China's territory, and this move seemed to have something to do with the *Agreement on Transfer of Civilian Nuclear Technology* signed by the U.S. and India. In May 2007, China refused to grant a visa to an official from South Tibet (a disputed area, called Arunachal Pradesh in India), giving the reason that South Tibet belongs to China. In 2009, this measure extended to the area of Kashmir. In July 2010 when Lieutenant General Jaswal, head of Indian Army's Northern Command, paid a visit to China at the invitation of Beijing, he was only given a visa note instead of a stamp on the passport as he was in charge of the defense of Kashmir, which led to the cancellation of visits by all Indian high-level officials.[7] From 2007, India began to deploy their most advanced warplane Su-30 MKI in Assam which is next to South Tibet. In December 2009, New Delhi announced that it would change its strategic defense policy to face the two-front wars, i.e. wars on the west line and the northeast line.[8] The same year, India was planning to send 60,000 more soldiers to the northeast and the northwest, and in November 2011, it declared that it would increase the troops by 100,000 and build a mountain legion and 4 mountain divisions.

Will the change of Sino-India relations in recent years arouse the fear that India is cooperating with America to implement a "Return to Asia" Policy and collaborate with countries in East Asia, Southeast Asia, and even South Asia to counterbalance China's rise, or that China has been so conceited and unruly in recent years that all the other countries should join together to contain it?

We will have a discussion on the following four issues.

Sino-India Boundary Issues

The China-India Joint Working Group has already had more than 14 talks on the boundary issue, but in vain. The key is that New Delhi will not compromise in either the east line or the west line. Both Zhou Enlai and Deng Xiaoping had considered using the actual control line as the boundary line,[9] i.e. the McMahon Line to the north of Arunachal Pradesh. This means that China will trade South Tibet for Aksai Chin in West India. The eastern section of the Sino-India boundary involves a disputed 90,000 kilometers,[10] while Aksai Chin is about 34,000 kilometers. Tawang in South Tibet is a holy place of Tibetan Buddhism as well as the place where 6th Dalai Lama in the 17th century was born, and so Beijing seems willing to be flexible in the sovereignty over this place. In the *Political Guidelines for Negotiation on Boundary Issues* was the rule that says resident populations should not be traded, indicating that China will not reclaim Tawang.[11]

In fact, although the Chinese troops attacked South Tibet in 1962, they ceased fire one month later and withdrew with no intention of permanent occupation. If the two countries recognize the Status Quo in the past 50 years and accept the actual control line as the boundary line, it will greatly contribute to improving bilateral relations.

As early as in 2003, India expressly indicated that Tibet was part of the Chinese territory, while in 2005 China recognized that Sikkim belonged to India. However, in recent years, the territorial disputes seemed to heat up again. In 2006, just before Chinese President Hu Jintao visited India, the Chinese Ambassador to India Sun Yuxi claimed that the land south of the McMahon Line belonged to China, and this started the argument. Boundary disputes of China with other countries were settled, such as Russia, Tajikistan, and Kyrgyzstan are all parties willing to compromise, but an agreement in the China-India boundary dispute is still far off. A new round of negotiations will be held soon, but India's firm stand makes a deal unlikely.

The Indian Ocean and South China Sea

The Indian Ocean and the Malacca Straits are the lifeblood of China. Almost 60% of the commercial ships passing through the Malacca Straits belong to China, and so it is reasonable and necessary for China to strengthen strategic activities in the India Ocean to ensure the safety of the waterway, which, however, poses threats to India's ocean strategy as the whole area is deemed to be India's turf. New Delhi is especially concerned about the String of Pearls Strategy which was put forward by the American strategic analysts in 2005. According to the String of Pearls Strategy, China cooperated with countries in South Asia to explore ports, such as Gwadar in Pakistan, Chittagong in Bengal, Hambontota in Sri Lanka, and Kyaukphyu in Myanmar, which could serve as supply bases and also allow China to monitor activities on the sea. They can also replace Malacca to become the relay stations for oil transportation, thus avoiding a potential problem.

On the contrary, India's Look East Policy[12] was incorporated into the free-trade promoting "10 plus 1" mechanism to enhance economic interaction with ASEAN as well as seek cooperation in security. This policy evidently reflects India's ambition to become a great power but also stimulates the nerves of Beijing. Moreover, disputes on the sovereignty of the South China Sea are becoming increasingly heated ever since last year and India's involvement has made them more complicated. Therefore, competition and exclusion of the two countries are becoming prominent on the vast waters from the Indian Ocean to the South China Sea. The Chinese Scholar Wu Yongnian holds that only by developing more extensive cooperation in protecting the thoroughfare for trade and energy in the Indian Ocean and Malacca Straits, can China and India protect their fundamental interests.[13] If the two nations can respect each other's interests on the basis of "mutual understanding and mutual accommodation," both can co-exist peacefully, but if both think that their turf is invaded and thus guard against each other, the situation will not be optimistic. In September 2007, America and India held the first such naval exercise; the same month, America, India, Japan, Singapore, and Australia conducted the largest military exercise in history; from late April till early May 2009, America, India, and Japan conducted a military exercise, all of which marks India's taking the road to the West Indian Ocean and collaborating with America and Japan to balance the potential threat of China.[14]

Nuclear Power of India and Pakistan

Beijing is quite unhappy with the *Agreement on Cooperation in Civilian Nuclear Power* concluded in 2006 and holds that India should not be granted the right of immunity which is against the guidance of the Nuclear Security Group. Since India did not join the Non-Proliferation Treaty, America should not export nuclear technology to it. In order to protest against this move of America, China provided Pakistan two nuclear reactors in March 2010. Beijing once thought that as the agreement was already concluded before China joined the Nuclear Suppliers Group (NSG), Pakistan should have the right of immunity even without the NSG's consideration, but actually China once requested that Pakistan be granted the right of immunity at the meeting held in New Zealand in June 2010 but this was rejected.[15]

In 1998, India and Pakistan conducted 5 and 6 nuclear tests, respectively. There was now a nuclear triangle between China and South Asia. Due to the Equalizer Effect brought about by the nuclear weapons, the weak party owns nuclear weapons and is no longer afraid of the strong party. As a consequence, the two parties are in even positions and this mutual deterrence helped to improve India-Pakistan and Sino-India relations.

Although India and Pakistan reinforced their nuclear equipment, including increasing the number of missiles and extending the missiles' ranges, and India built five nuclear missile submarines, of which the first, *The Arihangt*, was launched in July 2009. However, this cannot change the situation of mutual deterrence due to nuclear strategy. When America and Russia were cutting the number of strategic nuclear weapons, nuclear armament races in South Asia were becoming intensified, which is actually no good to the peripheral security of China. Therefore, it is the first priority for China and India to establish a military confidence-building mechanism, improve transparency of armament development and expand high-level exchanges to enhance mutual trust and dissolve doubts. In 2011, the two nations resumed bilateral defense exchanges, and in 2012, they conducted a third joint military exercise. It seems that both hope to get things back on track.[16]

Confidence-Building Mechanism

China and India's rise and the growth of their national strength inevitably affects the balance of power in the whole Asia Pacific region, which is determined by objective factors, but the positioning of the two nations in the future Asia Pacific political order depends on the subjective factors of the leaders of the two nations. There is much difference in attempting to influence other countries in a high profile manner or respecting other countries with a humble attitude. When powerful neighbor countries are rising, they should try to find opportunities for cooperation in facing international situations rather than comparing their strengths. The speaker has noticed that India and China, two of the BRIC (Brazil, Russia, India And China) Countries, share common views on global warming, cooperation in trade and economy, the fight against piracy and terrorism, and that the two nations are both new powers that receive the current regulations passively in the international system and are willing to take part in and reform the international system.[17] Therefore, both nations have the intention to influence the formulation of the future international standard, which is the basis for the exchanges of the two nations and may consolidate security relations between the two.

India and China will have more communications regarding a response to the situation of the Indian Ocean and South China Sea, naval deployment, nuclear power, and nuclear strategy, and this will prevent crises brought about by nuclear security and nuclear expansion issues.[18]

Conclusion

The rapid rise of India and China places a high demand on resources. As neighbors, the two countries should be supportive of each other and seek cooperation opportunities. To obtain oil resources, the gas companies of the two nations acquired 37% of the shares from the gas company of Syria in December 2005, and in December 2006, they acquired 50% of the shares from that of Columbia, which were good examples of equality and mutual benefits for the two nations. Unfortunately, when it comes to precious water resources, it seems that China did not account for the interests of their neighbors downstream. The dam to be built on the Yarlung Zangbo River will displease India, because the Yarlung Zangbo River in India is the Brahmaputra, and when the dam is built, the headwaters will be controlled by China. However, if a consultation is made before building to reach an agreement, there would be no doubts and concerns. This is also an issue that must be considered when formulating international strategy.

The Chinese scholar Tang Shiping pointed out that China's strategy in South Asia is not to contain India, but to ensure that the position of India in South Asia does not threaten China's interests.[19] Similarly, China must also prove that the rising China will not threaten the interests of India. This is what a responsible power should do.

Notes

1. Ding Wei 丁偉, *The "Grand Strategy" of China's Rise and Its Foreign Policies* 中國崛起的"大戰略"與外交政策 (Beijing: Social Sciences Academic Press, forthcoming).
2. The most controversial statement in this regard is John Mearsheimer's *The Tragedy of Great Power Politics* (New York: Norton, 2001).
3. Francine. R. Frankel, "The breakout of China-India strategy rivalry in Asia and the Indian Ocean," *Journal of International Affairs* 64, 2 (Spring / Summer 2011):14.
4. Joseph Nye, *Bound to Lead* (New York: Basic Books, 1990);
   Joseph Nye, *Soft Power* (New York: Public Affairs, 2004);
   Ting Wai 丁偉, "Reflection on China's soft power" 中國軟力量的思考, *21th Century Bi-monthly* 廿一世紀雙月 (Dec. 2009):6–11.
5. Shang Qinyu 尚勤餘, "China and India: Partners or rivals" 中國與印度：合作夥伴還是競爭對手, *South Asia Research Quarterly* 南亞研究季刊, no. 1 (2011):3.
6. David M. Malone, and R. Mukherjee, "India and China: Conflict and cooperation," *Survival* 52, 1 (Feb.–Mar. 2010):138.
7. Sujit Dutta, "Managing and engaging rising China: India's evolving posture," *The Washington Quarterly* 34, 2 (2011):132.
8. Jeff M. Smith, "Sino-Indian relations: A troubled history, an uncertain future," *Harvard International Review* (Spring 2011):110.
9. Srijit Ditta, p.131;

   Malone and Mukherjee, p.153.
10. Cheng Ruisheng 程瑞聲, "Sino-Indian boundary negotiations and the prospect" 中印兩國的邊界談判及其前景, in *China and India: Political and Strategic Perspectives,* eds. I. Saint Mezard and J. K. Chin, Center of Asian Studies, University of Hong Kong (2005), 43;

    Also refer to Frankel, p. 2–3.
11. "A Himalayan Rivalry," *The Economist*, Aug. 21, 2010, p. 17–20.
12. Zhang Li 張 力, "India's strategic rising and Sino-Indian relations: Questions, tendency and response" 印度戰略崛起與中印關係：問題，趨勢與應對, *South Asia Research Quarterly* 南亞研究季刊, no. 1 (2010):8.
13. Wu Yongnian 吳永年, "Ground, questions and prospects of Sino-Indian bilateral cooperation" 中印雙邊合作的基礎，問題與前景, *South Asia Research* 南亞研究, no. 2 (2007):23.
14. Zhang Wei 張威, Analysis on Indian Ocean strategies 印度海洋戰略析論, *Southeast Asia and South Asia Research* 東南亞南亞研究, no.4 (2009):20.
15. Refer to Frankel, p.8.
16. *Hong Kong Economic Journal* 信報, Nov. 14, 2011, p. A22.
17. Zhao Gancheng 趙幹成, "First exploration on security relations of Sino-Indian geopolitics" 中印地緣安全關係初探, *South Asia Research Quarterly* 南亞研究季刊, no. 2 (2011):2.
18. Lora Saalman, "Divergence, similarity and symmetry in Sino-Indian threat perceptions," *Journal of International Affairs* 64, 2 (Spring / Summer 2011), 190.
19. Tang Shiping 唐世平, "Game of Sino-Indian relations and China's south Asia strategy 中國—印度關係的博奕和中國的南亞戰略, *World Economy and Politics* 世界經濟與政治, no. 9 (2000):28.

16

Chapter

Deliberating a "Cross-Regional" Perspective: China, India, and the Emerging World Order

Jagannath P. Panda

The Premise

Contemporary diplomacy suggests that effective multilateral cooperation requires serious dialogue and a great deal of understanding between nation-states. This is important at a time when a new global order, very much multi-polar in nature, is evolving and global power relations are changing rapidly. The current world features a new sort of power politics which create new challenges and prospects for global governance. Against this background, two prominent global political powers — China and India — are poised to play vital roles, and any potential for cooperation between them is likely to influence the politics of the globe in a huge way. Despite their conventional differences on the age-old boundary issue and on various other bilateral and regional fronts, there are areas of greater convergence of interests between them at the wider global level. Their evolving understanding in global affairs and prospects to cooperate in cross-regional multilateral areas are a new development of utmost importance. The significance of their rise is currently shaping most global politics. China has arrived as the number two economy of the world and India has become the number four economy. New regional, cross-regional, and global issues and political themes, as well as directives, are shaping their relationship. The *India-China Joint Communiqué* of December 16, 2010 acknowledged this fact by stating: "India-China relations go beyond their bilateral scope and have acquired global and strategic significance."[1]

This paper explores the areas of possible cooperation and convergence of interests at the cross-regional level between China and India, specifically, in regional and cross-regional multilateral settings or groupings. It deals with the appearance, importance, and perspectives of Sino-Indian relations under a cooperative prism within the newly arrived cross-regional multilateral groupings like the BRICS (Brazil, Russia, India, China, and South Africa), BASIC (Brazil, South Africa, India, and China), and IBSA (India-Brazil-South Africa) arrangements. The paper argues that these new compelling steering mechanisms manifest the idea that the multi-polar world order sets new parameters for progressive foreign policy strategies and offers a new scope for the global convergence of interests, cooperation, and issue-based engagement. It further argues that the lately arrived China-India multilateral interaction at the cross-regional level is a prelude to a constructive vision of a new multilateral international order. Not only is global politics changing, but the rise of China and India prompts a new scope for collaboration and global interaction and engagement. As the December 16, 2010 *India-China Joint Communiqué* further indicates: "There is enough space in the world for the development of both China and India and enough areas for the two countries to cooperate."[2] The distinctness of this sentiment lies in the acknowledgment that the global preeminence of both China and India is rising; the two are regional neighbors and must try to coexist.

Framing the Discourse

The premise that unites China's and India's global conditions and motives is the developing world, and the nations being "emerging economies" from Asia. While both have time and again expressed the sentiment that they belong to Asia or the Third World and should be considered as developing countries on the rise, the crucial question is: Do the two countries have a reasoned strategy for the cause of the developing world, and if so, what is it? A coherent common strategy to maximize the developing-world cause between the two did not exist until recently. However, the recent growth of cross-regional parameters where the two countries are massively engaged with each other confirms their evolving global understanding. This is mainly for two reasons: One, both are realizing the benefits of having a mutual understanding at the global, or cross-continental or cross-regional level, in a rapidly evolving multi-polar world order; two, the rising importance of the developing world in global politics. While the idea of a multi-polar world structure is a thesis beneficial to both, what really unites them, at least temporarily, is the logic and vitality of the developing world.

The developing world dialogue has always been attractive, and has been a global reference grouping since the developing countries gained independence. Yet scholars "descry much continuity in a policy that has undergone rapid changes over a few decades — from the advocacy of violent means to peaceful progress, from ideological exclusivity to eclectic ecumenism, from egalitarian poverty to purpose-rational payoffs, from revolutionary idealism to realism, etc."[3] But if there are any progressive elements in the identity of the developing world formulation, it has been because of China's and India's advocacy of shared global objectives. Despite their historical hostility, both have been strong advocates of Panchasheel sentiments and exclusive examples of developing societies. Scholars place the China-India discourse within the spectrum of civilization's course. They argue that "the prime contradiction of our epoch while assessing the relationship between China and India needs to be reconceptualised as one between the forces of swaraj and jiefang (liberation), on the one hand, and [the] forces of hegemony, led by global capitalism, on the other."[4] This sufficiently indicates that there are many facets to China-India relations; one of these is the embryonic cross-regional dialogue which binds different continents in their multilateral relationship discourse.

The emerging global order is heavily dependent upon the Sino-Indian cross-regional discourse or engagement. Both countries have time and again acknowledged this understanding. For instance, while acknowledging that there is a "continuous democratization of international relations and multilateralism," the document *A Shared Vision for the 21st Century of the People's Republic of China and the Republic of India* states that the "bilateral relationship in this century will be of significant regional and global influence."[5] This is important at a time when the global supremacy of the U.S. is declining and speculation abounds as to which among the world's burgeoning nations will rise to power.

Conventional global politics suggests that building an alliance is the most effective way to check the dominance of certain countries and construct a balance in global power politics.[6] But this is a difficult enterprise in the post-Cold War era, where a number of powers possess nuclear strength, strong militaries, and project different national security strategies and diverse objectives. Two factors that have tactical implications in the current global politics are: Ideology and identity, apart from economic and political strength. While on one hand, these two factors restrict China and India from forming a credible alliance against any particular nation or region, they also help them to sit together and think maturely to have a combined opinion, groupings, and partnership against conventional Western dominance. The basic premise here remains that both China and India have been associating with each other for greater global bargaining power against Western hegemonic multilateral systems and financial institutions through BRICS, BASIC, RIC (Russia, India, and China), etc.

These groupings are central to the two countries' global profile as "developing countries" and "developing economies." In the quest to maximize wealth, security, and identity, both would like to bring necessary adjustments to their foreign policy strategy in order to integrate with the evolving global structure. Multilateralism through different modes and mediums has been the main crux of most of the contemporary power strategies and that is seen here as a result. Multilateralism is viewed as an ad-hoc alliance arrangement in the current global politics.[7] By associating with various global, cross-regional, or regional bodies temporarily or permanently, the engagement of China and India makes a statement that associating with adversarial powers is possible in the current global politics.

Cross-Regional Settings: Prelude to the Multipolar World Order

Cross-regional settings make up a relatively new phenomenon in world politics. Rising or developing powers rely on these premises to maximize their security and strategic interests in a world that is still dominated by Western powers. The aim and objective is simple in these settings: Through these cross-regional settings, rising powers try to forge a separate identity for themselves and seek to promote their own wealth, welfare, and security, and advocate for greater transparency in the global financial structure. One such grouping that has been successful to an extent in putting pressure on the global financial institutions is the BRICS grouping. The progress of the BRICS is the new linchpin of global politics, a prelude to the devolution of global power and the surfacing of a "multipolar" world order of politics. These nations help us to re-interpret the old definition of multilateralism in a new style. For instance, Robert O'Keohane has aptly defined multilateralism as a "practice of coordinating national policies in groups of three and more states, through ad-hoc arrangements or by means of institutions."[8] This perspective is a conventional one, but with the rise of the multipolar world politics, it permits us to interpret it differently. Under a rapidly emerging multi-polar world order, it implies an innovative involvement or partaking in the multilateral organizations at different levels and brings ensuing policy adjustments. Forming or attaching multilateral bodies at different levels — governmental or non-governmental, regional or cross-regional — is an essence of the current global politics. China and India seem to be implementing this approach.

Three recent groupings that have been in the limelight of the current global politics are BRICS, BASIC, and IBSA. They are particularly noted for their cross-continental associations. Both China and India are associated with BRICS and BASIC. China is not a part of IBSA which places India at the front in this democratic setting. Most of these groupings are still at a conceptual and abstract level, but their very existence has an immense impact over the current global politics. Their vitality springs from the participant countries being large societies, emerging economies, and developing countries. China's and India's impressive rise and distinct global rise as political actors has made these groupings more vital.

Impressive BRICS

BRICS has been the biggest talking point among the three. With the latest summit at Sanya in the Hainan province of China, BRICS completed three rounds of annual leadership summits and is heading for the fourth round in India in 2012. While many still question its relevance as the group consists of diverse powers in diverse continents with various strategic interests, the very fact that BRICS has emerged as a group and has been meeting regularly has confirmed, to some extent, that global politics is changing its hue with the lead of the developing economies of BRICS. Moreover, BRICS has never been static; it has matured into some sort of alliance that looks at key global political, economic and trade issues from the perspective of the developing world, and offers an emerging model for global economic cooperation and competition. While the BRICS economies appear to have little in common, these countries lumped themselves together for three primary reasons: The size of population, rapidly emerging economies, and the ability of their governments to seemingly incorporate their economies seamlessly into the global markets and accept certain facets of globalization.[9]

On the surface, both India and China appear to be the most tenable options in BRICS for future investments. Both markets have been the prime destinations for global investors. The post-Olympics Chinese market is riding a super cycle of investment, and keeps on building world-class infrastructure in prime destinations. Problems, however, remain in the political aspect of the China-India discourse. The leaders of BRICS countries are repeatedly talking about the rise of a new "multi-polar world order" with the lead of developing countries. While the economic aspect of this vision is never in question, the primary lingering doubt is: Apart from the economic similarities that the BRICS countries have, is there anything that can tie them together forever to form a stable multi-polar world order? How would the two leading powers of the group — China and India — approach the idea of a multi-polar world order? The answers to these questions are the problematic facets of China-India cross-regional or multilateral discourse. There is hardly a new or constructive perspective emerging at the highest leadership level to push the cross-continental understanding between China and India.

The basic success of BRICS and the vision of a multi-polar world order will depend heavily upon China-India cross-regional or multilateral understanding and accommodation of each other's interests in greater continental or global issues. Currently, BRICS works in the hope that it will work with mainstream global bodies like the United Nations (UN), G-20, and other multilateral bodies for a democratic and transparent global governance system. The current progress of BRICS narrates that its growth is southward. Powers like Mexico are being considered, to an extent, to be included in the BRICS club. Future expansion proposals suggest new representation from the Middle East, with Egypt coming to the grouping; this will have greater continental representation. There is optimism that BRICS shares a vision for inclusive growth and prosperity in global politics through South-South dialogue. What it requires is a non-confrontational approach among its members, especially between the two leading actors of the group: China and India.

The 2011 Sanya BRICS summit confirms that the emerging economies seek a more balanced global and financial system more than anything else and this has highlighted a shift in the power order away from the Western world. Precisely, the Sanya declaration states that "the governing structure of the international financial institutions should reflect the changes in the world economy, increasing the voice and representation of emerging economies and developing countries."[10] In fact, the Sanya summit was strategically important for a few reasons: (a) inclusion of South Africa made this grouping more solid across the continent; making it BRIC to BRICS; (b) gathering support for Russia's entry into the WTO; and (c) the idea of trading directly among the BRICS members and cutting out unstable globally convertible currencies. The summit in Sanya also pointed out Chinese seriousness for BRICS as a plausible alternative to the Western dominated global financial system.[11] More notably, Sanya BRICS summit implies a greater task for the developing countries, particularly for China and India to forge a credible understanding on both political and economic issues which will be central to the idea of a multipolar world order. Two concrete issues could be taken here as an example: One, the issue of the UN reform; two; trading directly among the BRICS countries without relying on the dollars. The Sanya BRICS summit did mention the "comprehensive reform" of the UN. China as a Permanent Five nation of the UN Security Council should take this issue as an immediate priority and help to reform the UN Security Council, where India along with developing countries from the African continents can have a permanent membership. Similarly, both India and China must take the lead in establishing development banks in BRICS countries which can open mutual credit lines to local currencies.[12] That will automatically put pressure on the supremacy of the U.S. dollar.

Almost representing 40% of the global population, and nearly a quarter of its economic yield, the BRICS countries are justified to have this ambition for themselves. In fact, the Sanya summit did emerge as a realigned force for a new world order, being contrary to Western dominance and a challenge of the supremacy of the U.S.[13] However, putting into practice the goals and objectives of the BRICS is always a difficult phenomenon. In fact, much of the BRICS agenda depends upon China and India's policy approaches. Over the last two decades, the pattern of China and India's economic growth has been impressive; while India has been growing massively at 6–9%, China too has shown its economic rise through 8–9.5% growth consistently every year. To their advantages, high savings and the young populations boost their economies further, where rests most of the global financial clout of the two Asian powers. But there are greater issues that the BRICS nations need to attend to, both to remove its internal difficulties and to strengthen intra-BRICS cooperation. Independently, most BRICS countries face vital challenges in maintaining growth on track. China needs to tackle the fledgling financial system and bring necessary political reforms to support its massive economy first. Russia would like to revive its economy and move to a more broad-based economy from one with a heavy tilt towards commodities. India would like to overcome its debt and investment risk proposals[14] as its farmers find it hard to take further loans; India's abysmally stumpy education system at the primary and secondary levels is also an obstacle to the country's long-term growth rate. Both India and Brazil need to do more in infrastructure development and ratchet up their education systems.[15] India seems to appreciate the Brazilian strides in social inclusion.[16] The new BRICS member South Africa needs to put its economy on track and find a long-term solution to stabilize its growth record. These are difficult objectives to achieve and will remain challenging targets for the BRICS.

BRICS and IBSA: Two sides of the same coin

These difficulties make the BRICS dynamics more challenging for both China and India, being the main economies in this bloc. Further, there are different perspectives between China and India with regard to BRICS and IBSA currently, which restricts their cross-regional association and the global multilateral cooperation, which remain central for a multi-polar world order. India takes the lead in IBSA as a leading economy and democracy. Rising as a club that was mainly stung by the Western powers' obstinacy at the Doha Round of trade talks, and more vitally to push the cause of the developing countries at the cross-continental level, it has been promoted by India as an institution of democratic countries.[17] India capitalizes more on IBSA than BRICS because the former provides a suitable option for India to tackle the "social aspects of globalization."[18] To India's advantage, IBSA also comprises two important powers from BRICS — Brazil and South Africa — which are strong economic partners of China. For India, IBSA is a "unique," novel initiative meant for "special" global causes.[19] In India's perception, the IBSA setting draws inspiration from the "common political model of being major developing democracies geographically located in three diverse and different continents."[20] China, for its part, seeks the merger of IBSA and BRICS as a consolidated voice of the developing world to establish a credible intercontinental approach to tackle Western dominance at various levels of global politics. In China's perception, the existence of IBSA as a separate grouping weakens the developing countries' cause.

BASIC as a strategic reality

BASIC is another initiative which suggests that China and India are engaged in an ad-hoc and temporary cause rather than trying to have a permanent and credible understanding to maximize their strategic interests against the Western-dominated global order. China-India politics within BASIC suggests that this multilateral engagement is mainly limited to the issue of climate change. BASIC was created in December 2009 at the United Nations Framework Convention on Climate Change (UNFCCC or FCCC) summit during the COP15 climate change summit in Copenhagen. This consultative mechanism is different from the regular consultation mechanisms such as G-7 and G-20. The politics just before COP15 sufficiently indicated that the developed countries would not initiate steps to reduce greenhouse gas emissions if the developing countries failed to do so, targeting mainly China and India.[21] Though in principle, the BASIC countries agree that climate change negotiations should be carried out under the framework of the UNFCCC, Kyoto Protocol, and the Bali Roadmap, they realize that there has to be some concrete understanding among them as a base for forming a credible grouping. However, the fundamental differences between China and India on the issue of emission patterns put this in doubt. The climate burden of the Chinese economic growth on the rest of the global economy is disproportionately large compared to that of India.[22]

While the developing/developed world divide promotes China-India cross-regional engagement largely, this engagement has to be built in concrete terms and issues, looking at their greater interests in a multipolar world order. The Brazil BASIC summit joint statement reiterated that there is a need to forge cooperation in achieving a sustained and inclusive result in future summits in the context of sustainable development and in accordance to the framework and guidelines of the UNFCCC. Most notably, China and India need to take an open and considerate approach on this as both are linked with many emerging economies and the developing world in different settings. On climate change, India holds the position that "any legally binding cuts for developing countries" should be strongly opposed. India is of the view that the Kyoto protocol generally favors legally binding agreements, which call for mandatory emission cuts by the rich countries and voluntary cuts by the developing nations.[23] China and India need to talk more about the Kyoto protocol and decide if the future climate summits could be catalysts for the developing countries. They need to discuss and carry a common understanding on three select issues: Unilateral trade measures, intellectual property rights (IPR), and equitable access to sustainable development. These issues are important in UNFCCC dealings, where both China and India should set examples in addressing these issues.

A concrete understanding and framework needs to be built into China-India cross-regional dialogue, to maximize issue-based interests and the cause of the developing world. For example, there is a need to establish an international "energy order" that will be fair and equitable to both the developing and developed countries. A commitment needs to be developed between China and India for "joint efforts to diversify the global energy mix and enhance the share of clean and renewable energy..."[24] The highly estimable joint work between Chinese and Indian scientists with regard to the International Thermonuclear Experimental Reactor (ITER) project sets the ground for new cooperation in the field of energy and resources between the two countries. Furthermore, there is greater scope for China and India to combine their agenda in reforming the global financial institutions to grant equal voting rights to the developing and developed countries. Both countries also need to take a clear position on issues like IMF quota share of at least 5% to emerging markets and developing countries and a significant increase of at least 3% of voting power in the World Bank for the developing world, while reducing the voting shares of developed countries. The two countries are in talks to expand strategic bilateral collaboration on important issues like climate change and energy. For example, the recently concluded first India-China Strategic Economic Dialogue held in Beijing reiterated that there is an urgent need for strengthening bilateral cooperation on energy efficiency and conservation as well as on environmental protection.[25]

The current China-India cross-regional understanding is quite extemporized in nature. The only positivity of this arrangement is that they have started sharing the desk together at broader cross-continental or cross-regional settings. In fact, not to be ignored, the important outcome of China and India's cross-regional association through the BRICS and BASIC indicates that Asian powers are at the center-stage of global politics. The rise of Asia has been the certain force in global power politics and this is primarily not because of China and India's economic rise, but more because of their growth as vital political forces in regional, cross-regional, and global affairs. Their individual role and influence has been impressive in BRICS, BASIC, and IBSA. Yet, there has to be a substantial bilateral mechanism between the two which will lead to talk and deliberation about cross-regional politics. Without a solid bilateral mechanism which will exclusively deal with multilateral or cross-regional, cross-continental issues, the China-India association at this level looks weak and hoary. Other cross-(sub) regional formulations further explain this hypothesis.

For instance, apart from BRICS and BASIC, two other initiatives in the last decade have generated optimism for greater China-India regional cooperation are BCIM (Bangladesh, China, India, Myanmar) for greater regional economic cooperation (known as the Kunming Initiative) and the CIR (China, India, Russia) trilateral framework of the Track Two initiatives, now on the way to becoming a Track One framework. All these (sub)-regional multilateral initiatives cover a wide range of political issues, in a regional, multilateral apparatus running within the global structural unilateralism still dominated by the U.S.[26] The strategic opportunity and limitation of the CIR formulation is that it is a result of the "post-Cold War international system" which states that the U.S. is still the "sole superpower" and holds "absolute superiority" in the current pyramidal structure of various major powers.[27] Though still at the initial stage of its rise, the CIR formulation is a compelling mechanism which brings together the three most vital powers: China, India, and Russia. It is seen more in the context that the U.S. wants "to prevent the rise of other large developing countries ... what it opposes is that the emerging countries represented by China, Russia, and India may conceivably challenge its hegemony."[28] Overall, two things are reflected in the China-India spectrum under the RIC formulation: First, both remain central to the idea and discourse of the multipolar world structure; second; RIS is one formulation that is meant to bring stability to the Asian region by keeping the Western powers out of the continent and establishing a solid understanding among the three elite powers: Russia, India, and China. In short, the main premises under which both India and China solidify their settings are their common critique of the "neo-liberal" rules and norms.[29] After so many years of their establishments, neither the BCIM nor the CIR initiatives have provided any credible solutions in resolving the fundamental differences between China and India on boundary issues. True, these are cross-(sub) regional initiatives, and meant for greater sub-regional issues, but the very fact that all these initiatives have not been successful in minimizing the antagonist perceptions among other members explains its limitations.

Need for Serious Review?

Be it BRICS, BASIC, or any other regional, sub-regional, or cross-regional setting, both China and India lead the drive in this multilateral setting and remain crucial players for the emerging world order. Formulating a "global strategy" that will remain suitable for the developing world remains the key aspect in Indian and Chinese diplomacy in these multilateral groupings, as both step up their calculated steps to gain in energy supplies, capture vibrant markets, and counter the Western-dominated systemic challenges in the process. Shen Qiat notes that "only by accommodating the interests of all sides, seeking common ground while shelving differences, and jointly pursuing cooperation can countries properly advance and deepen the reform of the present international financial and economic system."[30]

To see it broadly, cross-(sub) regional or cross-continental power relations currently are in flux because of China's and India's expansionist multilateral engagements. Aptly referred to as "new" actors in cross-regional politics; the two countries have been quite impressive in influencing the other continental powers in their fold. Their influence and presence have extended to cross-regional or cross-(sub)-regional areas at a time when the global business climate has improved among continents and powers. But their differing approaches and diverse thinking in BRICS, IBSA, and BASIC confirm that engaging through various regional and global multilateral settings or bodies is not necessarily a fitting medium for launching collaboration and stabilizing the relationship. BCIM and CIR are also pointers in the same narrative. There is a need for greater political understanding and maturity between the two countries on global and multilateral issues.

In a rapidly evolving multipolar world order, China and India are not only exhibiting greater confidence in their political influence but also adopting new creative approaches for various levels of engagement. The U.S. remains the constant factor in their foreign policy, and assumes "great salience" in China-India multilateral engagement, as these three remain the most dynamic powers in the current global politics. China and India need to rise to the occasion and realize that their strategic partnership at multilateral or global levels needs to be constructive and should aim at democratizing the current world politics. As the China-India document *Shared Vision for the 21st Century* states: The "Two sides believe that the continuous democratization of international relations and multilateralism are an important objective in the new century."[31]

Both China and India belong to the same strategic club when it comes to the global parameters. They are "developing countries" and share "identical views" on various pressing global issues like energy, climate change, etc. The current Third World and "South-South" dialogue between the two countries needs a critical review when both are poised to be the driving factors of the multi-polar world order. The exposition of China-India cross-regional engagements is not a recent one. The year 1954 began this process, when the two countries agreed to set aside their ideological differences in charting out the "Five Principles of Peaceful Coexistence." These principles were the paradigm basis of the 1955 Bandung Conference. Popularly known as the Panchasheel, the benchmark of these "five principles" was the code of "noninterference" and "mutual respect" in interstate relations, which provided a basis for multiple level collaboration between the two irrespective of their different ideological, political, and social systems. However, the two Asian civilizations did not fully grasp the novelty or the practical implication of Panchasheel principles and failed to implement them in their multilateral discourse.

In the current century, within the prism of globalization and multipolar politics, the course of China-India multilateral dealings seems to have touched new complexities. Globalization has become a facilitator and has contributed to lessening their mutual fear, but it has not completely downplayed the threat perception.[32] However, the process of globalization has facilitated the discourse of engagement at various multilateral levels. Coinages like "Chindia" or "China + India" have become popular. It is argued by some that the appeal of "Chindia" may not necessarily be restricted to the parameters of "economic integration under the aegis of globalization." Some experts see this concept in terms of "cultural and spiritual interconnectedness between the Chinese and Indian civilizations."[33] However, these are emotional appeals to divert the strategic competitive realities and rivalries that Sino-Indian relations carry at the bilateral and global levels. Concrete institutional mechanisms must be developed between the two countries in order to put all these emotional perspectives into practice. Economic integration and the dialogue of civilizational encounter is a minimalist argument to create a win-win formula between China and India as both have the global ambition of becoming superpowers. Also, the leadership stance that "there is enough space for China and India to live with each other" looks commonplace at the moment.

Objectively, both countries are yet to develop a common ground to manage the international financial institutions like the International Monetary Fund (IMF), the World Bank, the Asian Development Bank (ADB), etc. While the voting rights in the World Bank, the IMF, and the Bretton Woods organizations are more favorable to the Western and European countries, the response of both China and India to these issues has been limited, resting at the level of rhetorical statements. No common perspective between the two Asian neighbors seems to be developing on global oil and commodity prices, global economic imbalances, and trade protectionism. A wider consensus between them on environmental governance on a global scale is still missing. On the nuclear issue, China has been suspicious of India because of the Indo-U.S. nuclear deal. China, it may be noted, maintained a neutral and flaccid posture during the India-specific waiver process at the Nuclear Suppliers Group (NSG).

During Premier Wen Jiabao's tour to India in December 2010, the two sides expressed common interests and similar concerns on major regional and international issues. Multilateral issues such as climate change, the Doha Round, energy and food security, and international financial and economic reform were identified as particular areas for cooperation.[34] The two sides recognized that as the global economy stabilizes and recovers, China and India would strengthen communication and consultation within the G-20 framework, jointly facilitate the progress of global governance and advance economic globalization towards balanced development and shared benefits,. The two sides agreed to enhance cooperation within the BRICS framework.[35] These understandings have, however, been limited to official dialogue.

Fundamentally, both China and India oppose the current situation of the international financial institutions being more in favor of the Western or developed countries rather than the developing countries. However, there is greater scope for both countries to play a "constructive" role in reforming these global institutions, and for commitment and seriousness on issue-based cooperation. On climate change, both countries had an idiosyncratic approach until recently.[36] Differences in their energy consumption levels are a big issue between the two. Rhetorical statements have been made time and again about building a cooperative approach toward global issues like energy, maritime security, climate change, and various developmental needs rather than bringing about any concrete institutional mechanism exclusively meant to address these vital issues.[37] Not much has happened in creating an Asian block of oil-importing countries like China and India to strengthen Asia's position on global energy deals.[38] To put it simply, the formula of a developing world or developing economies, on which China and India try to forge their multilateral relations, looks inspiring probably because the neo-conservative idea of the U.S.-dominated unipolar world is fading away. But to magnify the China-India multilateral relationship in pushing a multipolar world aimed at checking the Western dominance may not be prudent currently. A set of concrete understandings must be developed between China and India at the bilateral, cross-regional, and global levels to address those emerging cross-continental or cross-regional issues in this regard.

Summing Up

In conclusion, it is not much of a surprise to state that China-India multilateral cooperation and engagement is based on the premise that the current global financial structure is dominated by the Western world. In a Western-dominated world structure, where China's and India's invocation of the "multilateral spirit" at the cross-regional and global level should have been a solid one, their current engagement is intended only to advance their own strategic and national interests using the shield of multilateralism. As both China and India enhance their global profile, they find themselves isolated in a complex power dynamics where the U.S. remains a constant factor in their bilateral engagement and association. The 2009 Copenhagen climate change summit showed that there are greater and broader issues where both should engage and cooperate in concrete terms in order to maximize their mutual strategic interests in a Western-dominated order.

The rise of groupings like IBSA, BRICS, and global bodies like the G-20, the breakdown of the Doha Round and the appearance of BASIC in the arena of climate change politics, all signify that both China and India lead the global politics along with other developing economies. With the emergence of multipolar politics, India and China have not only sought to enlarge cooperation in various multilateral or global issues but have also started openly acknowledging each other's global preeminence. Progressive politics between China and India suggests that there is scope for global partnership, which is evolving to a limited extent; the scope of this progressive trend is also restricted and conditional. In their cross-regional engagement in the current global politics, it is apparent that the central motive of engagement has been to maximize their own sphere of influence and achieve respective national interests in a Western-dominated global order.

Notes

1. *Joint Communiqué of the Republic of India and the People's Republic of China*, Bilateral Documents (Dec. 16, 2010), http://meaindia.nic.in/mystart.php?id=530516879.
2. Ministry of Foreign Affairs of the People's Republic of China, "Bilateral relations" (Aug. 22, 2011), http://www.fmprc.gov.cn/eng/wjb/zzjg/yzs/gjlb/2711/;

   Also refer to *Joint Communiqué of the Republic of India and the People's Republic of China*, 2010.
3. Lowell Dittmer, "China's rise, global identity, and the developing world," *China, the Developing World, and the New Global Dynamic*, eds. Lowell Dittmer and George T. Yu (Boulder, CO: Lynne Rienner, 2010), 222.
4. Manoranjan Mohanty, "China and India: Competing hegemonies or civilisational forces of swaraj and jiefang?" *China Report* 46, 103 (2010):104.
5. Ministry of Foreign Affairs of the People's Republic of China, *A Shared Vision for the 21st Century of the People's Republic of China and the Republic of India* (Jan. 15, 2008), http://www.fmprc.gov.cn/eng/wjdt/2649/t399545.htm (accessed Dec. 10,2011).
6. Stephen M. Walt, *The Origin of Alliances* (Ithaca: Cornell University Press, 1987).
7. Robert O. Keohane, "Multilateralism: An agenda for research," *International Journal*, vol. 45 (Autumn 1990):401–34.
8. Ibid.
9. David Underwood, "BRIC economies," *The Global Dispatches* (Mar. 1, 2010), http://www.theglobaldispatches.com/articles/bric-economies.
10. Ming Jinwei, "What can world learn from BRICS summit in Sanya?" *Xinhua* (Apr. 15, 2011), http://news.xinhuanet.com/english2010/china/2011-04/15/c_13829493.htm (accessed Jan. 15, 2012).
11. Jagannath P. Panda, "BRICS Sanya declaration: What it means to emerging global strategic calculus," *The Tribune* (Apr. 23, 2011), http://www.tribuneindia.com/2011/20110423/edit.htm#4.
12. "BRICS in search of a foundation," *The Economist* (Apr. 16, 2011), http://www.economist.com/blogs/banyan/2011/04/emerging_economic_powers (accessed Dec. 1, 2011).
13. Ibid.
14. Soumya Kanti Mitra, "India trails BRIC peers," *Financial Express* (Feb. 6, 2008).
15. Ibid.
16. Dr. Manmohan Singh, "Opening statement at the Plenary Session of the BRIC Summit" (Speech, Ministry of External Affairs, New Delhi, Apr. 15, 2010), http://meaindia.nic.in.
17. Sandeep Dikshit, "IBSA needs to step up pace on trade within the grouping and security," *The Hindu*, Oct. 18, 2011, http://www.thehindu.com/news/national/article2546692.ece.
18. Ibid.
19. Sandeep Dikshit, "IBSA must remain restricted to 3 countries: Manmohan," *The Hindu*, Oct. 19, 2011, http://www.thehindu.com/news/national/article2549580.ece?css=print.
20. Ibid.
21. "POYRY report," *China, India, South Africa, Brazil (BASIC): Crucial for the Global Environment* (con R-2011-011, Mar. 4, 2011):30.
22. James Jacob, "Copenhagen and the 'BASIC' countries: Some basic differences between the Indian and Chinese emissions," *Current Science* 99, 4 (Aug. 25, 2010):439.
23. "BASIC countries to frame common position on Kyoto protocol," *The Hindu*, Oct. 31, 2011.
24. Refer to Ministry of Foreign Affairs of the People's Republic of China, Jan. 15, 2008.
25. Ashwini Phadnis, "India, China pledge to deepen cooperation," *Business Line* (Sep. 26, 2011).

26. Zhao Gancheng, "China-Russia-India trilateral relations: Realities and prospects," *China Report* 45, 2 (2009):127;

Patricia Uberoi, "India-China initiatives in multilateral fora: Two case studies," *China Report* 44, 3 (2008):311.

27. Zhao Gancheng, "China-Russia-India trilateral relations: Realities and prospects," *China Report* 45, 2 (2009):128.

28. Ibid.

29. Zhao Gancheng, "China-Russia-India trilateral relations: Realities and prospects," *China Report* 45, 2 (2009):129;

Rong Ying, "Stabilising Afghanistan: The role of China-India-Russia trilateral cooperation," *China Report* 45, 2 (2009):150.

30. Shen Qiang, "Subtle changes of major power relations: A perspective on the reform of international financial and economic system," *Global Review* 1, 1 (Jul.–Aug. 2009):51.

31. Refer to Ministry of Foreign Affairs of the People's Republic of China, Jan. 15, 2008.

32. Jonathan Holslag, *China and India: Prospects for Peace* (New York: Columbia University Press, 2010), 31–32.

33. Tan Chung, "International standing," *Rise of the Asian Giants: The Dragon-elephant Tango*, ed. Patricia Oberoi (London: Anthem Press, 2008), 273.

34. Priyanka Pandit, Vidya Krishamurty, Jagannath Panda and R.N. Das, "Wen Jiabao's India visit: A strategic review," *Issue Brief* (IDSA) (Jan. 7, 2011):5.

35. Ibid.

36. Chietigj Bajpayee, "China-India relations: Regional rivalry takes the world stage," *China Security* 6, 2 (2010):7.

37. Ibid.

38. Ibid.